BLUEGRASS BRAWLERS

The Story of Professional Wrestling in Louisville

By John Cosper

Cover design by Daniel Carroll.
Back cover photo courtesy Jason Saint.

www.johncosper.com
www.eatsleepwrestle.com

In memory of Thomas C. Cosper, Sr.
Father, grandfather, great-grandfather, fireman, and wrestling fan.

LOUISVILLE, KY
Tuesday, Oct. 30

Handsome Jimmy Valiant
& Randy Savage
-vs-
The Dirty White Boys
w/Jimmy Hart
(No Time - No D.Q.)

INTERNATIONAL
TITLE MATCH
Eddie Gilbert
-vs-
Lanny Poffo

Kortsia Korchenko
-vs-
Tracy Smothers

Tommy Rich
-vs-
Kurt Von Hess

Rufus Jones
-vs-
Ric Rude

Steve Constant &
Tim Ashley
-vs-
The Nightmares

CHAMPIONSHIP
WRESTLING
Presents

ACTION RINGSIDE

LOUISVILLE WRESTLING

At The
LOUISVILLE
GARDENS

Watch
Championship Wrestling
WAVE TV Channel 3
Saturday Afternoon
12:00 til 1:00 P.M.

This program is presented weekly
in the interest of Professional Wrestling
by Championship Wrestling
Promotion reserves the right to make necessary
changes in the scheduled matches.

TABLE OF CONTENTS

The Davis Arena, current home of Ohio Valley Wrestling.

FOREWORD
Jim Cornette

From the time I discovered pro wrestling on television at the age of nine, I was a fan. After attending my first live wrestling event in May of 1974 at the Louisville Gardens, then called the Convention Center, I was a fanatic. Since then, my life has been inextricably woven around the grappling game as both a pastime and a profession. I was lucky enough to be the perfect age to catch almost all of the "glory years" of wrestling at the Gardens, either on TV, in person as a fan and photographer, or in my rookie year as a budding manager. Collecting programs, newspaper ads, video tapes and stories from the veterans, I considered myself an expert on Louisville wrestling--until I met John Cosper.

From this fortuitous meeting, I discovered that there was a vast amount of history of Louisville wrestling I didn't know about, most of it coming from the early decades of the twentieth century. While I remain confident that I know as much about the sport in Louisville during the 70s and 80's as anyone alive, there was an entire world of knowledge out there waiting for me about the earlier years, and it was revealed to me through John's incredible, painstaking research. Some of it made me feel like a sap--I had no idea that all the Courier-Journal newspapers for the century existed on microfilm at the Public Library until John told me, and I've lived in Louisville the majority of my life. But in addition, John's meticulous interviews, searches for records that may yield clues from places such as the Jack Pfefer collection at Notre Dame, and other methods of squirreling out and tracking down info have opened up the floodgates to paint as clear a picture of the importance of the Derby City to pro wrestling as any book ever published.

Jerry Jarrett opening up Louisville in 1970 and bringing in the Tennessee talent may have ushered in the

Modern era, but there is so much more that Louisville has given the world of wrestling--and you will read about it here. From Strangler Lewis' name to the start of the infamous conflict between Lou Thesz and Buddy Rogers, from the Buckingham to the Columbia Gym to the Armory and a few stray places in between, from Masked Supermen to the Green Shadow and the early days of tag team wrestling with Herb and Roy Welch, all the way to the "dark' days of the 60's that served as the precursor to the 70s boom, you'll read about it here. You'll also learn of the many offshoots of the Gardens tradition, some famous and some infamous, that still operate in Kentuckiana as we advance into the twenty-first century. John has done a great job in relating the stories, portraying the stars, and unearthing the unknown that shaped Louisville wrestling over better than 100 years, and this book makes a great case for the Derby City as one of the most impactful locations on the landscape of twentieth century pro wrestling anywhere in the country. I hope you enjoy reading it as much as I enjoyed taking a few trips on John's journey with him!

Jim Cornette
Louisville, Ky.
May, 2014

INTRODUCTION
December 19, 2012, Louisville, Kentucky

From the outside Davis Arena looks no different from the other metal-clad buildings that surround it in the industrial area of Shepherdsville Road. Step inside the front door of the home of Ohio Valley Wrestling (OVW), however, and one comes face to face with a series of sketches by local cartoonist Joe Stark, the same man who designed the OVW logo, of the men and women who made this place legendary: Randy Orton, Batista, Brock Lesnar, Cody Rhodes, Victoria, CM Punk, and the man once known as the Prototype, John Cena.

I'm sitting in the top row chatting with an old friend who has worked at Davis Arena for more than a decade. The weekly TV taping has just concluded, and a second TV taping, due to the upcoming Christmas holiday, is about to commence. Our conversation is interrupted when the emcee steps into the ring with an unassuming gentleman in a brown shirt and khakis.

The man in brown is Joe Wheeler, a referee who was a fixture in the Louisville wrestling scene for more than three decades. His in-ring career began years earlier when Jerry Lawler and the USWA would invade the downtown Louisville Gardens every Tuesday night. When Ohio Valley Wrestling first established itself across the river in Jeffersonville, Indiana, Joe was the man chosen to lead and mentor the referees who would call the action.

Tonight, OVW paused to pay tribute to a legend. Few knew his name, but those who did cheered him as loudly as any superstar.

OVW announcer Dean Hill took to the ring to pay tribute to a man he had known almost his entire career. He was joined by long time OVW stalwart Trailer Park Trash and the man known to OVW fans as the Wizard of Oz, the man behind the curtain, the founder of OVW and namesake of Davis Arena, Nightmare Danny Davis himself. Hill and Davis shared memories, inside jokes, and praise for a man who had worked side by side with legends past an present.

But it was the men and women just outside the ring who made the greatest impression on me. As the impromptu ceremony began, the curtains parted and the current superstars of OVW surrounded the ring.

There were twenty or thirty of them, most between the ages of 20 and 25. Among the many present at ringside that night was Jamin Olivencia, the top face in the promotion and a promising young champion; Total Nonstop Action (TNA) signee and Tough Enough alum Ryan Howe; the flamboyant, rising superstar Paredyse; identical twins and TNA signees Holly and Hannah Blossom; and tag champs Alex Silva and Sam Shaw.

Most of the young superstars on the outside of the ring had their hopes set on bigger things than Louisville. They dreamed of playing arenas that would dwarf the tiny Davis Arena and becoming household names. But on this night it was Joe Wheeler's turn to be the star. With every accolade spoken, with every memory shared, the young talent outside the ring cheered, screamed, clapped, and pounded on the mat to express their appreciation and gratitude for a humble referee from Louisville, Kentucky.

Respect is a rare commodity in today's culture. Respect for parents, teachers, and leaders is at an all-time low, and respect for the past almost non-existent. Strange as it may sound, the world of professional wrestling is a genuine exception to the rule. Respect isn't just valued; it's required. If you want to get anywhere in the world of professional wrestling, you must learn respect for the past.

Respect for tradition. Respect for those who have gone before: the managers, the trainers, the referees, and yes, the wrestlers. Respect for those who blazed the trails, who held the belts, who broke the ground, who paved the way for those who even now are preparing to inherit a long and proud tradition.

When arriving backstage for a show, it is incumbent on the younger wrestlers to greet and shake hands with the older wrestlers. Respect is expected. It is demanded. Those who refuse to comply are shown the door - or taught a permanent "lesson" in the ring.

Perhaps that is why the wrestling literary genre has taken off like it has. The respect of current superstars for the heroes of the past spills out to the fans. Admiration for the past leads to an enhanced enjoyment of the present and a deeper understanding of the sport (or, as some prefer, sports entertainment) that has delighted generations of fans.

It is in that spirit that this book about a city and a sport was conceived. Louisville, Kentucky has a long and proud tradition when it comes to professional wrestling. The list of names that have reached the big time by way of the Derby City, as Louisville is known, reads like a who's who of wrestling royalty.

The tradition of professional wrestling in Louisville dates back more than a century. A generation of fans can recall when the Wednesday TV tapings in Davis Arena featured names like Leviathan, the Minnesota Stretching Crew, and the Prototype. An older generation still remembers those Tuesday nights when Jeff Jarrett, Jerry "The King" Lawler, and other stars of Memphis wrestling would invade The Louisville Gardens on Muhammad Ali Boulevard downtown. Some can still recall the days prior when the National Wrestling Alliance (NWA) brought marquee names like Orville Brown, Lou Thesz, Wild Bill Longson, and Mildred Burke to that same building when it was still known as the Jefferson County Armory.

But Louisville's passion for wrestling dates back even further than the golden days of the 1940s. Long before John Cena arrived with dreams of being the champ, another legendary champ earned his name at the opera house downtown. Even before that champion was born, professional wrestling took root in Louisville thanks the carnivals and barnstormers of the late 19th century.

PART ONE
THE PIONEERS

The Jefferson County Armory, now the Louisville Gardens, circa 1921.

(Item no. ULPA CS 037572 in the Caufield & Shook Collection, University of Louisville Photographic Archives.)

BATTLE OF THE SEXES

Professional wrestling and its popularity were direct products of the Civil War. Both Union and Confederate soldiers found wrestling to be an entertaining way to pass the time in between battles. After the war, the best wrestlers found paid work performing for paid audiences, and a new pastime was born.

Wrestling shows of the period were a far cry from the Monday night tradition of today. Wrestling was a legitimate sport, with roots going all the way back to ancient Greece. At least, that's what we're led to believe.

Wrestling matches were contests of strength, skill, and endurance. It was not uncommon for matches to stretch on for hours. Fans would watch late into the evening, waiting for one man or the other to get the requisite number of falls to be declared the winner. It's hard to imagine an audience sitting through a three or four hour main event, but remember, this was the late nineteenth century. There was no television, no radio, and not a whole lot else to do on a Friday night!

At the same time the legitimate sport of wrestling was packing houses, a different style of wrestling evolved in the traveling circuses and carnivals of the day. Known as "At Shows" (short for athletic shows), these wrestling troupes included a few acrobatic daredevils who would thrill the audiences with their exhibitions. These wrestlers wore colorful costumes, took on marquee-worthy names, and put on shorter exhibitions with high flying maneuvers, dramatic twists, and yes, prearranged endings.

To keep up the illusion that the contests were legitimate, each At Show also had at least one shooter - a legitimate wrestler skilled enough to take on audience members brave enough to accept a challenge - and a hooker - an elite shooter skilled at holds and moves that could quickly and permanently cripple any challenger.

Louisville sports enthusiasts were able to follow the early action in wrestling from afar thanks to *The Courier-Journal*, Louisville's daily newspaper since 1868. Created by a merger between *The Louisville Morning News* and the *The Louisville Daily Journal, The Courier-Journal* began covering the sport of professional wrestling in the mid 1870s. The sport was in its infancy when notices of wrestling matches from New York, Baltimore, Chicago, and Cincinnati began appearing in the pages of *The Courier-Journal*. The public's fascination with it grew, and slowly, the sport made its way closer and closer to the River City. Then in 1880, Forepaugh's Circus rolled into Louisville, and a female wrestler gave Louisville fans one of the most memorable sport spectacles in the city's history.

Adam Forepaugh was one of the late 1800s top showmen, and his circus was the chief rival to P.T. Barnum's in the 1880s. Like Barnum, Forepaugh had an At Show in the midway, and one of his top attractions was a five foot three, 150 pound pixie named Ida Alb. Alb captured the attention of Louisvillians with her exhibition matches against fellow circus performer M'lles Marcia.

Alb's visit would have come and gone without any mainstream coverage had she not taken umbrage with allegations that she and her compatriots were hippodroming: staging athletic contests that had a predetermined finish. The allegations were true, of course, but they provided Alb with a chance to gain some press coverage for the circus and defend her business.

The June 1, 1880, edition of *The Courier-Journal* states that Alb issued an open challenge to any Louisvillian in her weight class to step in the ring with her. A day later, her challenge was answered by Albert Marc, a Frenchman and a highly skilled athlete in his own right. An agreement was signed at the New Southern Hotel on June 2. Both wrestlers would receive $50 for the match, and the winner would be declared the Kentucky state champion.

The match took place in front of a packed house at the Standard Theater. After an unexplained delay, a man appeared in the audience at twenty minutes until nine to read the rules for the match:

1. No holds below the waist allowed.
2. No scratching or kicking.
3. Contestants must wear soft-soled shoes or socks.
4. Finger nails had to be cut close.
5. When a contestant touched both shoulders to the mat, they would lose one fall.
6. Best three out of five wins.
7. One referee and two judges would be chosen from the audience.

Albert Marc was first to make his entrance, played to the ring by a band of African American musicians. Standing at five foot three inches with "black hair, black, sparkling eyes, and a good humored face," he was dressed in loose fitting white tights, a red shirt, and blue trunks.

With a flourish of music from the orchestra pit, Miss Ida Alb appeared, skipping lightly and pausing to blow a kiss to musicians. The "luscious damsel with a pert smile," was described by the poetic sports writer as far less dressed than her opponent. She wore red tights "which fitted like she had been poured into them with a ladle until the point of running over was reached." She wore a blue leotard over top of the trunks tight enough that "the human form divine was outlined as perfectly as the most fastidious anatomist could have desired." Ida was of equal height to her opponent but had a seventeen pound weight advantage, and her tight fitting costume revealed that the difference in weight was all muscle.

The competitors stood before their audience as the judges and referee were selected. Arthur Suarez, described by *The Courier-Journal* as being from France, was chosen to be Marc's judge. The rotund Suarez danced about outside the ring throughout the match, voicing his admiration for Alb and declaring he would challenge her himself given the chance. Alb's judge was a wrestler named H. Schulen. Sam Self acted as referee, and *The Courier-Journal* notes he performed his duties with "grace and occasional relapses of deep emotion."

Alb appeared to be nervous as the match began, while Marc was the picture of cool composure. They traded holds and flips with one another until Marc managed to take Alb down for what he thought should be the first fall. Alb protested her shoulders did not hit the mat, and the referee disallowed the fall. Alb went in for her best hold, but Marc slipped out and managed to get her shoulders pinned to the mat, scoring the first fall in thirteen minutes.

Marc was energized as the match resumed, while Alb looked tired. Marc caught her in a headlock, but Alb escaped by tossing him overhead. She tried to roll his shoulders onto the mat, but he escaped and the match continued. Alb repeated the maneuver and this time got both shoulders to touch as he rolled across the mat. Her judge demanded the referee score a pin fall in her favor, and Sam Self gave Alb the fall.

The audience was really into the match, cheering the competitors on as they began round three. Alb came out with a vengeance, looking to continue her momentum. She tossed Marc a few times and tried to claim her second fall, but Marc managed to wriggle free before she could pin him. When Marc rolled up on his side to avoid being pinned, Alb grabbed him around the waist, flipped him with a somersault, and landed face down on top of his chest, scoring her second pin in six minutes.

With his back against the wall, Marc came out with renewed vigor in the fourth round. He caught Alb in a headlock and tried to roll her on her back, but Alb kept her shoulders off the mat. With a loud laugh, Alb attacked

Marc, but Marc was ready for her and flipped his opponent, nearly scoring his second pin fall. Marc attempted the maneuver twice more to no avail, but he finally evened the score when he caught Alb in a back-neck hold and turned her over, pinning her squarely to the mat. Reluctantly, the referee scored the fall for Marc at fifteen minutes. It would all come down to one final fall.

By now the audience was completely in Alb's corner. The referee was too, but he resolved himself to call the final pin fairly. Alb came at Marc at full speed. Marc out-maneuvered her and tried unsuccessfully to go for the pin. In the tumult Marc grabbed her legs above the knee, an illegal move, per the terms of the match, and Schulen demanded the referee disqualify the challenger. Alb refused to win that way, stating that she wanted the match to end the right way, with a pin. The competitors battled on the mat, each trying to use their weight to seize the advantage and win the final fall. Marc grabbed Alb by the shoulders and threw her, rolling over on top of her with his full strength, but he failed to score a pin. They locked up again, and this time, Alb wrapped her arms through his and gave him the bridge throw, scoring the final fall.

The audience erupted with cheers. Marc and Alb shook hands and bowed to the audience. Alb then announced that she would challenge Marc to a second match on June 17 following an engagement in St. Louis. Marc accepted on the spot. Alb gave Sam Self a kiss, and the evening was over.

There's no further mention of Ida Alb in *The Courier-Journal* archives to tell who won the rematch or whether one even took place, but it would not be Ida's last match with a man, or her last brush with mainstream fame. According to *The Cincinnati Enquirer*, Ida agreed to another man vs. woman match in St. Louis versus a man named Charles A. Standbrook. Standbrook took the first fall against the much smaller woman, but Alb rallied to take the second and third falls and claim victory.

One has to take both accounts with a grain of salt. The At Shows were staged exhibitions with fixed finishes, and it was not uncommon for promoters to plant ringers in the crowd posing as locals to take on the wrestlers. What's more, *The Courier-Journal's* account of the contract signing notes that Marc wrestled in London with M'lles Marcia - Alb's main opponent with the At Show. Whether it was staged or not, she clearly left an impression on the Louisville audience not easily forgotten.

Ida Alb made at least one return visit to Louisville when she and M'lles Marcia arrived in late January of 1881 for an engagement at the Buckingham Theater as part of an exhibition of novelty acts. Tragically, on July 6 of that same year Ida was found dead in Milwaukee from an opium overdose. A one paragraph notice found in *The Nashville Tennessean* identifies her as a member of Forepaugh's circus. "It is supposed from things found in her trunk that she is a Cleveland girl," the article's final sentence begins, "but her real name could not be discovered."

Ida Alb would not be the last wrestler to die tragically at a young age, but she made her mark on the world of professional wrestling and the city of Louisville. She blazed a trail for male and female wrestlers, creating an appetite for the drama and the action of professional wrestling. More than 130 years later, that craving lives on in the fans who buy pay-per-views, DVR Monday Night Raw, and wait in line for the local promotions in and around Louisville.

"THERE CAN BE NO DRAW"

In the days before organized promoters took over the business, newspapers like *The Courier-Journal* acted as the promoters for big time fights. Newspapers were the only form of mass communication, and they served not only as the promotional vehicle for fight sports but as a central point for fighters and their representatives to arrange bouts with one another. One fighter would contact the newspaper with his or her challenge and send a deposit - typically around $250 - for half the prize money. An interested challenger would then contact the paper directly or through their representation with an answer and a matching sum of money. The newspaper held the money until the fight took place or was forfeited in which case the money would go to the party that did not withdraw from the fight. If no one stepped forward to accept the fighter's challenge, their money would be returned to them.

A year after Ida Alb won the battle of the sexes, a Louisville resident named Robert M. Pennell stepped forward and issued a challenge to the world. The young Hercules, as *The Courier-Journal* called him, offered to fight for any sum of money against any citizen of the United States or Europe brave enough to step into the ring with him. Pennell was well known in the city for his feats of strength, handling 200 pound dumbbells with the ease that most men handled fifty-pound weights, and he laid claim he was the strongest man in the world.

In August of 1881 a Chicago athlete named Charles Flynn answered the call. In a letter to *The Courier-Journal* printed on August 21, Flynn promised to send a representative to Louisville to negotiate the terms of the fight. The following day Edward Morrill, Flynn's appointed representative, met with Pennell at the Knickerbocker Theater in Louisville. They agreed to a Greco-Roman contest with each side putting up $250. The contest would take place on September 17 at Woodland Garden, a popular beer garden located on Market Street. The match stipulations were identical to those laid out in the Alb/Marc match, but a few additional rules were added, one of which stated the match could not end in a draw.

The city was abuzz with excitement about the upcoming match. When Flynn arrived in town on September 7, people were eager to learn all they could about Pennell's challenger. Billed as a champion wrestler of the Northwest, Flynn stood at five feet, nine and a half inches tall and weighed 182 pounds. Flynn was fairly new to the sport of wrestling, but in less than five years he had racked up a number of notable wins in his adopted hometown of Chicago. *The Courier-Journal* chronicled his history of victories up to the match in early 1881 when he defeated J. A. Morgan and laid claim to his championship title.

So confident was Flynn in his ability to win, he offered to double the stakes of the match to $500 a piece. Flynn also wanted the winner to take all the gate money, but Pennell refused, insisting the loser get one-third of the box office.

Flynn trained for two weeks in Chicago prior to his arrival and resumed training when he reached Louisville. He gave a public training exhibition on September 14, when he announced he would run a timed five mile race through Louisville's National Park.

A crowd of eight hundred, mostly young men, gathered at Woodland Gardens on the 17th, where Pennell and Flynn did battle on an open stage instead of inside a ring. What happened was an unexpected and disappointing finish. Pennell was clearly the stronger of the two, but Flynn proved to be the superior technical wrestler. After a mighty back and forth struggle the man from Chicago took the first fall. But after falling behind two falls to one, Flynn began looking for a quick exit from the contest.

The agreement signed on August 22 stated the match could not end in a draw. But as the agreement also stated that the contest would take place on September 17. The match began on the 17th, but at 12:10 AM on September 18, Edward Morrill called time and announced that his man had withdrawn from the contest.

The crowd was livid. They screamed for Flynn to finish the contest. The referee, hoping to appease the crowd, announced Pennell as the winner, but Pennell gallantly refused to accept the win. Ignoring the cry of the masses who wanted him to take the win and the $500, he told the crowd that Morrill had out-foxed him, and he agreed the match should end in a draw. But he also took the opportunity to demand a rematch, two weeks hence, for double the stakes - a $1000 purse! Flynn agreed to the rematch, and the evening was over.

The very next day, Flynn seemed to back off from the rematch, at least publicly. When pressed on the matter, Flynn said he had no objection to wrestling Pennell again in private, but he had no desire to face him in Louisville with the city's fans against him. Flynn had no immediate plans to leave town, stating he had made many friends and intended to stick around for a week or so, but the public rematch was out.

The next day, Flynn put up a deposit of $50 at *The Courier-Journal* to show he was sincere about the private rematch. He announced his intention to remain in Louisville until the races were concluded at Churchill Downs, home of the Kentucky Derby, and he reiterated his stance he would not face Pennell in a public exhibition.

Pennell remained mum on the chances of a rematch, but on September 22, he met with Edward Morrill at the Knickerbocker and agreed to a second match. The two met the following day to negotiate the rules, and Pennell went in with one non-negotiable: there would be NO draw this time!

On September 30, a crowd of more than 1000 gathered to watch the strongest man in the world take on the champion of the Northwest. A good number of bettors and sports enthusiasts from Peoria and Chicago came in for the match to cheer on Chicago's own, but the crowd was largely local and largely in Pennell's corner.

When the opponents disrobed, it was clear Flynn was in better shape than his opponent that night. He was also much cooler and patient than in their previous match as the two locked up. Pennell matched Flynn's caution, and both men took a defensive posture. Flynn took the early advantage when Pennell went for a neck hold, dropping him to mat, but when Flynn went for a hold, Pennell powered out and dropped Flynn on his shoulders, scoring a fall and drawing a roar from the partisan crowd.

Flynn came out more aggressively for round two. His scientific knowledge of the sport gave him the edge, and in ten minutes, Pennell was on his back, struggling to keep one shoulder off the mat. Flynn overpowered him, and the match was even at one fall a piece.

Flynn looked fresh as they began the third round just before 10 PM. Pennell, on the other hand, was showing serious signs of fatigue and suffering from sprained fingers. Pennell spent much of the round face down on the mat as Flynn struggled to flip him on his back. Unable to put his "Nelson grip" to use, Flynn ultimately used a neck lock to turn the stronger man over and take the third fall.

Pennell called for a surgeon during the third intermission and attempted to treat his badly damaged hand. It was of little use, and when Pennell answered the bell for the fourth round, he appeared "timid as a child." Flynn kept Pennell on the defensive, chasing him all over the stage. At one point, Flynn had Pennell pressed against the floodlights, and Pennell, afraid he might be tossed off the stage, was heard saying, "Don't hurt me, Flynn, don't hurt me." At that moment, Flynn flipped Pennell over one last time and scored the pin, taking the victory and ending the contest.

After the crowd left, the two competitors met in the presence of the judges, referee, and *Courier-Journal* representatives. Flynn received his prize of $1000 plus two thirds of the gate. Pennell admitted he had been soundly defeated and congratulated his opponent.

A minor scare happened during the match when a drunken man appeared at the window of Flynn's dressing room with a rusty revolver threatening to kill him. Edward Morrill alerted security, and the drunk was tossed out of the Gardens without his weapon.

Having won the battle, Flynn declared his intention to next challenge Chicago wrestler Duncan C. Ross. Pennell and Flynn would leave town together on September 7 for Chicago where they hoped there would be a run in with Ross.

It seems strange that two such bitter rivals would leave practically arm in arm in pursuit of their next challenge, but a year later, an article in *The Courier-Journal* shed a different light on their so-called rivalry. An unidentified wrestler gave *The Courier-Journal* what he claimed to be the real story of Pennell and Flynn: it was all a work.

According to the unnamed source, Pennell and Flynn came into Louisville playing a very common game. A wrestler of some repute would move into a town where people could be "easily gulled." The wrestler, now claiming to be a local, would issue open challenges that would be answered by a pre-selected opponent from out of town. The opponent would come to town, engage in a war of words with the challenger, and ultimately square off with him in a match.

What's more, the outcome of these matches was often decided on the fly. Observers would watch the betting on the matches, and depending on who had the most money bet by the third of fourth round, decide the finish based on who could win the more money. By doing so, the promoters and their allies could maximize their profits by betting on the perceived underdog.

"It is," the source concluded, "a settled fact that all the wrestlers, who are abusing each other, are very good friends in reality and put on the disguise of enmity to gull the people more easily."

Pennell and Flynn were long gone when their secrets hit the paper, but a new pair of barnstormers was in the midst of an even bigger feud. Duncan C. Ross was the new Louisville hero, and his out of town opponent was the biggest name in the sport.

THE SOLID MAN OF SPORT

Shortly after Flynn and Pennell left town, Duncan C. Ross moved in, making himself at home in Louisville. The champion of America, as he billed himself, wasted little time making a splash in his new hometown, wrestling a series of matches with a challenger named Lew Moore in late 1881 and earning the nickname The Louisville Terror. His efforts against Moore made him an instant hometown hero, but Ross had his sights set on bigger opponents and bigger stakes. Ross wanted a match with William Muldoon.

Hailing from New York, Muldoon was one of the biggest stars of his day. Billed as the "The Solid Man of Sport" and "the best preserved athlete in the world," the 250 pound Muldoon first took up the sport when he served in the Union Army during the Civil War. He was considered to be one of the very best grapplers in the Union.

When the war ended, Muldoon volunteered to fight for the French in the Franco-Prussian war. It was there Muldoon learned the Greco-Roman style of wrestling - a style that, despite its name, was actually developed in France.

In 1876, Muldoon moved to New York City, where he became a policeman. He also began wrestling in the saloons, and he quickly made a name for himself. Muldoon was a big draw, and he counted Thomas Edison, Harry Houdini, Teddy Roosevelt, and P. T. Barnum among his fans. He came to the ring dressed as a Roman gladiator, and he enjoyed showing off his physique in and out of the ring.

Muldoon was best known for a series of matches with fellow legend Clarence Whistler. In three separate contests, Muldoon and Whistler battled for a combined fourteen hours with one match lasting 8 hours straight.

When Muldoon did not respond to Ross's challenge, Ross issued another challenge to an old foe, H. M. Dufur. Dufur defeated Ross in the summer of 1880 in Dufur's home state of Massachusetts, but when he received the challenge from the The Louisville Terror, Dufur could not resist. "I am not disposed to let the little giant of 205-pounds-weight's challenge pass unheeded," he said in a letter to *The Courier-Journal*. Dufur mailed $100 earnest money to *The Courier-Journal* as a guarantee he would come to Louisville and take on the American champion.

The invitations to Muldoon and Dufur led to an unforgettable series of matches in 1882 embroiled in controversy, rumor, and scandal. The first of these matches was scheduled for April 1, 1882, at the Old Buckingham Theater. It turned out to be an April Fool of a kind, as Muldoon refused to show.

Muldoon sent his agent to the opera house (yes, the Buckingham was also the opera house!) that evening to inform the management and Ross of his decision to no-show, citing a disagreement over the money to be paid for the match. Muldoon's agent stated that he had agreed to the match with the understanding that John Macauley, the promoter, would receive one-third of the gate and the winning wrestler two-thirds. The contract signed by Ross and Macauley gave the promoter half and the winning wrestler half - a very different deal than the one Muldoon agreed to. A very disappointed crowd hung around outside until the lights were put out. It would not be the last time Muldoon would draw the ire of the Louisville crowd.

Ross met with Muldoon's representatives on the 2nd, and the match was re-scheduled for the 3rd. But Muldoon's no-show on the 1st had soured the public on the Solid Man of Sport. Rumors were swirling that Muldoon was not a legitimate wrestler, and allegations of hippodroming circulated the city. Other rumors suggested that Muldoon would not pay out if he lost or that Muldoon was prepared to cripple Ross permanently if Muldoon lost the match.

Despite the negative publicity, a "howling mob" packed the opera house that night to see if Muldoon would show. This time Muldoon showed up ready to fight, but he continued to draw the ire of the crowd by his actions. Muldoon objected to Ross's choice of referee, a newspaper man named Ben Ridgely, and the two ultimately settled on a man named George Knott, who it turns out knew nothing at all about the sport and its rules.

After Mr. Knott introduced the judges for the two competitors, he read the rules for the match. The rules agreed upon by Ross and Muldoon came from *The Police Gazette*, a seedy periodical that dated back to 1845. *The Police Gazette* was known for lurid crime stories of murder, sex, and scandal as well as engravings (later photos) of scantily clad women. By the late 1800s, it was also one of the most important sports publications in the country, contributing to the growth of both boxing and wrestling.

The Police Gazette rules stated that an opponent had to pin two shoulders and one hip or two hips and one shoulder had to be on the mat to score a fall. As soon as Knott finished reading the rules, Muldoon objected, drawing the ire of both Ross and the crowd. Muldoon spoke to the crowd and insisted the Gazette rules were not recognized by respectable people. Muldoon wished to follow the James Rules, which stated that two shoulders constituted a fall.

Knott didn't know what to do. He had Muldoon threatening to back out of the match if his demands were not met and an angry crowd screaming to start the match. Knott gave up his position and left the stage.

Once again, Ben Ridgely's name was suggested as the referee. This time, Muldoon inexplicably agreed. Ridgely proved to be just as ignorant as Knott about what to do, and despite the written agreement stating they would follow *The Police Gazette* rules, Ridgely overruled Ross and agreed to call the match by the James Rules - two shoulders equals a pin.

Muldoon had an unfair edge from the start. Not only did he switch the rules on Ross at the last minute, he had the distinct advantage of having wrestled Greco-Roman style. Ross had never wrestled Greco-Roman in his life, but he agreed to the stipulation and made no objection to the last minute rule changes. At long last, the confrontation between Muldoon and Ross would begin.

Muldoon won the first fall in five minutes with a neck lock. He won the second fall almost as quickly with the same hold. When it came to the third round, Muldoon began flaunting the rules again. Under the rules, when a man is thrown to his knees, he must get up and begin again. Muldoon ignored the rules, repeatedly tossing Ross to the stage and pinning him. At one point, Muldoon claimed to have scored eight falls on his opponent. Muldoon was finally awarded the victory.

Ross wasted no time challenging Muldoon to a rematch. This time they would wrestle Ross's way, and if Ross failed to throw Muldoon eight times in an hour, Muldoon would be the victor.

Muldoon answered Ross's challenge through *The Courier-Journal.* Stating his preference for the Greco-Roman style, Muldoon said he would do battle with Ross in the catch-as-catch-can style, but not in Louisville. The rematch, if it were to take place, would happen in Cincinnati. Muldoon's reply was accompanied by a brief comment from *The Courier-Journal,* which stated that the wise decision would be to let Muldoon go and concentrate on Dufur, "who is said to be a first-class wrestler in every respect."

Muldoon appeared at the Buckingham again on April 17, when a group of wrestlers were included in a variety show. As odd as it sounds to think of wrestling happening in a theatrical setting, it was really the only option in the 1880s. Indoor sporting arenas that play host to today's wrestling shows would not come into existence until the 1900s, when basketball and hockey made them a necessity. Thus the Buckingham became the ideal location to introduce Louisville to the sport.

Wrestling was the final feature on a bill that included a theatrical production, music, and "feats of strength" that included a man named James Messenger juggling cannonballs.

The crowd enjoyed the early acts, but it was the wrestling that packed the theater to the rafters that night. Muldoon took on two challengers in Greco-Roman style wrestling. Muldoon bested Louisville hero Robert Pennell in seven minutes, but Andre Christol, described in *The Courier-Journal* as "the prettiest wrestler in the profession" battled Muldoon to a draw in the fifteen minute time limit.

Two days later, H. M. Dufur finally arrived in Louisville. At first glance Dufur looked more like the owner of the local mercantile than a wrestler with his curly brown hair, blue eyes, and dark mustache. He was listed at five foot eleven and 190 pounds with a 43 inch chest, and he road into town with a perfect record in paid exhibitions: forty-five wins, no losses.

Dufur had come at the invitation of Ross, but he made it clear he wanted a piece of Muldoon as well. Dufur issued a challenge to the Solid Man in the collar and elbow style match "in an hour, a day or a week - in public or in private."

On April 20 Muldoon made a proposition to Dufur and Ross: Muldoon and Andre Christol would each take on one of their rivals in a style of Dufur and Ross's choosing. Ross and Dufur consented, and the matches were set for April 23.

Prior to the three match card, Dufur and Ross met at the Masonic Temple to see who was the better man. The competitors wrestled multiple styles in a best three out of five format. Ross won the first fall in five minutes. Dufur came back and won the second fall in only two and a half minutes. Ross won the third fall in three minutes, and Dufur took the fourth in only thirty seconds. The final fall lasted two and a quarter minutes, and Dufur took the fall and the victory. Counting the ten minute breaks between rounds, the entire affair lasted less than an hour, and the match drew the largest crowd yet for a wrestling match in Louisville.

The match and its newspaper coverage were overshadowed by *The Courier-Journal* story exposing the proliferation of hippodroming in the sport. The article not only exposed the Pennell and Flynn series as a fraud, but claimed that Muldoon himself was known for hippodroming, but not without excuse.

The source stated that Muldoon began his career as an honest wrestler, but his superior skill began to cost him bookings. No one wanted to wrestle a man they could not beat, and if Muldoon didn't get booked, he couldn't make money. Muldoon began agreeing to end matches in draws to let his opponents save face.

Muldoon's expertise in the Greco-Roman style was often used as part of the ruse. Muldoon would sometimes drop a fall in a different style in order to put his opponent over as a legitimate contender, but Muldoon would take another fall in the Greco-Roman style as well as the deciding fall in the match.

The same evening these allegations appeared in the paper, Muldoon, Ross, Dufur, and Christol engaged one another at National Park. Muldoon squared off with H. M. Dufur in the first match. Dufur won the coin toss and chose to face Muldoon in the "collar and elbow" style wrestling. The referee chosen for the match was inexperienced and far from knowledgeable about the sport. Muldoon took advantage of this by cheating every chance he got. He wore a tight fitting sweater instead of the loose fitting attire required by the rules of collar and elbow wrestling, and he refused to maintain the proper stance for the chosen wrestling style.

Dufur made repeated protests, but the inexperienced referee declined to correct Muldoon. Time expired, and Muldoon took the opportunity to brag and boast to the crowd, further cementing his position as the first true heel in Louisville wrestling history.

The second match was a Greco-Roman affair between Ross and Christol. Ross initially was a no-show at the park, sending word through his second, a Mr. Johnson, that he was opposed to wrestling on a Sunday. The crowd began to turn against Ross, and one of Ross's friends raced to Ross's house and dragged him back to the park.

Muldoon made himself the referee and time keeper for the second bout. Ross was clearly the better man that day, tossing Christol around as if he were a small child, but the local favorite only managed a four falls to three victory. Close observers showed the score as ten to one in favor of Ross, but the dirty dealings of Muldoon gave Ross the narrow victory and left Louisvillians with a bad taste in their mouths. The champ left town after the match, and Louisvillians bid him good riddance.

Dufur and Ross were to have one more match on April 24, but Dufur forfeited his $25 earnest money and called off the match, citing injuries from the matches he had already fought that week. Despite the withdrawal, Louisvillians had grown fond of Dufur, and it was clear he was welcome to return.

On May 11, Dufur issued a challenge to Ross through *The Courier-Journal*. The two met on May 27, and local favorite Ross won a thrilling match five falls to four.

When Dufur and Ross was the last big match Louisville would see for two years. Clarence Whistler had a match in 1885 at the Buckingham Theater, and William Muldoon - who became the first true professional athlete when he decided to wrestle full-time in 1885 - would defend his championship against Englishman Thomas Cannon in 1888. Muldoon retired in 1890, undefeated for his world championship, and later became the first athletic commissioner for the state of New York.

Despite the bad taste that Muldoon and the hippodroming allegations left on the public, the sport of wrestling grew in popularity. By the late 1880s a committee formed in Louisville to create the River City Athletic Club, an organization that would promote both wrestling and boxing in the city. The Louisville YMCA also offered wrestling and other fight sports, keeping the sport alive for city residents. Amateur exhibitions were common throughout the rest of the nineteenth century.

The Courier-Journal kept wrestling fans up to date on the top matches across the country, but professional wrestling was largely absent from Louisville through the turn of the century. Muldoon's retirement left the sport without a top name, but newcomers like Evan "The Strangler" Lewis from Wisconsin and Farmer Burns from Iowa would soon fill in the gap. Burns also became the top trainer of new talent, and by the turn of the century, a new generation was ready to take over.

THE NEW CENTURY

The sport of wrestling was hotter than ever at the beginning of the twentieth century. While New York, Chicago, and St. Louis were quickly established as the central hubs for the sport, Louisville began playing host to matches in the early 1900s.

The Courier-Journal covered the sport with the same seriousness and attention as horse racing. A 1903 article in *The Courier-Journal* by Professor Anthony Barker hailed wrestling as "the only natural exercise" and explained in photos many of the basic holds and techniques of the sport. A 1905 article in the same publication noted the sport's growing popularity in the city and praised its athletes for being "cleaner" than prize fighters. William Muldoon was well known for his commitment to sober and healthy living, while his contemporary boxing legend John L. Sullivan was known for his commitment to the bottle.

Barker cited Frank Gotch and George Hackenschmidt, the top stars of the turn of the century wrestling scene, as men of virtue who shunned not only alcohol and tobacco, but caffeine. Six years later, these "men of virtue" would shame the entire professional wrestling community with their controversial rematch in 1911, a match that was "fixed" when Gotch paid one of Hack's sparring partners to injure him prior to the match.

As Gotch and Hackenschmidt crisscrossed the country on the road to their first collision, it was inevitable that the Louisville wrestling scene would have a revival. In December of 1905, Ed Parsons, a New Yorker who claimed he was the only person in the world who could "walk, run, dance, and jump on his head," got the ball rolling when he issued a challenge via *The Courier-Journal* for a wrestling match. Professor Alfred P. Maas, a "well-known strong man," answered the challenge via the paper, and professional wrestling returned to the River City (yet another nickname for Louisville).

In December of 1906 another challenge hit the papers, this time from Alex Swanson of New York. Swanson came to town with his manager, William H. Barton. Marvin Hart, a prize fighter from Louisville, stepped forward to answer the challenge. Swanson lost the match to hometown favorite Marvin Hart in a stunning upset, but as with all great bouts, a rematch was quickly scheduled.

In January of 1907, Barton returned to Louisville with a new challenger for Hart, Jake Snyder. Barton explained that a "misunderstanding" between Swanson and himself caused the two to part ways, and Barton chose Snyder to be the substitute in the rematch.

Snyder boasted that he would throw Hart three times in sixty minutes, and the terms of the match stated that if Hart secured just one pin on Snyder, Hart would be declared the victor. Snyder took the first fall, but Hart took the second, ending the match and claiming the victory.

Both sides wasted little time scheduling a rematch. This time it would be a straight match, two out of three falls, to settle the matter between the combatants. Once again, Barton's man would come up short, losing two falls to one to Marvin Hart.

The feud was a profitable one for Barton in the long run. While fans concerned themselves with wins and losses, promoters and wrestlers concerned themselves with just one thing: money. The Louisville matches were good money, and Barton saw a golden opportunity. He would soon become one of Louisville's first true wrestling promoters and popularize the sport in the city.

When Barton began promoting fights in 1905, his venue of choice was the new Buckingham Theater. Built in 1894 the "Buck," as it was also known, was located at 223-227 W. Jefferson Street, the same block as the original Buckingham Theater that hosted Muldoon and Ross in the 1880s. The Buckingham Theater began life as the Grand Opera House and was still referred to by locals as the opera house. Seating capacity in the theater was around 1600, and the stage was thirty-one feet wide by thirty-eight high by forty deep.

The Buckingham was re-named the Jefferson in 1919 and then the Savoy in 1922. Wrestling's first Louisville home became a series of adult clubs and businesses before being razed in 1989. The Kentucky International Convention Center now occupies the space once held by the Buckingham.

Wrestling was one of many attractions to take place at the Buck. When Barton began promoting fights, the fights were usually the last feature on a bill that might include a play, a burlesque show, vaudeville acts, and feats of strength.

One of the more unusual matches in the city's history took place on New Year's Day in 1909 when a man from South Africa named Huperfulagas wrestled a bull. Huperfulagas claimed to be a descendant of Zulu royalty, and he proposed to take on a live bull bare-handed. Huperfulagas assisted the promoters in picking his opponent from the Bourbon Stockyards on New Year's Day. Huperfulagas expressed no fear entering the match, proclaiming he would not be in the slightest danger, while the bull, he vowed, would not suffer more than "temporary discomfort."

Huperfulagas squared off against the bull the night of January 1, 1909, wearing traditional native Zulu attire "somewhat modified to meet the local ordinances." The results of this match did not appear in the January 2, 1909, edition of *The Courier-Journal*, leaving us to speculate just how much discomfort the bull and his opponent actually suffered.

In February of 1910, wrestling royalty came to town in the form of the women's world champion, Cora Livingston. Livingston entered the professional wrestling game at the insistence of her husband, wrestler and promoter Paul Bowser. Billed at 5 foot 2 and 135 pounds, Livingston came to town offering a $25 challenge to anyone who could last ten minutes in the ring with the champ.

A Philadelphia native named Ada Rich took up the challenge on Livingston's first night in town and went the distance. There was some dispute as to the legitimacy of the time keeping, but Livingston kept her word and paid the $25 to Rich in the ring.

Livingston offered a re-match to Rich with a $50 prize if Rich could last a full 15 minutes. Rich accepted the challenge, and the match took place February 16 at the Buck.

Women's matches were uncommon at the time not just in Louisville, but across the country. Many state athletic commissions barred women's wrestling, seeing it as an obscenity more than a sport. Livingston would carry the championship title for women's wrestling until her retirement in 1935. Livingston blazed the trail for future legends like Mildred Burke, the Fabulous Moolah, and the WWE Divas of today.

In December of 1912, a young referee named Heywood Allen arrived in town. Allen would become a key member of William Barton's staff and one day start his own promotion. He arrived in town with William Demetral, whom Barton booked for a series of matches. Born in Steno, Greece, Demetral proved to be a big draw and would make numerous appearances in the city over the next decade.

In January of 1913, Yussif Hussane arrived with his manager Billy Sandow. Known as the Terrible Turk, Hussane was a legitimate "hooker," a wrestler skilled in holds and moves that could cripple a man, who purportedly hailed from Bulgaria. Hussane was not the first "Terrible Turk," nor was he the last, and it's very likely he was not actually from Eastern Europe. A number of wrestlers billed themselves as Terrible Turks in the late 1800s and early 1900s, and the majority of them were American or Mexican born wrestlers who happened to have spectacular mustaches.

Hussane was one of the few wrestlers who wrestled barefoot, making it harder for an opponent to get him into a dangerous toe hold. He quickly became a fan favorite with the Louisville crowd, a rarity for a Terrible Turk as foreign-born wrestlers were usually pushed as heels.

Dr. B.F. Roller was another top draw in 1913. A physician in real life, Roller was one of many men to lay hands on the coveted world's championship in the coming years.

One of the most intriguing characters to appear in the coming year was Chris Callender, who wrestled under the name "The Mysterious Conductor." The Conductor faced a number of top stars, including Demetral, whom he defeated with skill, speed, and a mastery of jiu-jitsu.

Despite numerous appearances in Louisville and other cities in the early 1900s, it's unclear from newspaper records just what kind of "conductor" Callender portrayed in the ring or whether the mysterious one wore a mask. We can safely conclude, however, that Callender was on the forefront of wrestlers who would create larger than life images for themselves, paving the way for the masked wrestlers and mystery characters that followed.

In late January of 1913, a newcomer arrived from Wisconsin who would really shake things up. His name Robert Friedrich, but until his arrival in Louisville, he wrestled under the name Bob Fredericks. Had he arrived a week earlier than he did, it might have remained Bob Fredericks. Louisville would give him a new name that would change the world of professional wrestling forever.

THE STRANGLER

In the late 90s, Louisville's Ohio Valley Wrestling became known for churning out some of the biggest names in professional wrestling. John Cena, Brock Lesnar, Randy Orton, Big Show, and CM Punk all spent time in Louisville honing their craft on the way to multiple world titles. Prior to the OVW days, it was Jeff Jarrett's wrestling promotion that brought future champions Stone Cold Steve Austin, The Rock, Kane, and The Undertaker through town on their way to the top. Even Hulk Hogan made regular Tuesday night visits to Louisville Gardens prior to becoming a star in New York. Long before any of these future stars graced the River City, another legend was born on the stage at the Buckingham Theater.

Born in Port Edwards, Wisconsin on June 30, 1890, Robert Friedrich was a natural athlete who excelled in all sports, including baseball. One of many legends spun about the future world champ involves a baseball road trip when the team found itself short of the funds needed to travel home. Friedrich accepted a challenge from a local wrestler, hoping to win enough prize money to get the team home. Friedrich won the match, and Friedrich suddenly found himself on a new career path.

Friedrich took to the road using an Americanized version of his name. Bob Fredericks became a good draw across the Midwest, but when he arrived in the Kentucky territory in early 1913, he ran into a problem: Barton and Allen already had a Bob Fredericks wrestling for him.

According to wrestling historian Steve Yohe, Allen and Barton had invited the real Fredericks to Louisville. When Fredericks failed to respond to the invitation, it created a small problem, as Allen and Barton had already announced that Bob Fredericks was coming. When the date arrived and Fredericks did not show, Barton and Allen had to send someone out as Bob Fredericks - an easy solution in the days before mass media. The promoters slapped the moniker on another wrestler named Bob Managoff, who impressed the Louisville fans in a hard fought loss to the Terrible Greek, William Demetral.

A week later the real Bob Fredericks arrived, and the promoters found themselves in a predicament. They already had introduced Managoff as Fredericks. While there was no television at the time, there were enough regulars in the crowd that would know a switch had been made if the real Fredericks went out using Managoff's new name.

It's unclear who actually gave the Bob Fredericks his new name. In later years Heywood Allen, William Barton, and even Bob Managoff would all claim responsibility. It's hardly surprising they would all take credit, since the Strangler would soon become the number one name in professional wrestling across the country.

While credit for the name change is in dispute, the origin of Fredericks' new name is not. Since Fredericks was from Wisconsin, the decision was made to name him after another famous grappler from the state, Evan "The Strangler" Lewis. Thus on January 24, 1913, Bob Fredericks entered the ring for the first time under the moniker Ed "Strangler" Lewis.

Only 21 years of age, standing six foot one and 208 pounds, Lewis made a huge impression on the Louisville crowd, winning his first match in the Bluegrass over Bob (Managoff) Fredericks in convincing fashion. A scary moment in the match had the two grapplers toppling over the edge of the Buckingham Theater stage into the orchestra pit, with Lewis ending up on bottom. But both men were able to continue the match, and Lewis made quick work of Fredericks with his soon to be famous stranglehold.

Strangler Lewis was an instant hit with the fans, packing houses in Louisville and Lexington, where Lewis decided to make a home for himself while in the Bluegrass.

Various accounts have Lewis either attending class or teaching at the venerable University of Kentucky while his wrestling career took off.

In March of 1913, Lewis competed in Lexington in a match that had more in common with late twentieth century sports entertainment than early twentieth century wrestling. Lewis faced off with the Polish strongman Stanislaus Zybszko. The match had a one hour time limit, and the stipulations stated that if Zbyszko could not win two of three falls in that hour, he would forfeit his winnings at the gate.

Zybszko would score one pin fall, but Lewis would win the match, denying Zbyszko a second fall by slipping out of the ring and running from his opponent. Lewis's tactics foreshadowed those of the great heels that would follow in decades to come, and his actions were met with hostility by the Lexington crowd. However, referee Heywood Allen declared that Lewis's actions were legal and he was within his rights.

In April Lewis defeated Demetral in straight falls, taking out the feared grappler with his stranglehold. It was Lewis's biggest victory yet, but Demetral would even the score a month later. Lewis was "weakened" for the second contest by a bout of indigestion, and the Terrible Greek took full advantage.

On September 29 in Lexington, Lewis and Demetral met for the third time. Lewis was now the American Heavyweight Champion by virtue of a victory over Dr. B.F. Roller on September 18. The two grapplers came at each other hard and rough, drawing repeated warnings from the referee to fight fair and stay within the rules. Lewis and Demetral were too hot blooded to listen. After fifty-five minutes referee (and fellow wrestler) Jack Stone awarded the first fall to Lewis for Demetral's rough tactics. Demetral persisted in using Lewis's own stranglehold, a hold barred for that match, and the two wrestlers retired for their mandatory rest after the fall was declared for Lewis.

Lewis and Demetral would never return to the ring. The bad blood came to a boil, harsh words were exchanged, and the two men came to blows in the dressing area. Lewis and Demetral were arrested, and the match was called off.

The following day, Lexington Mayor J. E. Cassidy shocked the community when he banned all wrestling matches from Lexington. "These matches have been pulled off here without getting permission of anyone," said Cassidy, "but from what I hear regarding them they should not have been allowed. Broken ribs, stranglehold, eyes gouged out, and the toe-hold, which I am told makes these monsters of bone, flesh, and muscle cry like little children, does not sound very respectable to me."

Lewis and Demetral were each fined fifteen dollars for disorderly conduct. In spite of the fines and the prohibition, Lexington promoter Jerry Wall declared his intention to hold another match between the two within ten days. Wall insisted there were no laws in Kentucky banning wrestling, and that the opera house had a license to hold such exhibitions.

In the days that followed, a number of Lexington citizens spoke out, asking the mayor to reconsider his ban. Cassidy would not overturn the ban himself, but decided to put the matter to the Board of City Commissioners. The commissioners voted unanimously to lift the ban, and wrestling resumed in Lexington.

On October 21, 1913, Lewis and Demetral met at the Lexington Opera House. Lewis was injured during the match when he fell off the stage into the orchestra pit, and Demetral was able to claim the victory and steal Lewis's title.

Six months later in April of 1914 Strangler and Demetral met again in Lexington. After both men scored a pin fall, the match was once again called off when

Strangler and the Greek began slapping each other, ending the fight in another melee.

Promoters and wrestlers in the barnstorming days of Pennell and Flynn knew there was often more money in a re-match than the initial conflict. They were not opposed to letting matches end with no decision because there was more money to be made in a second match. Given the increasingly violent nature of their series and the lack of a clean finale to settle the score, it is unlikely Lewis and Demetral were playing for another paycheck. Theirs was not a rivalry created to sell tickets. The two legitimately hated each other.

Ed Lewis kept his home in Lexington for some time, but he would eventually move on to bigger cities and bigger conquests. When World War I broke out, Lewis enlisted in the army like many in his profession. It was during his time in the army that he became close to Billy Sandow, whom Strangler may have met in early 1913 when Sandow came to town with Yussif Hussane. Sandow and Lewis served their country teaching hand to hand fighting techniques to America's soldiers. Following the war, Sandow would act as Lewis's manager, and the two men, along with promoter Toots Mondt, would change the face of professional wrestling forever.

History has proven time and time again that the right name can make all the difference to a career. Although they were talented men with undeniable skill and charisma, it's unlikely that Rodney Anoa'i, Phil Brooks, Mark Callan, and Paul Levesque would ever have been as big if they had not been rechristened Yokozuna, CM Punk, The Undertaker, and Triple H. And can anyone imagine that Terrymania would have been even a fraction of the phenomenon that Hulkamania became?

Everyone was afraid of the Strangler, just as they were afraid of Yokozuna. But how often does one feel intimidated by a man named Bob? Or Terry? Or Rodney?

Bob Fredericks might have become a great and legendary name had he arrived in Louisville a week or soon earlier. He, like those named above, had all the talent and charisma to be a legend, but Bob Fredericks doesn't carry the aura or the mystique of Ed "Strangler" Lewis. Bob Fredericks needed the Strangler name.

Wrestling needed Ed "Strangler" Lewis. His rise to fame came at a crucial time in the development of the business. Frank Gotch retired as champion, refusing to drop the belt and pass the proverbial torch to anyone, leaving the industry without a headliner. In the coming years, Lewis would be one of the names to reestablish the business and paving the way for generations to come. Regardless which of the parties involved bestowed a new name on Bob Fredericks, it was a decision that made all the difference for the man and the business that made him famous.

THE CHAMPS WERE HERE

Ed "Strangler" Lewis was one of the biggest wrestlers to ever launch his career from Louisville. He was a larger than life figure whose star transcended the world of sports. Lewis spent a good deal of time in the company of movie stars and sports heroes. He even counted legendary boxer Joe Louis as one of his closest friends.

But Lewis isn't the whole story of the pioneer days in Louisville. Over the next several years a parade of champions would pass through town giving the fans in Louisville a front row seat to the world title picture.

In early 1914 a new promoter named George Beuchel began hosting wrestling at a new venue, the Jefferson County Armory. The Armory offered several advantages over the opera house, not the least of which was the opportunity to surround an actual ring with seats and put the action in the center of the room.

The move was not without controversy, and a number of court hearings were held from to discuss the legality of hosting events at the Armory and whether the fee paid to the brigade stationed at the Armory was sufficient. In the end the promoters won out, and wrestling moved to the building it would call home for the next eighty years. The building, later dubbed "the Madison Square Garden of the South," would eventually lose its military moniker in exchange for its more famous and lasting name: Louisville Gardens.

In February of 1914, Beuchel offered up the biggest card yet seen in Louisville featuring two huge matches: Wladek Zbyszko vs. John Friborg and Charley Cutler vs. Mamutoff.

Unlike Ed Lewis, Wladek Zbyszko and Charley Cutler were already known names before they reached Louisville. Zbyszko, a Polish strongman, was the European champion who would test his mettle against the Swedish champion Friborg. Friborg had put together an impressive three year run, including a win over the Mysterious Conductor, but it was Zbyszko who, along with his brother Stanislaus, left 96 mauled and mangled men in his wake during a recent tournament to determine the European championship - a title Wladek won when his brother stepped aside, allowing Young Zbyszko to claim the European title.

Cutler was an even bigger name, a six foot three, 220 pound grappler from Chicago with a reputation as one of the best in the business. For the time, Cutler was one of the biggest men in the business, but he would face a much larger foe in the six foot seven, 320 pound Russian giant. Mamutoff was reported to be one of the Czar's personal guards, and he made a huge impression walking the streets of Louisville in his military uniform. He lacked the experience and skill of Cutler, but the question remained whether skill alone could defeat a giant.

The heavyweights did not disappoint in their Louisville debut. Zbyszko was too powerful for Friborg and dispatched the Swedish champion in straight falls. Zbyszko's strength was on full display as he powered out of a number of holds during the match. Cutler had a tougher time with the Russian giant, whose strength kept the smaller man on the defensive, but it was Cutler's signature move, the toe hold, that gave him the edge. Once the toe hold was locked in, the giant was defenseless, and Cutler won in straight falls.

On February 18 two more huge names squared off at the Armory when Wladek's big brother Stanislaus arrived to face Dr. B.F. Roller. The match had world title implications thanks to the retirement of Frank Gotch. Whoever won the battle at the Armory would most likely be recognized as the new world's champion. Dr. Roller took the offensive early in the match, taking the fight to Zbyszko, but the Pole seized the upper hand and surprised his opponent by using the toe hold. After Roller conceded the first fall, Zbyszko gave Roller's foot another hard twist before letting go. The first fall lasted more than an hour, but the second only twenty minutes. Zbyszko had laid his claim to the world's title.

Unfortunately for Stanislaus, he did not lay claim to the belt. Frank Gotch arranged for a title bout between Fred Beell and Americus in March. Americus took the victory and Gotch's belt.

Zbyszko next squared off with Ed "Strangler" Lewis in Lexington. It was a loss for the would-be champ, but not because of Lewis's skill in the ring. Under the terms of the match, if Zbyszko failed to throw Lewis in an hour, he would forfeit all his winnings. Lewis stayed on the run throughout the match, jumping in and out of the ring, taking the victory in heel-like fashion.

The big climax to the Armory wrestling season featured Yussif Hussane and Stanislaus Zbyszko. Hussane won the right to challenge Zbyszko by virtue of a victory over Dr. Roller at the Armory, and a match was arranged between Hussane and Zbyszko the night of the Kentucky Derby. The match took on greater significance when Zbyszko took the world title from Americus on May 7 in Kansas City.

Strangely enough, the result of the match doesn't appear in *The Courier-Journal* archives, but given the history of the world title it's clear Zbyszko walked away from Louisville with the victory and the title.

Zbyszko moved on after the Derby show, but Hussane, Demetral, and Cutler remained a part of the Louisville scene through the rest of the year. George Beuchel put on some outdoor matches during the summer months, and Allen and Barton continued to put on exhibitions at the Buck.

One of the odder tales to come out of 1915 involved a European wrestler named Isando Bey. Beuchel booked Bey for a match against former champion Americus, but the match nearly didn't happen because of

Bey's inability to speak English. Traveling alone, with some letters written in English from his manager, Bey accidentally boarded the wrong train in Cincinnati on his way to Louisville. By a stroke of luck, the "wrong" train, the Baltimore and Ohio, happened to be headed to Louisville, and Bey arrived in time to make the match. He lost in straight falls.

In early 1915 Yussif Hussane thrust himself back into the title picture with victories over Americus and Karl Lemle at the Armory. Hussane's victories put him on a collision course with the new world heavyweight champion Charley Cutler. Beuchel booked Hussane and Cutler for the 1915 Derby Eve show, starting a tradition of Derby week fight shows that would last for several decades. Their match ended in a draw after three hours and thirty-seven hard fought minutes.

William Barton, meanwhile, scored a major coup at the Buck when he booked one of the top young talents in the country, Joe Stecher. Born in Dodge, Kansas, Stecher took the wrestling world by storm when, at age 16, he stepped out of a crowd and nearly defeated the great Dr. B.F. Roller. Stecher had extremely strong legs, and used them to great effect with his signature finishing hold, the body scissors.

Stecher appeared at the Buck on March 12, 1915, in a bout against Hassan Ali. Ali was clearly not in Stecher's class, and Stecher won in straight falls - five minutes and two minutes - using his dreaded scissor hold.

On July 15, 1915, Stecher shocked the world when he scored two falls in seventeen minutes to defeat Charley Cutler for the world heavyweight championship. When Stecher returned to Louisville in 1916, he made his debut at the Armory with the title around his waist. It took only eight minutes and twenty seconds to defeat Italian John Perelli with the body scissors.

The 1916 Derby Eve show, held the night before the Kentucky Derby, featured a championship match between Stecher and Yussif Hussane for the world title. Stecher had already defeated Hussane twice. The first time was in Stecher's hometown, when Hussane was traveling with wrestler/promoter Farmer Burns. Stecher was the volunteer from the crowd who took on Hussane, and when Stecher slapped his body scissors on Hussane, Hussane got himself disqualified for biting Stecher's leg. Hussane lost the second in only nine minutes in a bout that would cement Stecher's legend as a "mat wonder."

Hussane left everything he had on the mat that night in front of 6000 people, but Stecher left no doubt regarding his superiority. The body scissors did their worst, and Stecher retained his title over the Louisville favorite.

The 1917 Derby Eve show featured a showdown between Wladek Zbyszko and John Olin, who had come close to unseating Stecher during a December 1916 match. Like the match between Wladek's brother and Dr. Roller two years prior, the match had world championship implications. A month prior to the match, Joe Stecher refusing to re-enter the ring during a title match with Earl Caddock in Omaha, Nebraska. Stecher dropped the title to Caddock. Caddock signed up to serve his country after the US entered World War I, and both Zbyszko and Olin considered the title up for grabs.

Zbyszko defeated Olin in a back and forth match that thrilled the fans in attendance, but Zbyszko did not get his hands on the title. The title picture would remain cloudy and in dispute until 1920, when Stecher ended three years of controversy by defeating Caddock.

Less than a decade after Frank Gotch left the business without a single superstar, four new faces emerged to carry the business forward. Joe Stecher, Wladek Zbyszko, Earl Caddock, and Ed "Strangler" Lewis were fast becoming household names as the country went to war. When the war came to a close, they would be at the forefront of what many consider the first golden age of wrestling.

GOLD DUST

Wrestling season did not return in early 1918 as it had the previous four years. The United States was now embroiled in World War I, and many of the young men who thrilled audiences across the country with their wrestling skills were already in the service of their country. More and more wrestlers would find themselves drafted into service before the year was out, and lengthy promotions were no longer practical. But that didn't stop promoter George Buechel from putting two mammoth Derby Eve matches.

On April 9, 1918, *The Courier-Journal* announced a match for the world championship would be held on Derby Eve at the Kentucky State Fairgrounds. Two Louisville favorites would do battle: Wladek Zbyszko from Poland, and Kentucky's own Ed "Strangler" Lewis. The press coverage hyped the match as a must-see event. The two men had recently battled at Madison Square Garden in New York before a crowd of 25,000. The fairgrounds were not equipped for a crowd that size, but as many as 15,000 would find seating available.

Now represented by manager Billy Sandow, Strangler was advertised as "The Kentucky Whirlwind," and his strangle hold was hyped as being a formidable weapon. Sandow created a whole new back story for the Strangler, selling him as a former instructor from the University of Kentucky, a far cry from the paper mills and warehouses where the real Robert Friedrich once earned a living. Zbyszko, on the other hand, was a power wrestler with the strength to overcome and escape almost any hold. It was a dream match by any standard.

Anticipation for the match grew as the Derby drew closer. *The Courier-Journal* covered a tune-up match for the Strangler against Joe Stecher, in which Strangler was able to break Stecher's favorite move, the scissor hold.

Meanwhile, Zbyszko's representative Jack Curley began to campaign for Lewis's stranglehold to be banned.

Lewis won the match by decision, after the two wrestlers had each won a fall. Asked to comment on the match, referee Packey McFarland wrote a commentary for *The Courier-Journal* expressing his belief the match was on the up and up.

"I believe the wrestling match last Friday night at the Horse Show Pavillion [at the State Fairgrounds] was honestly contested," he wrote. "There probably was some exhibition stuff sprinkled around in the performance, but on the whole I believe both men were trying their best to throw each other."

A year later, Zbyszko returned for the 1919 Derby Eve show. This time, the Pole would do battle with Joe Stecher. Both men came into the match having served their country in World War I. Stecher represented the Navy, and Zbyszko the Army. (Zbyszko was from Poland, but had become a naturalized citizen.) Both men were in top form, and Zbyszko had avenged the previous year's loss by scoring two victories over Strangler Lewis during the previous year.

The 1919 Derby Eve show took place at the Armory, and H. E. Mechling, director of the local YMCA, was selected to be the referee. The action was hard and fast, but the outcome was not quickly settled. It took an hour and 48 minutes for Stecher to seal the victory over Zbyszko and claim the heavyweight championship of the world.

In those days, every territory in the country had a heavyweight champion of the world. There was no unified body governing the sport, and every promoter had his own world champion. In truth, Stecher was widely regarded as one of the top claimants to the world title, but that title would remain in dispute until January 30, 1920, when Stecher defeated Earl Caddock at Madison Square Gardens in New York City to become the undisputed champion in what many believe to be the last true legitimate wrestling match in the sport's history.

Stecher returned to Louisville in April of 1920. After defeating Strangler Lewis in Lexington, Stecher met Yussif Hussane at the Derby Eve show. The Strangler was also on the card, wrestling Raymond Cazeau, a war hero from France. Both Stecher and Lewis were victorious that evening.

Two years later, Lewis would once again be the center of controversy when Edward Heverin of Louisville's Southern Athletic Club agreed to host a match between Strangler Lewis and a man named Carl LeBeige at the Jefferson Theater. Heverin was initially promised a match between William Demetral and one of the Zbyszko brothers, but when Zbyszko proved unavailable, he booked Lewis instead.

Heverin was not a wrestling fan and only agreed to give wrestling a chance when he saw that his patrons were interested in the sport. When he discovered that LeBeige was in fact John Olin, a former world champion, he smelled a rat.

It isn't clear what happened during the match to anger Heverin, but the Athletic Club president was so upset, he issued a statement in the paper on March 12, 1922, apologizing for the match and declaring it to be the last wrestling match his club would ever promote. "Our first and only venture in the wrestling game has convinced us that we are not wrestling promoters, and it is our intention to adhere strictly to boxing in the future," he wrote.

By the time Heverin had his encounter with the Strangler, he and Sandow had forged a working relationship with Toots Mondt, a wrestler turned promoter from New York. Known as the Gold Dust Trio, the three were at the forefront of the movement to transform wrestling into the spectacle we now know today. Not only were they instrumental in the movement to worked matches, Mondt was the first to promote wrestling as a packaged show, creating the model the territories that would soon proliferate the continent. Instead of one time matches being promoted here and there, promoters formed stables of wrestlers who would work one area and put on a series of shows. Wrestlers could then be swapped in and out of those stables from time to time to keep things fresh, creating new rivalries and story lines.

The change to a more entertaining form of wrestling was as much about survival as it was profit. When World War I ended, wrestling was no longer the only game in town. Baseball was on the rise, and football was not far behind. Promoters knew that the days of marathon matches lasting into the wee hours of the morning were over. People wanted faster matches with exciting moves and dramatic finishes. They wanted heroes and villains. They wanted entertainment. The veil of secrecy in the wrestling business (or kayfabe, as the wrestlers called it) held fast for nearly seven more decades, but from wrestling's earliest days, even the 1880s, the vast majority of matches were in fact worked.

To the fans, hippodroming was a bad word. To promoters it was best for business.

That's not to say there were not legitimate matches from time to time. In the days before the National Wrestling Alliance, promoters were notoriously distrustful of one another, and with good reason. On multiple occasions, shady promoters would send a shooter or hooker into the ring against another promoter's champion in an attempt to steal the other promotion's championship belt via a shoot match - a legitimate wrestling match where one or both wrestlers use real holds in order to score a victory.

In 1931 Sandow and Lewis lost control of the world championship in such a double cross. The two feigned taking the high road long enough to get Lewis a match with the new champion, a former Olympian named Ed Don George. George entered the match with Lewis believing that it was just another work and that Lewis would do the

54

job for him. When George stepped into the ring, he was stunned when Lewis gave him an ultimatum: "Do we give the fans a great match or do we wrestle?" Knowing he could never truly out-wrestle the Strangler, George put on a great match, did the job and surrendered his belt.

One man who experienced the true power of the Strangler was John Pesek. An accomplished wrestler in his own right, Pesek was booked to lose against an aging Strangler in Pesek's hometown of Kansas City. When Lewis showed up at the arena out of shape, drunk, and very ill, Pesek sent word to Lewis's locker room. He refused to do the job for Lewis in his condition, especially in his hometown.

Six minutes into their two of three falls match, the drunk and ill Strangler pinned Pesek with ease. In between falls, Pesek sent an apology to Lewis. It was no use. "Tonight, we are wrestling," said Lewis in reply. He won the second fall in even less time.

Men like Ed "Strangler" Lewis were greatly valued by promoters because they were dangerous enough to dissuade most wrestlers from trying to pull a screw job, taking the title by force or by cheating. These matches, on the rare occasions when they happened, nearly always disappointed an audience. Either they turned into marathon snooze fests, like the 1954 match between Mildred Burke and June Byars in which Byars, acting on behalf of Burke's ex-husband Billy Wolfe, tried to forcibly take the women's title from the long time champ; or they ended quickly and violently, leaving one competitor unable to walk normally for the rest of his life.

There were few men who could truly go toe to toe with Ed "Strangler" Lewis in a legitimate contest, but the legendary hooker put the business ahead of his ego. The Gold Dust Trio led the charge to transform the sport they loved into a new form of entertainment. For better or for worse, it was men like Strangler Lewis who saved the sport from vanishing all together and inspiring the changes that would make wrestling's popularity grow across the nation, including his adopted home of Kentucky.

PIONEERS AMONG PIONEERS

In 1962 Bobo Brazil became the first African American wrestler to earn a claim to the heavyweight world championship by defeating Buddy Rogers. Brazil refused to accept the title, however, because Rogers was injured, and while Rogers' injury was later revealed to be (probably story line) fake, the NWA never officially recognized Brazil as world champion. Thirty years later, former Florida State football player Ron Simmons broke the glass ceiling Brazil only touched, becoming the first African American to hold the world championship.

Simmons' victory ended more than a century of struggle by African American wrestlers to reach the top of the industry. From the late 1800s and into the 1950s, African American wrestlers struggled to achieve the success their white contemporaries enjoyed. On rare occasions, African Americans were given matches against Asian or Mexican performers, but for the most part, they were only allowed to wrestle against other men of color.

One of the few promoters to see box office potential in African American wrestlers was Heywood Allen. In the mid 1930s Allen began including African Americans on the card at the Savoy Theater (formerly the Buckingham). It was an opportunity Louisville native and African-American Jim Mitchell needed to make his dream of becoming a professional wrestler come true.

Mitchell's wrestling dream began with a match in Indianapolis for Jack Reynolds, a fellow Louisvillian and wrestler. Years after, Mitchell claimed he rode his bike all the way to Indianapolis for the match. He wore a mask in those early years and went by the name The Black Panther, long before the controversial activist group would adopt the same name. He quickly found regular work as a curtain jerker (wrestler-speak for wrestling in the opening match of the night) for Allen at the Savoy.

The dapperly dressed young man impressed fans from the start, and it was clear the Black Panther was destined for big things. In 1934 he left town, traveling to the West Coast, where, according to Online World of Wrestling, he became the first African American to wrestle in a "big league" ring. Like most African Americans, he was forced to wrestle only other minorities when he arrived in California, but his skill and popularity eventually earned matches against top white stars like the Masked Marvel.

Back in Louisville, Allen took it upon himself to create a "Negro World Heavyweight Championship," an honor he bestowed on an African-American wrestler named Gentleman Jack Claybourne. Claybourne was an international star, having traveled to England, Australia, and Canada. *The Courier-Journal*, publicized him as one of the few men to ever "whip" Joe Louis. On July 22, 1941, he defended his championship at the outdoor Sports Arena against fellow African-American wrestler Haille Samara.

Haille Samara was actually Seelie Samara from Fort Valley, Georgia who, like so many other wrestlers, received a name tweak courtesy of Heywood Allen. Samara was billed as the former bodyguard of the emperor of Ethiopia and a native of Africa. Back story aside, Samara was an outstanding performer in the ring who, like Mitchell, became a main event performer in the US, Canada, and Australia.

Claybourne defeated Samara on July 22, but two weeks later, Samara took the crown from Claybourne.

Samara headlined two more outdoor matches for Allen that summer. On August 26 of that same year, he successfully defended his newly won title against the Black Panther, who returned home to a hero's welcome. Then on September 2 he defeated Jack Claybourne for the second time.

In May of 1942, Samara dropped the belt to King Kong Clayton on a packed Derby Eve card at the Armory. That same night, Bill Longson defended his title against

Sandor Szabo; Mildred Burke defeated Mae Young to keep her unbeaten streak intact; and rising star Lou Thesz (renamed Don Louis Thesz by Heywood Allen) battled Chief Little Wolf to a draw.

Not bad company for the African American stars.

Samara would re-take the title in November. He returned two years later as Seelie Samara to defend the title from Eddie Jackson.

Despite the racism that dominated their time, the early African-American wrestlers worked as babyfaces whenever they wrestled white opponents. In a time when fans believed everything was real, it was far too dangerous for an African-American to work as heels, particularly in the South. A few dastardly acts by a despised heel could turn anyone into a fan favorite no matter what their skin color. It wasn't until the 1960s when former NFL star Ernie Ladd entered the ring that an African-American was able to wrestle successfully - and safely - as a heel.

Samara, Claybourne, and Mitchell were pioneers in an era of pioneers. Claybourne, who joined the service during World War II, continued to break ground as an African American, wrestling on cards with Strangler Lewis, Montreal legend Yvon Robert, and Whipper Billy Watson. Samara continued to main event cards across the country. Before he retired, he would step in the ring with Jim Londos, Everett Marshall, and Lou Thesz.

Mitchell also found success wrestling against white competitors. His most famous battle took place in 1949 at the Olympic Auditorium in Los Angeles when Mitchell faced the infamous Gorgeous George. A tense crowd erupted in violence when George tossed Mitchell from the ring and refused to let him back in. George pushed and kicked his opponent in the face, trying to keep him from crossing back between the ropes. When George kicked Mitchell in the face, a fan leapt between the ropes and went after George. A riot broke out, and several fans were injured - including one fan who took a knife in the shoulder.

Mitchell spent a lot of time in southern California, but like many men of the era he wrestled all around the world, collecting souvenirs everywhere he went. Mitchell was fond of smoking pipes, and when he returned in 1954 for the annual police benefit show, Mitchell told a reporter for *The Courier-Journal* he had over 4,000 in his collection.

Mitchell returned to Louisville again in 1954, where he was welcomed with open arms by the other Allen Club alumni. While segregation divided the city outside the Armory, Mitchell was treated as an equal back stage, receiving warm hugs and welcomes in the locker room from his opponent and others. Two years after the police show, Bobo Brazil followed in Mitchell's footsteps, wrestling in Louisville against local hero Stu Gibson.

Bobo Brazil is often referred to as the Jackie Robinson of wrestling, the man who shattered the color barrier in professional wrestling. But Brazil's path to the top was well-paved by the legendary African American grapplers who dared to dream they could one day be main event stars. By the 1970s performers like Rocky Johnson competed on an equal playing field with Jerry Lawler and the other Memphis talent at the Louisville Gardens, the same arena where Samara, Claybourne, and the Black Panther paved the way for future African American stars.

Waiting in the wings for his father to finish those matches with Lawler was Rocky's son Dwayne. Years later, Dwayne would get his chance to wrestle in Louisville Gardens for the Memphis promotion. He would go on to become one of the biggest stars in wrestling history.

William Muldoon, the Solid Man of Sport.

(Reproduced from the original held by the Department of Special Collections of the Hesburgh Libraries of the University of Notre Dame.)

The Savoy Theater, formerly the Buckingham Theater, where Ed "Strangler" Lewis was born in 1913. Photo circa 1941.

(Item no. ULPA R_05819_n in the Royal Photo Company Collection, University of Louisville Photographic Archives.)

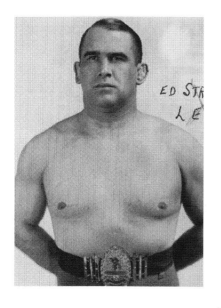

Ed "Strangler" Lewis.
(Reproduced from the original
held by the Department of
Special Collections of the
Hesburgh Libraries of the
University of Notre Dame.)

"Black Panther" Jim Mitchell.
(Reproduced from the
original held by the
Department of Special
Collections of the Hesburgh
Libraries of the University of
Notre Dame.)

Masked wrestlers and angels were all the rage in 1940. A pair of ads for the Allen Athletic Club from that year.

The perks of being promoter: putting your photo on top of Lou Thesz in your weekly ad. From 1941.

The Legendary Mae Young. (Reproduced from the original held by the Department of Special Collections of the Hesburgh Libraries of the University of Notre Dame.)

Cowboy Bill Longson, aka Masked Superman II.

(Reproduced from the original held by the Department of Special Collections of the Hesburgh Libraries of the University of Notre Dame.)

Inside the Armory (Louisville Gardens) circa 1950.
(Item no. ULPA R_11750_n in the Royal Photo Company
Collection, University of Louisville Photographic Archives.)

Program for the 1953 Police Benefit Show, featuring Baron Leone.

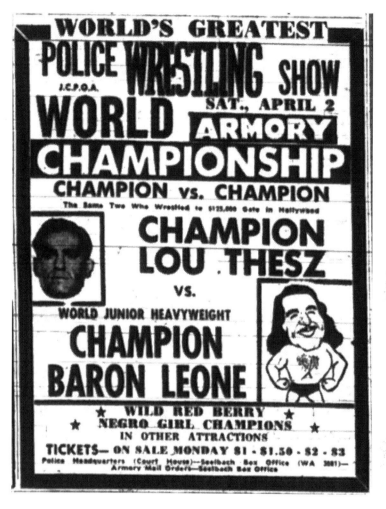

Ad for the 1955 rematch between Thesz and Leone in Louisville.

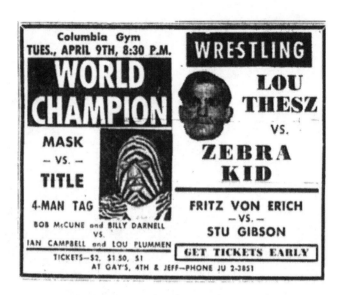

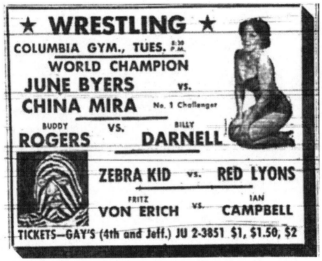

Two of the last ads for the Allen Athletic Club in 1957 before
Francis McDonough's death.

PART TWO
THE ALLEN ATHLETIC CLUB

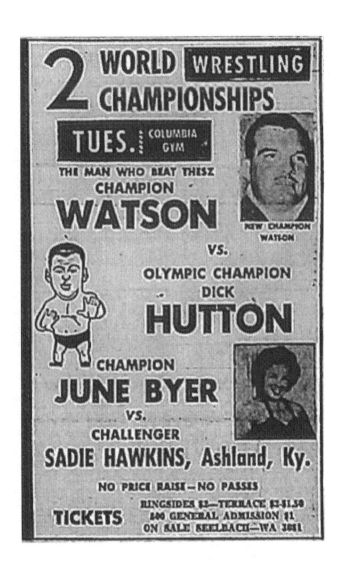

HEYWOOD ALLEN

In the early 1920s, change was in the air in downtown Louisville. The Buckingham Theater became the Savoy Theater, and the wrestling business that once thrived at the Buck went into a decline. The Derby Eve shows that featured some of the greatest legends of the early twentieth century vanished, and the Tuesday tradition at the opera house disappeared with it.

In the late 1920s, wrestling moved into the Gayety Theater for weekly Wednesday evening shows. In the early 1930s, the Savoy (Theater) Athletic Club and Blake Amusements both promoted wrestling shows in town and around Derby time, but the glory days of packed houses at the Buck were long gone.

Wrestling also had a new competition thanks to the growing popularity of boxing and the growing influence of the local boxing promotions. Kentucky Athletic Commissioner Johnson S. Mattingly had a close relationship with the Louisville boxing promoters, and boxing began to fill the void left by wrestling, including the Derby Eve Show. In spite of these setbacks, wrestling's brightest days were still ahead in Louisville. A man who began his career in the ring as an official for William Barton had dreams of establishing his city as a premiere destination for wrestling's brightest stars.

If anyone deserves credit for establishing Louisville's identity as a wrestling city, it's Heywood Allen. "Kentucky's Greatest Showman," as The Courier-Journal described him, was a "dapper little man with a stentorian voice and the heart of a lion." In his younger years, Allen worked as a "circus wrecker." When the major circuses traveled from town to town, they would occasionally run up against direct competition from some smaller shows. Circus wreckers like Allen were hired to bring in some strong arms and "wreck" the smaller circus, forcing them to pack up and leave town so the larger show wouldn't suffer from the competition.

It's likely Allen was first exposed to the sport through his association with the circus. Professional wrestling remained a staple of the circus side attractions well into the twentieth century, and the At Shows with their colorful characters and daredevil high fliers were the true forerunners of what we now call sports entertainment.

Allen left the dubious world of circus wreckers for the more respectable world of wrestling in the early 1900s. Allen found work as a referee and called matches for all the legends - Lewis, Stecher, Cutler, Zbyszko, Hussane, Demetral. He called both wrestling and boxing matches and promoted both equally in the 1910s and 1920s. When Barton stepped out of the picture it was Allen who sought to restore wrestling to its former glory. Allen promoted fights at the Savoy Theater for short-lived promotions like the Savoy Athletic Club and Blake Amusement Company. Then in 1935 Allen put his name on the marquee by establishing his own wrestling promotion, the Allen Athletic Club of Louisville.

On June 3, 1935, the Allen Athletic Club held its inaugural wrestling program at the Swiss Park Open Air Arena, which was located between Preston and Lynn Streets near downtown Louisville. A crowd of 1000, including 882 paid admissions, was on hand that evening generating a total gate of $485.44. Heywood Allen, Jr., was on hand to officiate the main event in which Indiana University wrestling coach and "junior middleweight" champion Billy Thom retained his title against Alexander "Cyclone" Burns in a re-match from that year's Derby Eve show. The card featured mostly local talent, including a "Louisville vs. Kentucky" match that ended in a draw, but for Allen this was only the beginning. Allen made sure the crowd knew the parking at the arena was free and that two policemen "who expect no tips" would be on hand to keep watch over the fans' vehicles.

Allen held weekly wrestling shows on Tuesday nights at the Columbia Gym. Located on 4th Street just south of York, the Columbia Gym would one day be the place where young Cassius Clay, who became Muhammad Ali, started training to become a boxer. Allen had visions of seeing the top names in the sport return to Louisville, but he knew that would not happen over night. He used a number of solid local talents to fill out his shows in the early days and beyond.

Cecil "Blacksmith" Pedigo was one of the locals who became a fan favorite. Born in Glasgow, Kentucky in 1902, Pedigo's career was nearly cut short by a bad back injury suffered during the 1920s. Against all odds, Pedigo came back from the injury. He wrestled in Ohio and Michigan as well as the Bluegrass State. Years later, Pedigo's name would come up frequently in the Gardens, when old timers would tell the young fans, "None of these guys were as tough as the old guys like Blacksmith Pedigo."

"Kid Scotty" Williams was another local and a long time Allen associate. He was part of the inner circle known as "that old gang of Allen's," and he worked both as a wrestler and a referee. He remained with Allen through his retirement in 1947.

Perhaps the most infamous of the early Allen regulars was the heel "Gorilla" Grubmeyer. Billed from New Jersey, Charles Eastman was in fact a native of Chicago who earned the moniker "Gorilla" thanks to his naturally unpleasant face. Grubmeyer, who also wrestled as "Frankenstein" is best known not for his in-ring work, but a tragic event outside the ring. On May 20, 1944, he murdered his wife Geraldine in their Michigan City, Indiana home before killing himself, leaving a 15 month old infant behind. The story was all but forgotten until 2007, when Chris Benoit followed in Grubmeyer's bloody footsteps, killing his family and then himself.

Allen's hopes of attracting bigger names eventually paid off. The legendary Ray Steele, a former carnival wrestler and legitimate hooker, became a regular in the early 1940s. Steele not only held a world title for a year but proved his toughness in winning a mixed boxing-wrestling match against Kingfish Levinsky in only 35 seconds. Other notables from the 1930s and 40s include CWF founder Cowboy Clarence Luttrell, the Dusek Brothers, the Savoldi brothers, "The Nebraska Tigerman" John Pesek, Yvon Robert, Ray Eckert, Bobby Managoff, Jr., Tex Riley, Dorve Roche, Herb Welch, and Herb's brother Roy, who would one day run the Memphis territory that Jerry Jarrett expanded into Louisville.

Allen's efforts saw results at the box office, but he frequently clashed with the Kentucky Athletic Commission and struggled to regain the respect his sport once had. In 1938 he lashed out at Kentucky Athletic Commissioner Johnson S. Mattingly, claiming that the reason boxing was always featured at the Armory on Derby Eve was because of a sweetheart deal Mattingly made with the Ziegler Athletic Club, who promoted boxing in Louisville. Mattingly denied the charges vehemently, but Allen insisted he had a copy of the signed agreement in his office.

Surprisingly, Allen was able to book the Armory in 1939 for Derby Eve. Jim Londos returned to Louisville for a match against Joe Savoldi on May 5, 1939. The match had a somewhat controversial ending, with Heywood Allen, Jr., awarding the third fall to Londos after Londos used an illegal move off the ropes to pin Savoldi. But as another promoter would famously say decades later, controversy creates cash, and Allen cashed in to the tune of $3500 that night, a huge increase from his initial gate in 1935.

Allen rode the success of the 1939 Derby Eve show into the 1940s. In a time when many wrestling promotions struggled to keep an audience, the Allen Athletic Club would thrive. Louisville would ride out World War II on the backs of freaks and masked marvels before bearing witness to the dawn of a new golden age in wrestling.

Heywood Allen was riding high in the spring of 1941. A huge crowd packed out the Armory for a star-studded show in February, and fans continued to fill the Columbia Gym week after week. Allen had momentum, and he hoped to capitalize on that momentum with an even bigger show featuring Bronko Nagurski, a former member of the Chicago Bears who had recently won the world championship. After featuring newly crowned world champion Nagurski in a match at the Gym, he announced an elimination tournament to choose a worthy challenger to the champion at the 1941 Derby Eve show.

A number of big names came into town to fight at the Columbia Gym, including Everett Marshall, Dorve Roche, Jim McMillen, Emil Dusek, and Joe Dusek, "The man all Louisville hates, a public enemy if there ever was one!"

The biggest draw in the tournament, however, was the man Allen billed as Don Louis Thesz. Lou Thesz, as he was known to the rest of the world, was not yet the larger than life, bigger than any promotion super star he would become after World War II, but he was well on his way. Thesz began his Louisville record by going on a tear, winning week after week and surviving challenge after challenge.

Fans knew they were headed for a big something special when Thesz and Everett Marshall finally met. Marshall was the bigger name to the Louisville fans, having rolled off 26 victories with no defeats the previous year. Louisville fans were looking forward to an explosive finale, and Allen was looking forward to a big payoff.

Allen was sure that a title bout between tournament champion and Nagurski would be enough to secure the Derby Eve date at the Armory. Unfortunately for Allen, state athletic commissioner Johnson S. Mattingly had other plans. Before Allen could make his pitch, Mattingly had booked the Armory on Derby right out from under him. Mattingly and Harry Wolff, president of the Sportsmen's Boxing Club, had their own show already in the works featuring a main event between Sammy Angott and Canadian lightweight champion Dave Castilloux.

Allen remained diplomatic at first, asking Mattingly to allow him to book the Armory on Thursday night, May 1, the night before the Derby Eve show. A wrestling show the night before the big boxing show would no doubt cut into the boxing show's pay day, and Mattingly and Wolff had no desire to see their revenues cut. Mattingly denied Allen's request, telling him he could still run his regular show on Tuesday, April 29, three days before Derby Eve and pay day for Louisville fans.

Mattingly believed the matter was settled, but he learned otherwise when he received a notice from the Louisville Fiscal Court. Allen had put in a request to book the Armory on May 1 and 2, and the Fiscal Court was giving Allen serious consideration of his request. Mattingly reiterated his stand that a wrestling show would not go on the night before the boxing show, but Allen had history and tradition on his side. The Fiscal Court ruled in Allen's favor, granting him sole control of May 1 and 2.

Allen continued his diplomatic course, insisting he would give up the Friday night show if Mattingly would allow him to run a show on May 1. But Allen made a fatal mistake in this game of chess. On April 15, the night Bronko Nagurski first came to town, he took the mic to vent his frustrations with Mattingly. Allen's comments were not recorded by The Courier-Journal, but they were enough to give Mattingly the advantage he needed. When Allen refused to recant his statements, Mattingly pounced. Tuesday night, April 22, right after the weekly show at the Columbia Gym, Mattingly informed Allen that he was out of the wrestling business.

Mattingly had Allen backed into a corner. Allen had control of the Armory on May 1 and 2, but Mattingly, as State Athletic Commissioner, pulled Allen's license. He had no choice but unconditional surrender. The day after losing his license, Allen agreed to relinquish all claims on the Armory for Derby Eve and the night before. He would run his regular Tuesday show on April 29. Mattingly, having gotten his way, reinstated Allen's license.

Allen put on a great show the night of April 29, in which Lou Thesz would battle two of the Dusek brothers, scoring a pin fall on Emil and going to a draw with Joe. Heywood Allen could only dream what the box office could have been if he had held the show in the Armory on a Friday.

Allen wasn't done reaching for the Derby brass ring, however. On Friday, May 2, Allen released his "Derby Dessert" card for Tuesday, May 6 at the Columbia Gym featuring Ray Steele and Dorve Roche. He then announced plans on May 11 to hold a late Derby Eve show at the Armory with the fight Louisville was waiting for: Lou Thesz vs. Everett Marshall.

On Friday, May 16, Allen suffered another major publicity blow when *The Courier-Journal* printed a front page story about his son. Heywood Allen, Jr., was a fugitive of justice. On November 28, of the previous year, Allen plead guilty to a charge of petit larceny for stealing a suit valued at $27.50. Allen previously was convicted in another case where he stole a wallet containing $21.25 from an M. A. Cornette* of 1130 S. Second Street.

On February 5, Criminal Court Judge Loraine Mix released Heywood, Jr., for a day to visit his mother, who was ill. Judge Mix was known for allowing prisoners the opportunity to visit sick relatives on the condition they did not drink and return the next day. Mix allowed these visits for more than four years. The program had boosted morale in the prison, and Mix had had up to 30 men released on one day passes at a time. A few had tried to run after being let out, but all were caught quickly. Unfortunately for the kind-hearted judge, and other prisoners hoping for similar passes, Heywood, Jr., left prison and went straight to the train yards. He never even stopped to see his mother.

The judge and the Allen families kept the matter quiet. Mix had made a lot of families happy with his prisoner release program, and he did not want one bad egg to spoil it for others. They kept the story out of the public for three months before a *Courier-Journal* reporter discovered the story.

Allen, Sr., did his best to dissociate himself from his wayward son, telling *The Courier-Journal*, "I have washed my hands of him long ago." The father also speculated that his son might have joined the army, having previously served in the National Guard.

The truth of the matter was a little less romantic than joining the army. Heywood, Jr., planned to relocate to Georgia, change his name, and start a new life for himself, but on February 24, he fell off a box car and severely injured himself. He checked into an Atlanta hospital under the name J. H. Wilkerson and wound up spending most of his time out of jail in a hospital in Atlanta.

When Heywood, Jr., heard about the bad publicity he had caused for Judge Mix, he knew he had to go back. He didn't want the judge or anyone else to suffer any repercussions because of his actions. He left the hospital on May 18 and made his way back to Louisville.

On Monday, May 26, Heywood, Jr., was back in jail, having turned himself in. Despite his earlier pledge to revoke a probated two year sentence that would have sent Junior to the state penitentiary, Mix welcomed the runaway back and agreed to let him serve only the remaining nine months on his original sentence. "I always knew he would come back anyway," said the judge, not at all sounding like a man who cut a deal with the boy's father. Heywood, Jr., apologized for all the grief he had caused. He vowed to serve out his sentence and return to his previous profession - working as a wrestling referee for his old man.

Mix's prisoner release program became a casualty of the scandal. Heywood, Jr., had brought the program too much negative publicity, and despite all the good he had done, Mix could not justify releasing any more prisoners.

Allen's Derby Eve Show went off on Thursday, May 22, 1941. A disappointing crowd of only 2000 endured the heat inside the Armory, where the cooling system was not quite working, to see Lou Thesz earn a title shot by defeating Everett Marshall. The following Tuesday, Thesz issued his challenge to Bronko Nagurski for the heavyweight championship. The match would take place at Allen's Sports Arena in Louisville on June 2.

A rough spring would give way to a fruitful summer, as the Allen Sports Arena would become the place to be Tuesday nights. Thesz lost to Nagurski on the first night. That same night, Allen introduced the Louisville crowd to a masked wrestler named the Monster Man. He was the second masked wrestler introduced in less than a year, and he would help the Allen Athletic Club pick up where they left off in the spring, drawing huge crowds eager to see what face lies beneath the mask.

* I was actually with Jim Cornette in the Louisville Free Public Library when we came across this story. A. Cornette is not a known relative of the promoter, but Cornette laughed at the irony. "Wouldn't be the last time a promoter stole from a Cornette," he said.

WHO WERE THOSE MASKED MEN?

As the 1940s began, the national wrestling scene was in a slump. The business once dominated by Strangler Lewis, Joe Stecher, and the Zbyszko brothers was suffering from a serious lack of star power. Too many claimants to the world title and too much in-fighting among promoters deprived the business and its fans of any true champions or heroes, making life difficult for promoters like Heywood Allen. But in the fall of 1940, the Allen Athletic Club would give the fans something better than a hero they could love: a villain they could really hate.

Eight months prior to the debut of Monster Man, a villainous masked man with a heroic sounding name appeared. His name was Masked Superman, and he burst onto the scene appropriately enough just before Halloween. Masked Superman made his mark with victories over Johnny Marrs and Gordon MacKenzie, but it was his third victory that established him as a true star.

Allen brought world champion Orville Brown came into town on November 12 to square off with Rudy Strongberg, who had earned a title shot thanks to a series of victories in the River City. But that night, the crowd came largely to see if Michele Leone - still a decade away from his record-breaking match with Lou Thesz - could unmask the notorious Superman. Masked Superman dropped the Italian star in two straight falls. It was a spectacular match, and the unstoppable masked man outshone the champion.

A week later, the crowd grew to 2000 fans when Allen brought the Swedish Angel to town. That same night Rudy Strongberg earned a shot at Masked Superman by defeating Gordon MacKenzie. Strongberg would become the fourth man to fall to Masked Superman a week later.

With every victory, the boos for Masked Superman grew louder and stronger. By mid-December, the Columbia Gym was seeing near capacity crowds hoping to witness the unmasking of the new villain. 2250 were present the night Jim Wright fell to Masked Superman, and more than 1000 were turned away. In January 1941 the crowds grew even larger, topping 2500 for the first show of the new year.

On January 21, 1941, Mike Sexton became the first man to score a pin fall on Masked Superman. Sexton would lose the next two falls and wind up another victim of the masked juggernaut. One week later, Dorve Roche had to cough up a $100 donation to the infant paralysis fund (a fund set up to fight the scourge of polio) when he failed to fulfill his promise to unmask the Superman. The audience could hear Roche's knee crack during the third fall, and those who didn't clearly heard the woman who cried out, "He's broken his leg!" Attendance that night was one shy of 2400, and $321.75 of the $1560 gate was also donated to the infant paralysis fund.

Masked Superman appeared to be unstoppable, and on February 11, 1941, he got his shot at the ultimate prize when he faced Orville Brown. The Armory would play host not only to a men's title bout, but a women's match between world champion Mildred Burke and her redneck rival Cousin Elvira Snodgrass. A record crowd of 7123 was on hand, and over 600 people who refused to stand in the balcony were given refunds.

After watching Burke defeat Snodgrass, the main event took place. Masked Superman scored the first pin fall and appeared to be on his way to claiming the world title, but all that changed during the second fall when Orville Brown managed to unmask the Superman. Masked Superman turned out to be Hans Schnable, and as Hans Schnable, he was as helpless as Superman in a room full of Kryptonite. Brown scored the second and third pins in a very anti-climactic finish.

No doubt inspired by the success of the Masked Superman, Allen introduced another masked wrestler in at Parkway Field, the home of Louisville's then professional baseball league baseball team, the Kentucky Colonels. The new villain's name was Monster Man, and he defeated Herbie Freeman in his first bout with his signature finishing move, the "Jungle Grip." Monster Man defeated George Zaharias, husband of famed women's athlete Babe Zaharias, and Ray Eckert in subsequent weeks, but his reign of terror came to an end after only four matches. Monster Man lost to Jim McMillen via a disqualification and when the mask came off it was Warren Bockwinkel - billed as Frankie Bockwinkel by Heywood Allen - beneath the hood.

On August 3, 1941, Allen advertised his next masked warrior in the Sunday paper, the Green Shadow. The weekly ad hyped the newcomer, saying, "He's terrific... women faint, men scream, children become hysterical when he turns on... persons with weak hearts... well, they better not go to see him."

The Green Shadow defeated Bobby Roberts in his first bout. A week later, he defeated two men, Louisville regular Tex Riley and former bull fighter Carlos Rodriguez, when Roy Welch failed to show for a match against Rodriguez.

The Green Shadow had the longest run of all the masked men, popping in and out of town from August of 1941 through January of 1942. Every time he came to town, Allen's Sunday ad hyped that the unmasking was at hand, but the Green Shadow successfully downed a series of challengers and kept his face covered.

Finally, on January 13, 1942, Herb Welch got the better of the Green Shadow. After dropping the first fall, Welch took the second and third, and a crowd of 2200 braced itself for the moment of truth. The Green Shadow tried to slip out, but Welch's men grabbed him and held him while Welch revealed the Green Shadow to be Eddie Malone. Eddie was in fact Pat Malone, a fearsome wrestler who trained one of the sport's most infamous animal stars,

Ginger the wrestling bear. He would also play an important role in the Jeff Jarrett promotion almost forty years later.

The same night Malone lost his mask, a fourth masked man appeared, Superman II. Like his predecessors, Superman II would go on a winning streak, knocking off Am Rascher, Ben Lowell, Ray Steele, Ivan Grandovich, and K. O. Koverly. His win streak earned him a title shot against Orville Brown, and once again, Brown would attempt to unmask a Superman at the Armory.

At the time, Brown was recognized as world champion by the National Wrestling Association and the Midwest Wrestling Association. Sandor Szabo was recognized by the Eastern Wrestling Association. Many fans were hoping that Brown would meet Szabo in a unification match, but two months before the Louisville match, Szabo lost his title claim to Cowboy Bill Longson in St. Louis, Missouri.

After a star-packed undercard that saw Chief Little Wolf defeat Joe Dusek and young Lou Thesz defeat Mike Sexton, the crowd was ready to see Brown do the honors and bring an end to Superman II.

Brown and Superman II split the first two falls. Brown took command in the third, tossing his opponent around and even out of the ring. It was then that Superman II shocked the crowd, removing his purple mask and revealing his true identity - Bill Longson, world champion as recognized by the Eastern Wrestling Association.

Longson jumped in the ring with his mask in hand, turned it into a noose and choked the champion. Referee Billy Love tried to rescue Brown, but it was too late. Brown wound up on his back, and Longson took the third fall, becoming the "undisputed" world champion.

Wrestling historian Steve Yohe is quick to point out the inconsistencies regarding the world titles, most of which were fabricated by promoters as a tool to draw in the fans. Nevertheless, Longson's unmasking proved to be a shocking finale to an exciting run for masked men in Louisville.

Longson returned on Friday, May 1 for another stellar Derby Eve show. Longson defeated Sandor Szabo two out of three falls. Mildred Burke defeated Mae Young to retain her own crown. And rising star Lou Thesz battled Chief Little Wolf to a draw. Longson would be a mainstay in Louisville in the coming years. As one of the few wrestlers who would not be called upon to serve his country during World War II, he proved to be a steady draw in an era that would be dominated by women, older wrestlers, and so-called freaks.

WORLD WAR II

Thanks to Lou Thesz, Superman II, and other emerging stars, business was on an upswing as the United States entered World War II, but by the time Superman II was unmasked at the Armory, many of the young grapplers who had helped to draw people back to the Gym were being called into the service.

Angelo Savoldi signed up with the Navy. Joe Millich, whose Jewish ancestry became a selling point after Germany declared war in the Jews, was called into service on a week he was scheduled to wrestle. Even Lou Thesz, whose knee injury should have kept him out of the service, got the call up from Uncle Sam thanks to a bitter ex-wife and her politically well-connected family. Talk about the fury of a woman scorned!

The wrestling business would see a downturn during the second World War, but it would not be as steep as the one it experienced during the first World War. The public would still get its fill of the sport thanks primarily to the freaks, the ladies, and the old guys too broken down to be fit for service.

Bill Longson was one of the few top stars who did not find himself in uniform. A native of Salt Lake City, Utah, Longson suffered a broken back at the hands of Man Mountain Dean in 1939. He recovered from the injury and won a return match with Dean, but the injury would keep Longson from being called into service by Uncle Sam.

As a result of his injury, Longson held the world championship throughout most of the war years and even after. A few wrestlers managed to take the title from him in that stretch, including Ray Steele, Sandor Szabo, Yvon Robert, and Bobby Managoff, but the title kept coming back to Longson, who lost the belt for the final time in Indianapolis against his arch-rival Lou Thesz in 1948.

Longson spent many Tuesday nights in Louisville before and after the war, defending his title against the likes of Ray Eckert, Rolland Kirchmeyer, Dorve Roche, and Warren Bockwinkel. He also dropped 2 out of 3 falls, the second via disqualification, to Ed "Strangler" Lewis in Louisville during one of his visits without the title.

Longson would make appearances in Louisville well into the 1950s, headlining Heywood Allen's final night as promoter and numerous Derby Eve shows. He successfully defended his title in 1947 against Lou Thesz shortly before Thesz began his eight year reign at the top of the business.

Longson was a steady draw during the war years in Louisville and beyond, a hated heel who could always draw heat. But like so many promoters across the country, Allen realized he needed more than one major star to put butts in the seats. It was the perfect opportunity for a group of wrestlers known as the freaks to make their mark.

One of the first such "freaks" to make his way to Louisville was the Texas giant known as Hippo Wiggins. Hippo appeared at the Sports Arena on August 26 and was billed at 6'6" and 390 pounds. To honor his arrival, anyone weighing in the neighborhood of 300 pounds or more was given free admission as Hippo's guests.

A week later, Hippo was billed at 413 pounds when he returned to face Herr Fredric von Schacht. Either Allen decided to exaggerate Hippo's astronomical girth, or Louisville's reputation as a food city stretches back long before the days of the Louisville Originals.

In the fall of 1941, Allen brought an even bigger star to town. Maurice Tillet was born in the Ural Mountains of Russia to French parents. As a child, he earned the nickname "The Angel" for his sweet, handsome face, but around age 17, Tillet's handsome features began to transform into something other. He was diagnosed with acromegaly, a condition caused by a benign tumor on the pituitary gland. Acromegaly causes the bones to overgrow and become thicker than normal, giving the victim larger than normal body features. Unable to follow his father's footsteps into engineering because of his physical condition, Tillet entered the world of professional wrestling, and the French Angel was born.

Tillet arrived in town to do battle against Ray Eckert, a much-hated heel in the Louisville wrestling scene, with Ed "Strangler" Lewis acting as guest referee. Tillet was only 5'7" tall, but at 270 pounds he still cut a terrifying presence in the ring. His very appearance repulsed the fans, particularly the ladies. The newspaper covering the match even led with the headline "Wives see 'Angel,' think hubbies came from Heaven."

Despite their abject hatred for Eckert, some fans actually felt pity for the man once the Angel got hold of him. Eckert appeared as helpless "as a grape in a nutcracker" once the Angel applied his deadly bear hug. Eckert took the second fall, but the Angel won the third, a victory for himself and the fans of Louisville who had waited so long for Eckert to be taught a lesson.

The success of the French Angel led to a number of copycats, the most successful of which was the Swedish Angel, Phil Olafsson. The creation of legendary promoter Jack Pfeffer, the Swedish Angel captured the MWA World Championship from Orville Brown in Kansas City back in 1941. Brown would cut his reign short and re-take the title back six days later.

The Swedish Angel made his Louisville debut in 1940, a year before the French Angel, scoring a victory over Dan Mahoney. He returned in 1944 to defeat Laverne Baxter, who was unable to finish after suffering the effects of the Angel's bear hug. The Swedish Angel lost a title shot in June of that same year to Bill Longson at the Columbia Gym.

A different group of angels also made a big splash during the War. Billy Wolfe was the top promoter of women's wrestling in the country from the 1930s through the 50s, and Wolfe's estranged wife, Mildred Burke, was at the height of her power as champion. Wolfe seized the opportunity while the men were away to send his stable of beauties out across the country, wowing men and women alike with their skill any place women's wrestling was allowed. The sport was banned in Indiana, but Kentucky and Heywood Allen were open for business.

Burke's marriage to Wolfe was always more a professional arrangement than a love relationship. Wolfe had the connections and the clout to get Burke high paying bookings, keeping her in furs, diamonds, and all the finer things she loved so much. Wolfe was notorious for sleeping with as many of his women as he could arrange, and Burke had a long term relationship with Wolfe's son, her grown step-son.

Millie became a star attraction in Louisville, doing battle with fellow Wolfe signees like Elvira Snodgrass, Mae Young, and Gladys "Kill 'Em" Gillem, The women usually appeared on the undercard, but when Mildred was in town, they sometimes were the headliner.

Allen used foreign-born and foreign-named wrestlers to draw in a crowd too, especially those on the other side of the war. Count von Zuppe, a 165 pound German wrestler with a mustache and a monocle, was the kind of heel the anti-Nazi fans could really hate. So too was Frederic von Schacht, whom Allen billed as a Nazi Stormtrooper. The Germans had natural heat and proved to be the perfect foes for the American heroes who also took the ring.

From 1941 through the end of the war, a number of sailors, soldiers, and other servicemen made appearances in the ring. Some of the top names included Pvt. Hoosier Jackson, Sailor Olsen, Sailor Dick Lever, Sailor Watkins, Soldier Thomas, and Corporal Freddy Corodona.

Were they really service men? Were they really sailors, soldiers, and marines? Were the Nazi wrestlers actually Nazis - or even German? At the end of the day, it didn't matter. Wrestling, like other sports and radio programs, was a welcome distraction from the horrors of war. Kayfabe still was the rule of the day, and fans didn't bother to ask themselves if it was real or fake. Fans wanted an escape. They wanted to forget about the war for a few hours and enjoy themselves. Wrestling was both a distraction and a cathartic release, with real-life heroes battling soldiers, sailors and the like in defense of truth, justice, and the American way.

By far the most unique wrestler to entertain the Louisville crowd during the war made her debut on June 30, 1942, in the Sports Arena. Trained by Roy Welch, the young lady, who went by the name Ginger, briefly battled sportswriter Buddy Atkinson with no decision. Atkinson, who considered himself to be a daredevil, spent most of the match running from his opponent before finally hanging it up. One can hardly blame the 120 pound writer for chickening out, considering Ginger, his opponent, was a 305 pound Canadian black bear.

Ginger the Bear stepped in the ring with Floyd Bird that same evening. Bird didn't run. He also didn't win, taking the fall for his fearsome opponent. Bird might not have been pleased to job (wrestle speak for lose) for Ginger, but Bird was no fool. You just don't shoot on a 305 pound bear.

MYTH BUSTING

A business like professional wrestling is, by its very nature, filled with tall tales, myths, and legends. Two of the most talked about legends took place in or around Louisville during the 1940s. Neither one is completely true.

In Joe Jares's book *Whatever Happened to Gorgeous George?* (a phenomenal survey of the wrestling industry first published in 1974), Jares claims that Mildred Burke and Elvira Snodgrass drew a crowd of 18,000 in Louisville. If it were true, it would rank as the largest crowd ever drawn by a women's main event, and one of the largest crowds ever drawn at the time the book was published.

A close examination of the wrestling results from *The Courier-Journal* shows that's just not true. Burke and Snodgrass only wrestled once in Louisville that year, on February 11. The main event that night saw Orville Brown unmask Masked Superman. Burke and Snodgrass were part of the undercard, and while the crowd of 7123 was impressive, it was less than half the number reported by Jares.

During the summer of 1941, when Jares claimed the match took place, a number of shows were held out doors at Heywood Allen's Sports Arena on Burnett Avenue between Floyd and Preston, but Burke and Snodgrass never appeared in any of the outdoor shows.

Burke and Snodgrass met again on February 1, 1944, headlining the regular Tuesday night show for the Allen Athletic Club. The house wasn't listed in the paper for this meeting, but given they met at the Columbia Gym, it's safe to say they did not draw 18,000 that evening.

Another popular story surrounds a car ride that ended in Louisville. The story appears in Lou Thesz's autobiography *Hooker.*

When Lou Thesz returned to wrestling after World War II, he made a deal to buy out Tom Packs of his promotion in St. Louis. Packs had been in business since 1922, running one of the most successful promotions in the country. Thesz jumped at the chance to have more control of his career and his booking, and so he bought into the promotion with a few partners.

Thesz was a regular in the River City before the war, and he would become a regular attraction - and the biggest name in the business - in the decade that followed. As the Golden Age of Wrestling dawned, Thesz put himself in the driver's seat. He had full control of his career and the careers of many others, including his longtime rival Buddy Rogers.

Thesz and Rogers could not have been any more different. Thesz was a true wrestler, a legitimate threat in the ring and one of the few remaining hookers in the business. Thesz feared no man, and no one dared try to double cross him in the ring. Simply put, there was no one left in the business who could take him in a real fight.

Rogers was part of the new breed, the performers who succeeded on their flamboyance and personality in the ring. He was the original nature boy, a cocky, bleach blonde heel whose act would be imitated countless times in the years to come, most notably by Ric Flair. He was also one of the first to regularly incorporate high flying maneuvers into his matches, changing the style that future wrestlers would follow for generations to come. He knew how to get under the skin of any crowd in any town, and that made him money at the box office.

Rogers had become the top draw in the St. Louis promotion in Thesz's absence, and the two men were booked to face off in Louisville. It would be Thesz's first appearance in the ring since the war ended. Thesz met Rogers at the train station in St. Louis, and the two men hit the road together.

Thesz was excited about the booking. A sellout crowd was expected, and a sellout meant a great pay off for the two. But Rogers began to complain about Heywood Allen's choice of referee for the match.

"The promoter has even brought in Ed Lewis to referee our match. Why do we need that fat old has been? The money they're paying him should be going into our pockets."

Rogers had no clue who Ed "Strangler" Lewis was. Not only was he a legend who owed his career to Heywood Allen and the Louisville promotion, he also happened to be Lou Thesz's hero, mentor, and dear friend.

Thesz gave Rogers an ear full, telling him what the Strangler had done to break ground for Thesz, Rogers, and the hundreds of others who made a living in the ring. Rogers could tell he messed up, and he tried to play it off as a joke. The damage had been done, and Rogers would pay the price for his arrogance.

On arriving in Louisville, Thesz spoke with the promoter about the match. While it would have been more logical for business to let Rogers, the new blood, win over the returning soldier, Thesz made it clear he would not put Rogers over - not in Louisville, not ever. The finish was changed, and Rogers, who was no match for Thesz in a real fight, had no choice but to agree.

Thesz and Rogers would wrestle many times over the years. Some nights Thesz won outright. Other nights they battled to an epic draw. But never, in all the years Rogers and Thesz faced off, did the Nature Boy beat the champion. Thesz would never allow it - and all because of one fateful car ride.

Thesz's story checks out when you check the win-loss-draw records of the two men. Thesz either defeated or drew with Rogers every time, but he never lost. The one part of the story doesn't hold water is where and when it took place. Thesz and Rogers didn't meet head to head in Louisville in 1946.

On March 26, 1946, Rogers defeated Ralph Garibaldi at the Columbia Gym two out of three falls. That same night, Lou Thesz went over La Verne Baxter two out of three falls. The following night, on March 27, 1946, the two wrestled to a hard fought draw against one another in Evansville, Indiana.

Rogers had a booking prior to the Louisville match in Atlanta, GA on March 22, so it's unlikely he would have been in St. Louis for the car ride Thesz described. It seems much more likely that the infamous car ride Thesz wrote about took place on March 27, when Thesz and Rogers would have driven from Louisville to Evansville for their first ever match.

Thesz and Rogers had their first Louisville match on December 9 at the Armory. The winner was slated to receive a title match against Bill Longson, who had recently taken the title from Thesz. The pair gave the Louisville fans a show and battled to a draw, leaving Longson to do battle with the Volga Boatman, a 6'7" 330 pounder.

If Thesz was confused on the place and time of his famous fight with Rogers, one can hardly fault him for getting a few facts mixed up. Men like Lou Thesz and Buddy Rogers lived on the road, and after so many years and miles, the dates and places all blur together. With that in mind, here's one more story of historical significance that - if true - has a Louisville connection.

Thesz and his partners found enormous success when they took over St. Louis from Tom Packs, but Thesz was not the only show in town. Sam Muchnick, one of Thesz's travel partners, opened his own promotion shortly before World War II. He went on hiatus during the war, but as soon as the fighting was over and the men began coming home, Sam resumed his own promotion in earnest.

Muchnick brought in a lot of the old timers for his shows, but he was fighting an uphill battle. Thesz was the number one draw of his day, and Muchnick didn't have an answer for the champ's drawing power. He caught a break in 1948 when he signed Buddy Rogers, who proved to be a big draw for Muchnick, but it would take something bigger than the Nature Boy to save the his promotion.

In 1948 Muchnick called a meeting in Waterloo, Iowa with five other promoters - Tony Stecher of Minneapolis, Max Clayton of Omaha, Al Haft of Columbus, Pinky George of Des Moines, and Orville Brown of Kansas City. The result of that meeting was the founding of the NWA, National Wrestling Alliance, a coalition of promoters who agreed to share talent, honor each other's boundaries, and help one another defend their territories against "outlaw" promotions that ran against them.

The NWA grew to 13 members in its first year. Each promotion had its own talent and its own champions, but collectively they recognized one world champion, Orville Brown.

Despite his affiliation with the NWA, Muchnick was still losing to Thesz. Thesz had plenty of talent with star power to stay independent, but as time went on, the stress of running a promotion and headlining the promotion wore him down. When he was ready, Thesz struck a deal with Muchnick. They would be equal partners, 50-50, with Muchnick running the office and Thesz handling the wrestling shows.

Bringing Thesz into the fold was a major coup for the Alliance, but there was one issue yet to be settled. Thesz wore a world championship belt that could legitimately be traced back to Frank Gotch, but the NWA had its own champion in Orville Brown. A unification match between Thesz and Brown give the Alliance one world champion, but neither Thesz nor Brown was willing to take the fall. The two had a bad history dating back to 1936, and it was a matter of pride to both men that they retain their title.

In a legitimate contest, Brown was no match for Thesz. He didn't have the skills Thesz had, and Brown knew if Thesz came after him, he had no chance in the ring. But in the interest of doing what was best for business, Brown and Thesz agreed to a unification match in St. Louis, scheduled for November 25, 1949.

The match undoubtedly would have done big business and added new legitimacy to the infant NWA, but as fate would have it, the match never took place. On November 1, while driving from Des Moines to Kansas City, Orville Brown and his business partner Bobby Bruns were in a terrible car accident. Both men survived, but were critically injured. Brown was paralyzed on one side of his body.

According to Lou Thesz, he was in a hotel room in Louisville when he received the phone call from Sam Muchnick. While Brown's long term future was still uncertain, it was clear the match on November 25 would not happen. Thesz knew it was only a matter of time before he was declared champion.

The accident caused a bit of bad publicity for Brown and the NWA. Brown and Bruns were partners in real life but rivals in the ring. The fact that two men believed to be mortal enemies were in a car accident was a big blow to the sport's believability. Fortunately for the NWA, they had a champion with a legitimate wrestling background, an old school hooker who could take on all comers in a straight up fight.

On November 27 at a meeting of the NWA membership, Thesz was named the undisputed heavyweight champion, a title he would hold until 1956.

Orville Brown would recover the use of his legs, but he was never the same physically. He attempted a comeback, but the pain from his accident never went away, and Brown was forced to hang up his boots.

"A SEVEN FOOT ORGY OF FEAR"

In the 1950s, when wrestling was in its golden age and Lou Thesz was at the peak of his power, he laid out a number of ground rules for promoters who wanted to book him. He had a strict rule that he would work three weeks and be off one. His earnings were ten percent of the money taken at the gate plus transportation. And to protect the dignity of his world championship title, Thesz would not appear on a bill with women, midgets, wrestling bears, or other carnival acts.

Although Thesz makes no mention of it in his autobiography *Hooker*, one has to wonder if a 1947 stop in Louisville played a part in the "no carnival acts" dictum. Thesz was on hand to wrestle Warren Bockwinkel, who wrestled that night as Frankie Bockwinkel. A crowd of 7300 spectators (larger than any basketball crowd that same season, *The Courier-Journal* noted) packed the Armory that night, a crowd worthy of the two legends such as Thesz and Bockwinkel. Yet the crowd assembled that night didn't come to see Thesz and Bockwinkel. Nor did they brave the January cold to see up and coming female wrestler June Byers. They came to see the alligator.

The alligator, a very real seven foot long live reptile, faced off against Gil Woodworth. Woodworth, billed as being from the Florida Everglades, claimed he had never been afraid of alligators as a child. After watching the young man prove his worth against the deadly beasts, Ross Allen, owner of the Silver Springs reptile farm in Florida, told Woodworth he was a natural born alligator wrestler. Woodworth also claimed he had doubled for Johnny Weissmuller on a Tarzan movie filmed at Silver Springs.

On January 21, 1947, Woodworth and a seven foot alligator found themselves on the bill with Thesz, Bockwinkel, and Byers at the Louisville Armory. The evening began with a match between male competitors Felix Miquet and Olie Olsen. Miquet got the win in less than eighteen minutes, and the men cleared the ring for the ladies. Byers and Dotson were two of Billy Wolfe's girls, part of the growing company of female wrestlers that Wolfe unleashed on the country in the 40s and 50s. Byers "daintily" tore into Dotson and claimed the win in just under thirteen minutes.

Thesz and Bockwinkel put on a real show, according to *The Courier-Journal*. Thesz won the hard-fought match in two straight falls, but his accomplishments and all before were just a warm up. The crowd came to see an alligator.

Prior to the match Woodworth gave the crowd a short lecture on alligators. His speech, which emphasized that alligators have 1000 pounds of pressure in their powerful jaws, served to both educate the fans and set the stage for the battle to come.

Having set the stage for the match, Woodworth's opponent was brought to the ring. The always colorful *Courier-Journal* described the beast as "a seven-foot orgy of fear." Woodworth demonstrated his lack of fear during the ensuing match by sticking his head in the creature's mouth.

"He didn't keep his head in there long, did he?" said one of the young men watching the show.

"Which is better than I would have done," said his girlfriend.

As terrifying as the alligator appeared to be, Woodworth showed no fear, taking to the ring and taming the wild creature. Woodworth escaped the beast, retired to the back, and returned in formal wear to finish the night by getting married.

Much of the crowd gathered for the evening's wrestling had left by the time Woodworth and his bride, Perma Crook of Rippley, Tennessee, took their vows. Justice of the Peace Herman Jorris presided over the vows, and June Byers pulled double duty by acting as Miss Crook's maid-of-honor.

Many fans believe the wedding of the Macho Man Randy Savage and Miss Elizabeth was the first wedding to take place in the squared circle. However, Woodworth and Crook's wedding proves that there's really nothing new story-wise in the world of pro wrestling. Weddings have been a part of wrestling since at least 1939, when George Wagner, aka Gorgeous George, married his wife Betty in the ring. The wedding was such a huge draw, George and Betty were married several times more at numerous arenas across the country.

Woodworth and Crook did not beat Gorgeous George, but they beat Savage and Miss Elizabeth to the altar by 44 years. They also beat Jake "The Snake" Roberts and his wedding crashing cobra to the punch by the same margin by having an alligator involved in the evening's festivities.

Woodworth appeared on the network TV game show *What's My Line?* in 1953, where Steve Allen, Bennett Cerf, Laraine Day, and Barbara Kelly attempted to guess his occupation as an alligator wrestler. It is unclear what happened to Woodworth and his bride beyond that event. Regardless what happened to him, he always had his memory of Louisville and the night he not only got hitched, but upstaged the greatest wrestler of the golden era. Small wonder Thesz never wanted to appear with a gimmick act again!

The alligator match would be one of the final gifts Heywood Allen gave to the people of Louisville. On February 9, 1947, *The Courier-Journal* reported that he was leaving the wrestling business. Allen sold his interest in the Allen Athletic Club to co-owner Francis A. McDonough, Jr., and a farewell show was scheduled for February 18.

A crowd of 5000 people packed the Armory for Allen's last show. World champion Bill Longson was on hand, defeating Felix Miquet (whose brother Francois would become famous as Corsica Joe) in two out of three falls. Babe Sharkey and Ed Meske won victories over Miguel Torres and Ralph Garibaldi, respectively, and Mickey Gold drew with Joe Millich.

Governor Simeon S. Willis received an invitation for the special event, along with a group of men referred to in the paper as the "Ole Gang of Allen's." The gang included McDonough, Charley Schullman, George Lewis, Paul Neal, Pat Murphy, Clarence Brenzel, Kid Scotty Williams, Ray McDonough, and Billy Love. Other regional promoters and NWA dignitaries also came to pay tribute to Allen.

McDonough sent word out to the community hoping to find Allen's oldest living fan. The honor went to a man named Robert T. Brown, who recalled one of Allen's first matches as a bout between William Demetral and Jack Stone during Demetral's first trip to town in 1912.

Allen worked matches in Louisville for 42 years. He bore witness to the birth of Ed "Strangler" Lewis, held court over the first golden age with Stecker, Caddock, and Zbyszko, weathered two world wars, the National Wrestling Association, the birth of the National Wrestling Alliance, and the rise of perhaps the greatest champ of all, Lou Thesz. The fire Allen ignited in Louisville sports fans would far outlive his career and his life, and the fruits of his labor can be seen in the rabid fan base that still packs Davis Arena every Wednesday.

Heywood Allen passed away in Louisville in 1958.

THE POLICE BENEFIT SHOW

When a wrestling promotion changes hands, it often means disaster. New managers, eager to do things their way, sometimes encounter friction with either the talent or fans. It's not uncommon for the end of a regime to spell doom for the promotion. Thankfully for Louisville wrestling fans, the man who took over for Heywood Allen picked up where his mentor left off and carried the ball even further.

Francis McDonough was no stranger to the wrestling business. Prior to World War II, he rose to become a press agent for the Allen Athletic Club. He served his country in the army during the war and returned to Louisville and Allen's world after. When he assumed control of the Allen Athletic Club in early 1947, fans hardly noticed a change in the cards. In the late 40s and early 50s, national stars like Lou Thesz, Whipper Billy Watson, and Bill Longson continued to mix things up alongside local stars like veteran Blacksmith Pedigo, Hoosier Golden Glove winner Stu Gibson, and Mel Meiners, aka the Schnitzelburg Giant. Meiners, who did not stay in the business long, was a devout Catholic, a devoted husband, and the father of fourteen children. One of those children became one of Louisville's most popular television and radio personalities.

Weekly shows continued at the Columbia Gym with major cards moving to the Armory several times a year. McDonough continued to feature women's wrestling, utilizing Mildred Burke, June Byars, Mae Young, and more of Billy Wolfe's top talent. Like Allen before him, he frequently ran programs with masked wrestlers like Diablo, Diablo II, the Zebra Kid, and the Great Zorro.

But McDonough wasn't content to simply carry on the status quo. In the early 1950s McDonough also began to experiment with television, broadcasting live for the first time on WHAS in 1952. One year earlier, McDonough and the Louisville Police put on the first in a series of hugely successful shows that would trump the Derby Eve shows of the last - the annual fundraiser for the Louisville Police Widows and Orphans Fund.

In many ways, the annual police show exceeded the success of the Derby Eve Shows of the past. Not only did the shows draw top talent and huge crowds, they became a huge fundraiser for the Police Widows and Orphans Fund.

The March 29, 1952 show grossed $22,677 and drawing 9281 fans, including 500 orphans who came as guests of the police. That night, Lou Thesz defeated Enrique Torres in the main event two falls out of three, despite complaining of a serious injury during the match. Ed "Strangler" Lewis, who had become Thesz's mentor and travel partner, was in the champion's corner.

The card also featured a thirty minute draw between Ray Eckert and Bill Longson and the usual mix of national and local stars. Sgt. Buck Moore of the Louisville Police Department participated in two matches and would go on to feature in Police Benefit Shows the next several years.

In May of that same year, Baron Michele Leone headlined the Derby Eve Show. The Baron was one of the biggest stars in the country, and unlike most "Italian born" wrestlers, he actually was born in Italy. Leone made a few stops in Louisville more than a decade earlier, most notably as one of Masked Superman's early victims.

Leone made his way to the West Coast, where he became one of the top heels in the business. Sporting a mustache and long, dark hair, he took on the title of Baron and carried himself with a regal air, but it was the United States's entry into World War II that would really put him over the top. Leone, as an Italian citizen, could not be drafted into the service, and his Italian heritage helped him get over as a much hated heel. Leone was so successful with his Baron persona, he was booed in a match against a German during the war.

Nineteen days after the Derby Eve show, Leone faced Thesz in Los Angeles for the world championship. The match took place on May 21, 1953 at Gilmore Field in Los Angeles and drew 25,256 fans. It marked the first time a wrestling match ever earned a $100,000 gate, with total receipts reported as $103,277.75. Thesz defeated Leone in two out of three falls to take Leone's Olympic version of the world title and solidify his status as the undisputed world's champion.

In 1953 it was Leone's turn to headline the Police Benefit Show. Leone defeated Jim Doby two falls to three at the end of an intriguing night of matches. Earlier in the show Mae Young fell to Gloria Barratini, who filled in for women's world champion Mildred Burke. Like Burke and Young, Barratini was managed by women's wrestling innovator Billy Wolfe. She was a classically trained opera singer with a phenomenal voice whom Wolfe billed as heiress to a $200,000 fortune.

Burke was reported to be "ill" and unable to wrestle, but it's more likely her no show had something to do with her rapidly imploding relationship with Wolfe. By 1954 the two would officially split, and a shoot match for control of the title and the women's wrestling business would take place between Mildred Burke and one of Wolfe's lovers, June Byars.

An Australian tag match - so called because the match was best two of three falls instead of one fall - featured long time Louisville regular and former world champion Wild Bill Longson. Fans remembered Wild Bill Longson's reign at the top during and after World War II, and there was no love lost for the cheating heel when he appeared at the benefit show. Stu Gibson was a local, a former Golden Glove winner from the Hoosier state. The two defeated a number of duos throughout 1952 and likely came into the match as favorites.

Longson and Gibson faced a pair of masked wrestlers, the Great Torro and the Great Zorro, who entered the night with the most fascinating back story. Born Jacob Grobbe in Leiden, Netherlands on January 28, 1924, Grobbe spent much of his early life on the run and in hiding. Grobbe was a Jew, and when the Nazis invaded his homeland, he joined the Dutch resistance. Grobbe was fluent in seven languages and was able to speak Frisian - a dialect spoken in Northern Germany - without an accent. His language skills helped him evade capture and survive.

Near the end of the war, Grobbe found himself on in an American military camp for displaced citizens. Rather than wait to be sent home, Grobbe stole the identification papers of an American soldier and sailed to America on a troop ship.

Grobbe made his way to Tacoma, Washington, where he assumed the soldier's name Howlett and became a police officer. Officer Howlett worked out at a gym frequented by a number of professional wrestlers, who persuaded him to give the sport a try.

Grobbe made his debut in 1946 in Tacoma and was soon traveling the country. From 1949 to 1952 he worked for Al Haft and Jack Pfeffer, and Grobbe adopted a number of ring personas, masked and unmasked.

Grobbe's life took another strange twist in the mid-1950s. Grobbe's wife turned her husband in as an illegal immigrant following a domestic argument between the two. Grobbe was told if he allowed the government to deport him voluntarily, he could petition to return to the States two years later. Grobbe took the deal and spent several years wrestling in Australia, New Zealand, South Africa, and France.

After returning to the states, Grobbe was recruited to the WWWF in New York. The Great Zorro transformed into the hated German heel Hans Mortier. He became one of the top stars for Vince McMahon, Sr., and his partner

Toots Mondt acting as the chief rival for long time champ, Bruno Sammartino.

The 1953 police benefit show drew a record crowd of 9,384 and raised $22,123 for the Widows and Orphans Fund. The 1954 show, featuring a main event between Lou Thesz and Mr. Moto, drew a more modest 9,055.

In 1955, McDonough shot for the moon by booking one of the most sought after rematches in the country - Lou Thesz vs. Baron Leone. The first $100,000 gate should have led to greater box offices in the rematches, but a less than whole-hearted effort by the Baron, who was forced to take the loss, hurt future revenues. Nevertheless, Leone and Thesz did what they could to draw money together.

The pair brought their rivalry to Louisville on April 2, 1955. Once again Strangler Lewis was on hand, and he was welcomed as a returning hero. Strangler gave an interview to *The Courier-Journal*, where he reflected on his past in Louisville and the way Barton and Allen turned a "country bumpkin" into a mega star.

The night of the match, however, it was guest referee "Wild Red" Berry who stole the show. Berry, who earlier in the night defeated Chris Zaharias in a match, was known as a skilled talker, a man who bragged he had committed every word of four syllables or more in the dictionary to memory.

After Thesz and Leone split the first two falls, Berry drew the ire of the Baron by awarding the third and final fall to Thesz. The Baron ripped Berry's shirt off and retired from the ring, but Berry got the last words in through the newspaper.

"Baron Leone is a sophisticated rhetorician," said Berry, "who is inebriated by his own verbosity and gifted with an egotistical imagination that does at all time start a series of interminable, insufferable arguments to malign his opponents and glorify himself."

Asked to clarify his comments, Berry said, "It's too bad Leone isn't an octopus so that he can love himself with twelve hands instead of one."

The media loved Berry and his big words, and the talented speaker went on. "I am enabled by congeneric concatenation and physical perspicuity to confabulate all nefarious cupidity." Berry declined to translate the statement, saying he "found it expedient to terminate this discussion because of an immediate necessity to avail myself of locomotion by steam or diesel on track."

With those words, Berry headed for the train station and left town. In future years, Berry's gift for words would make him one of the top heel managers in business, setting the bar for fast talking managers like Bobby Heenan, Jim Cornette, and Paul Heyman to one day try and match.

Thesz and Leone didn't match the six figure gate from three years earlier, but a record crowd of 9,500, including 1,200 underprivileged kids and orphans, made it a one of the biggest successes in the history of the Armory.

The Thesz-Leone match proved to be the pinnacle of the Allen Club's run in Louisville. McDonough continued to bring in top names like Thesz, Fritz Von Erich, Buddy Rogers, June Byars, and the masked Zebra Kid while still relying on local workhorses like Stu Gibson. Then in the spring of 1957, McDonough passed away.

After McDonough's death, the NWA stepped in to keep the city going. The best talent available out of the St. Louis office continued to make weekly visits. Even Sam Muchnick himself came to town for a night at the Columbia Gym to oversee an NWA tag team championship match.

In July of 1957, Georgie Lewis, the cigar-chomping announcer and longtime voice of the Allen Athletic Club, announced that a new "area" in wrestling was about to begin. Lewis had a Yogi Berra-like gift for words, but his announcement wasn't garbled completely. A new era was about to begin in a new area. Al LeCompte, a former baseball player with the Kentucky Colonels, purchased the Allen Athletic Club. He kept the name, but he moved the promotion to the Armory on a permanent basis.

Just two months later, the Allen Club moved its Tuesday shows to the Kentucky State Fairgrounds. By the end of the year, Louisville had gone dark. After 22 years, the Allen Athletic Club was done, 45 years after its namesake first arrived in town.

A TALE OF TWO CITIES

From the early 1900s the Louisville wrestling faithful had a front row seat to the very best professional wrestling had to offer. The list of main event stars for the first six decades of Louisville wrestling is packed with wrestling hall of famers: Joe Stecher, Ed "Strangler" Lewis, Cora Livingston, Orville Brown, "Wild Bill" Longson, Lou Thesz, Buddy Rogers, Mildred Burke, and so on. But in the early 1960s, events in two other cities - Lexington, Kentucky, and Indianapolis, Indiana - would lead to a major change in Louisville's wrestling fortunes.

Less than a year after the Allen Club shut its doors, Wee Willie Davis announced he was opening a new promotion called Goldenrod. Davis, a 6'10", 400 pound behemoth, was a former wrestler and a movie star, best known for playing himself in the 1949 film "Mighty Joe Young." An avid horticulturalist, Davis named the promotion Goldenrod Wrestling.

With the Allen Club's exit from the business, Louisville fell under the Indianapolis promotion led by Jim Barnett. Barnett's career began in Chicago, where he worked for one of the original members of the NWA, Fred Kohler. By the late 1950s, Barnett had his own territory, including Detroit and Indianapolis, and was booking talent for Vern Gagne's upstart AWA promotion out of Minneapolis.

Barnett was a highly successful promoter, and his territory was thriving. Then, without any warning, Barnett left the country in 1963, leaving Dick the Bruiser and Wilbur Snyder's WWA to take over Indianapolis and Louisville.

The why and how of Barnett's departure depends on who you ask. According to Shannon Ragland, author of the book *The Thin Thirty*, the sudden exodus of Jim Barnett is a twisted tale involving a Hollywood legend and the University of Kentucky football program. *The Thin Thirty* focuses on the story of the 1962 University of Kentucky football team. Coached by Bear Bryant disciple Charlie Bradshaw, the team's numbers dwindled from 88 players to only 30 due to the heavy handed way Bradshaw ran his team.

The book also chronicles a scandalous series of events involving Jim Barnett and the Wildcats football team. It was always a poorly kept secret that Barnett was gay. According to Ragland, Barnett and his partner Lonnie Winters purchased a house on Lakewood Drive in Lexington, Kentucky. The two became fans and boosters of the University of Kentucky athletic programs, and in 1959 they began hosting weekly dinner parties for members of the University of Kentucky football team.

Barnett had a standing dinner invitation for the players every Sunday evening. Steak, lobster, shrimp, and booze were provided free and in generous quantities. With very little money to their names and a scant menu available on Sundays at their dorm, Wildcat Manor, the players became regulars and "Jim and Lonnie's" house, unaware of their hosts' true intentions.

If you want all the details, I suggest you look up Ragland's book to read more for yourself. The long and short of it is, the parties led to Jim and Lonnie offering players money in exchange for certain favors. It was easy money for the players willing to go along, but it put the players in a compromised position that Barnett may have later used for his own monetary gain.

The story becomes even more salacious when, in 1960, actor Rock Hudson enters the story. Hudson was the very ideal of the heterosexual male in the movies, but he was a closeted homosexual up until his death. After paying a visit to Kentucky with Elizabeth Taylor, he found Lexington to be the perfect getaway where, in pre-tabloid America, he could live as he pleased. Barnett met Hudson during one of his Lexington visits, and soon Hudson became a regular on Lakewood Drive.

The players involved never let word slip about what was going on for fear their own activities might come to light. Barnett also had close friends in the Lexington Police Department, a connection that helped him keep things under wraps.

The party continued through the 1962 football season, the year of the Thin Thirty. Ragland claims it was during this season that Barnett used his influence over the players to fix a game, the second to last of the season against Xavier. Despite their thin roster, the Wildcats were favored by three touchdowns over lowly Xavier. Their performance on the field was so bad, with nearly everything going wrong, journalists immediately smelled a rat. Barnett was known to have ties to the Chicago gambling community, and when rumors about what was happening on Lakewood Drive began to circulate, Barnett was also linked to the cheating scandal.

When *Sports Illustrated* ran an exposé on the Kentucky football program in 1963, Barnett decided the party was over. Barnett and Winters skipped town and the country, setting up shop in Australia. The move proved to be a boon for the Australian wrestling business. Barnett had connections with the Australian airlines, which meant he could fly anyone he wanted into the country for nothing. Soon Australia was the hottest promotion on the planet, and Barnett was helping to make future stars including Memphis legend Bill Dundee. Barnett finally returned to the states in 1969, where he set up in Atlanta and began to build the promotion that would one day become WCW.

Barnett sold the Detroit end of the territory to The Sheik, a legendary wrestler and promoter and one of the first proponents of the hardcore wrestling style. According to those who worked out of Memphis in the 1970s, Barnett sold the Indianapolis end to Dick the Bruiser and Wilbur Snyder but was never paid for it. Indianapolis wrestling historian Chris Parsons disagrees. On his website rasslinrelics.com, Parsons reveals a very different version of Bruiser and Snyder's ride to power.

At the time of Barnett's departure, Bruiser and Snyder were the tag team champions of the AWA, the American Wrestling Association. The AWA was the brainchild of Vern Gagne, a highly regarded shooter and fierce rival of Lou Thesz. As Thesz's reign was winding down in the late 50s, Gagne believed he should be the heir apparent to the champ. Gagne became frustrated with the politics of the NWA and struck out on his own. He partnered up with Wally Karbo, a longtime associate of Tony Stecher in Minneapolis, and they established their own promotion.

The AWA quickly took over Minneapolis and began to spread its influence throughout the Midwest. They crowned their own world champion - usually Gagne himself - and began to produce their own colorful collection of superstars. Gagne did battle with legendary heels like Mad Dog Vachon and Baron Von Raschke - a German Nazi portrayed by shy farm boy Jim Raschke from the University of Nebraska.

Dick "The Bruiser" Afflis and Wilbur Snyder were former NFL stars who used their status as football stars to becomes heroes in AWA. Dick the Bruiser was a native of Indianapolis who played football for the University of Nebraska and the Green Bay Packers. When his football career ended, he established himself as a barroom brawler character working for Vern Gagne. After becoming an established star in his own right, Bruiser returned home to open the WWA with Snyder in Indianapolis.

On his website, Parsons compiled a series of newspaper articles that indicate Bruiser and Snyder struck out on their own and ran against the established promotion in Indianapolis in 1964. Bruiser and Snyder's departure caused the AWA to strip them of their tag team titles, but within a matter of months, the WWA shows were out-drawing and out-grossing Barnett's AWA promotion.

It is possible that Barnett sold his interest in Indianapolis to Balk Estes, who worked with Barnett and was listed as the promoter in the AWA ads that ran against the fledgling WWA. The sale to Estes could have been the motivator for Bruiser and Snyder to strike out on their own. It is also possible that Barnett sold to Bruiser after realizing he could not compete with the upstart promotion. While the exact details remain a mystery, Parsons's research shows that it took less than a year for the old AWA promotion to give up and close shop. Shortly after the WWA's takeover, Bruiser and Snyder agreed to become an AWA affiliate and regained their tag titles.

The tale woven by Ragland and Parsons is as sordid as any you'll find in the twisted world of professional wrestling. It's the kind of scandalous mystery you expect to find behind the scene's of one of the world's strangest businesses. But longtime Ohio Valley Wrestling trainer Rip Rogers tells a much simpler tale about Barnett's sudden departure.

"Bruiser pushed a guy out a window and said, 'Get out of my town,'" says Rogers. "That's why Barnett left the country."

For what it's worth, Danny Davis of OVW backs Rogers's version of events.

The WWA recognized the AWA champions, but they also had their own champions, heavyweight and tag team. Bruiser promoted himself as the star of the WWA, just like Gagne did with the AWA, and he carried the heavyweight title much of the time. He carefully protected his image on television by preventing any match or wrestler who might upstage him from airing on WWA TV. According to Lou Thesz, when the former NWA champ came into town and did a match for television that brought down the house, Bruiser not only prevented the match from airing, he had the tape erased.

Despite being a heel who couldn't care less about being cheered, Bruiser was a hometown hero in Indianapolis. The Indiana fans loved him, and the WWA thrived until the late 1980s, when the WWF conquered the wrestling world.

As much as Indianapolis loved Bruiser and the upstart WWA, the same could not be said in Louisville. Working with Wee Willie Davis, Bruiser and Snyder scheduled weekly appearances Louisville, but the attendance sagged and the box office died out.

It didn't help matters that the WWA never established a lasting television presence in Louisville. For all his strengths as a promoter, Bruiser never put a high priority on television. Bruiser didn't get his shows on Louisville TV, fans were unable to keep up with the local action, and attendance went into a steady decline. When Louisville stopped making money, the WWA stopped coming

"He was lazy!" says Rip Rogers about Bruiser. "He didn't want to travel more than he had to. He had Chicago and Indianapolis. He was making good money in both cities. And he didn't want to cater to the crazy southern wrestling audience in Louisville if he didn't have to."

If Louisville made money for the WWA, they might have never left, and the landscape of professional wrestling might look very different today. The AWA might have established a stronger foothold in the South, and Vince McMahon, Jr., might have found his dream of nationalizing the WWF in the 1980s a little more difficult. The WWA left a critical hole in the wrestling map when they vacated Louisville, and that opened the door for invasion in the early 1970s.

It would be easy to dismiss the late 60's as a time when nothing significant happened in Louisville wrestling. There was no television, and after a while no live events either. But no matter how "bad" something may look on paper, every wrestler, every era, and every promotion was someone's favorite.

To many Indiana wrestling fans, including late night talk show host David Letterman, Dick the Bruiser remains a hero. The AWA grew to become a national power, rivaling the NWA. AWA television expanded coast to coast, as did their territory. AWA stars became household names from the Midwest all the way to San Francisco. The promotion would later become the launch pad for the likes of Mean Gene Okerland and Hulk Hogan.

Louisville was the exception rather than the rule when it came to the AWA. Like a jilted teenage lover, they missed their old girl, the NWA, and no matter how great the next girl was, the Louisville fans were never going to like her as well. In time, Louisville would get over the disappointment and embrace a new girl from the South, but not before the city was witness to the debut of yet another legend.

It was during the brief span when the WWA held weekly shows in Louisville that Dick the Bruiser introduced the world to a young man who would become one of the biggest names of the 70s and 80s. He is one of the most beloved and most hated figures in the entire history of the business, and like Ed Strangler Lewis before him, he first met the public in Louisville, Kentucky.

Ray was only ten years old when the wrestling bug bit him. He discovered the sport watching TV in Chicago. He had a neighbor, a police officer, who was also a wrestler, and when that neighbor took young Ray and a few friends to see the matches live, he was hooked.

At age fifteen, Ray and his mother moved to Indianapolis. Ray began to put on wrestling shows himself, small time affairs that recreated much of the pageantry and theater of the real thing. Ray dropped out of school in the eighth grade and took a job at a local car dealer. He also earned money doing every little odd job he could pick up at the Armory in Indianapolis where Dick the Bruiser's crew worked every week. He set up the ring, carried the bags for the wrestlers, sold Cokes before the show, walked wrestlers to the ring before their matches, sold more Cokes during the matches, and on a good night, he earned an extra five bucks washing The Shiek's car when he was in town.

Ray was twenty years old when he received a call at work from Dick the Bruiser on January 10, 1965, informing him to be at the TV station on Tuesday for interviews. Ray took lunch that Tuesday at the time given him by Dick Bruiser. When he arrived, he was surprised to learn that he was now the manager for Joe Tomaso and Guy Mitchell, a pair of masked wrestlers known as the Assassins. Joe wasn't in attendance for Ray's first TV taping, but Dick wanted to go ahead and film them anyway. They threw Joe's mask on a mannequin, Guy did all the talking, and Ray's career as a heel manager was officially under way.

After the filming wrapped, Bruiser gave Ray a new order. "At 6:00, be at the Holiday Inn on 31. We're going to Louisville."

Ray met up with Bruiser and the rest of the crew at six for the ride south. Upon arrival, Ray was officially "smartened up" to business by Bruiser. It was no surprise to Ray that the sport wasn't real, but it still put him off guard when Bruiser told him if he revealed the secret to anyone else, both Bruiser and his partner Wilbur Snyder would break every bone in his body.

With Joe Tomaso unavailable, Ray had to go to the ring with Guy as the other half of the Assassins for a match against Moose Cholak and Wilbur Snyder. The teenager, still very green to the whole business, tied his mask on tight, an action he would deeply regret when Moose decided to unmask him in the ring. Ray later learned that masked wrestlers who were likely to be unmasked wouldn't actually tie their masks on, but pull them tight and tuck the laces up under the mask. When Moose, who was 6'5" and over 350 pounds, grabbed hold of the young wrestler and tried to yank the mask off, he nearly took Ray's head off. Moose finally broke the laces and yanked off the mask, saving the match and Ray's life.

Ray slipped out of the ring and staggered into the audience. Big mistake. A toothless woman burned him by putting her cigar out on Ray's neck. The cops grabbed the woman, and Ray escaped to the locker room.

Ray had a ringside seat for the next fight of the night, one that took place backstage. Johnny Valentine was scheduled to face Bruiser in the ring, but Valentine refused to go out. He had earlier gotten into an altercation, punching a fan and a police officer, and rather than go out and face arrest, Valentine barricaded the locker room door. The police were on the other side, pounding on the door, while Ray watched a desperate Valentine from a bench, too scared to move.

Finally Wee Willie Davis decided to take action. Davis grabbed a fighting stick, went into the dressing room, and beat Valentine over the head until he hit the ground. The cops got the cuffs on Valentine and escorted him from the building.

On the drive back to Indianapolis, Ray recalled seeing a horrible truck wreck and a man on fire, rolling on the ground and screaming for help. They arrived at the Holiday Inn around 2 AM, and Ray received his pay out - a whopping five dollars from the notoriously tight Bruiser. Ray assessed his situation carefully. He had driven four hours in the freezing cold to Kentucky. He had been burned by a cigar. He had seen a man beaten to a pulp for real in the locker room and carted off in handcuffs. All this for a lousy five dollars.

Ray knew, then and there, this was what he wanted to do with his life.

In his memoir, Ray would describe Kentucky as the place they invented the toothbrush. "Any place else, and they would have named it the 'teethbrush.'" It was zingers like that that made Ray a household name - though the name he used in the ring was not his real one.

At the end of that fateful phone call on January 10, Bruiser addressed the young prospect as Bobby when saying goodbye. Thinking Bruiser made a mistake, Ray called him back. Bruiser assured "Bobby" that there was no mistake. Ray Heenan was now Bobby Heenan. He would soon become "Pretty Boy" Bobby Heenan, managing a number of tag teams and wrestlers before ultimately earning the nickname that would stick with him the rest of his life: Bobby "The Brain" Heenan, namesake of one of the greatest stables in WWF history, the Heenan Family.

In the words of Paul Harvey, now you know the rest of the story.

1973 ad for wrestling at the Gardens (then known as the Convention Center) featuring Jackie Fargo and Jerry Jarrett.

Action Ringside program featuring Jerry Lawler, Bill Dundee, and Paul Orndorff.

THE **KING**
vs
THE **SOULMAN**

This is the match that the fans have been demanding. The prize is the N.W.A. Southern Heavyweight Championship belt and these two wrestlers have to meet one another again for their rankings in the national ratings. The winner will be advanced in the rankings and probably get a shot at Harley Race for the world title soon. Both wrestlers won previous victories over Race and plan to use each other as a stepping stone to the World Championship.

PUBLISHED WEEKLY IN THE INTEREST OF PROFESSIONAL WRESTLING........AND AS A SERVICE FOR THE FANS ATTENDING AND WISHING A SOUVENIR OF THE LIVE MATCHES.

OFFICIAL WRESTLING PROGRAM

ACTION RINGSIDE!

35¢

VOLUME I
NUMBER 9
WEEK OF
SUNDAY
APR 17, 1977

Action Ringside featuring Rocky Johnson and Jerry Lawler.

121

P R O G R A M

★

★ RICK MARTEL

JARRETT PROMOTIONS PRESENTS CHAMPIONSHIP WRESTLING

Program featuring future WWF star Rick Martel.

The notorious manager Jimmy Hart.
(Photo courtesy Jim Cornette.)

Teeny Jarrett and Jimmy Valiant.
(Photo courtesy Jim Cornette.)

Jim Cornette snapped this action shot of Jerry Lawler a split
second before the soda thrown by a fan hit him in the head.
(Photo courtesy Jim Cornette.)

Andy Kaufman showing off his Intergender Championship belt at Louisville Gardens.

(Photo courtesy Jim Cornette.)

The legendary Dutch Mantell, known to younger fans as manager Zeb Colter. One of the few wrestlers with a match enshrined in the Smithsonian.

(Photo courtesy Jim Cornette.)

Superstar Bill Dundee, who continues to wrestle all over the world, including an early 2014 date for IWA Mid-South.
(Photo courtesy Jim Cornette.)

Dean Hill and Frank Morrell (aka the French Angel). Morrell had an infamous altercation backstage with a wall. He lost.

(Photo courtesy Dean Hill.)

The first ladies of pro wrestling in Louisville: Thelma
Cornette and Teeny Jarrett.
(Photo courtesy Jim Cornette.)

Newly minted manager Jim Cornette, ready to conquer the wrestling world.
(Photo courtesy Jim Cornette.)

The Fabulous Ones, one of the most popular and successful tag teams in Memphis wrestling history.

(Photo courtesy Jim Cornette.)

Dean Hill under the care of Jerry Lawler's personal dentist, Dr. Isaac Yankem, D.D.S. from Decay-tur, Illinois. Dr. Yankem would evolve into one of the WWE's greatest big men, Kane.

(Photo courtesy Dean Hill.)

Dean Hill with third generation wrestler Flex Kavana. You may have seen him wrestle for the WWE and appear in a few movies, but not under that name.

(Photo courtesy Dean Hill.)

PART THREE
MEMPHIS

Louisville, Ky.
Tuesday, April 12
8:00 P.M. *1983*

A.W.A. World
Heavy Weight Title Match
No Referee in Ring
Nick Bockwinkle
-vs-
Jerry Lawler

Southern Tag Team
Title Match
The Fabulous Ones
-vs-
The Moon Dogs w/Hart

Stagger Lee
-vs-
Bobby Eaton w/Hart

Mask At Stake
Rock & Roll Express
-vs-
The Galaxians w/Cornette

Duke Myers -vs- Dutch Mantell

Sonny King -vs- Carl Fergie

Thursday, April 14, Tell City, Ind.
Bryan Taylor Sports Center
Sponsored by Optomist Club & Ath. Dept.

Thursday, April 21, Mt. Washington, Ky.
Bullit East High School
Sponsored by Athletic Boosters

Thursday, April 21, Cave City, Ky.
Caverna High School
Sponsored by Athletic Dept.

CHAMPIONSHIP
WRESTLING
Presents

ACTION
RINGSIDE

WRESTLING CARD

LOUISVILLE
WRESTLING

At The
**LOUISVILLE
GARDENS**

Watch
Championship Wrestling
WAVE TV Channel 3
Saturday Afternoon
12:00 til 1:00 P.M.

This program is presented weekly
in the interest of Professional Wrestling
by Championship Wrestling
Promotion reserves the right to make necessary
changes to the scheduled matches.

Louisville Gardens wrestling program, 1983. The masked Galaxians included Danny Davis, who later founded OVW in Louisville.

"FROM MEMPHIS, TENNESSEE"

By the end of the 1970s, the Vietnam War would end, disco would rise and fall, *Star Wars* would change movie going forever, and Tuesday night at Louisville Gardens would be one of the hottest tickets in town. But as the decade began, wrestling in the city of Louisville was all but non-existent. Three hours south, an aspiring wrestler and promoter was poised to change that.

The Memphis wrestling territory, as it is most commonly known, belonged to Nick Gulas and Roy Welch and was run out of Nashville, Tennessee. Gulas was a well-respected promoter and the front man for the promotion, but behind the scenes it was Welch who really ran the show. Welch was a former wrestler himself and no stranger to Louisville, having wrestled numerous shows for the Allen Athletic Club decades before. Welch was also responsible for one of the promotion's most significant hires - Christine Jarrett.

Miss Christine, or Teeny, was a single mom with a great deal of pride and drive. The fiercely independent single mother began her wrestling career by selling tickets for the Nashville shows at Jarman's Shoe Store. Nick Gulas and Roy Welch found her to be indispensable, and they brought her into the main office. She worked hard for Gulas and Welch, and she wanted to see her son find his own success in any industry except wrestling. Unfortunately for Teeny, her son Jerry wanted nothing more than to be in the wrestling business.

Against Teeny's wishes, Jerry began training with Tojo Yamamoto, a long time hand in the Memphis territory and one of its most hated heels. Tojo brought Jerry into the business the old fashioned way, letting the boy take his licks in the ring night after night and slowly "smartening him up" to the business. Jerry Jarrett took to the road with Tojo and the gang, sometimes working as a wrestler and other nights as a referee. At every opportunity, the young father and husband sought new opportunities to advance in the promotion and make more money.

By 1970 Jarrett was booking for Gulas and Welch at the Mid-South Coliseum in Memphis, but the ambitious young promoter had his sights set on expansion. With the blessing of Gulas and Welch, Jarrett pulled out some road maps and looked for cities within a day's drive of Memphis to target. First and foremost, Jarrett wanted Louisville.

In Jarrett's mind Louisville, Lexington, and Evansville, Indiana were natural extensions to the southern territory. It had been thirteen years since Louisville had its own dedicated promotion, and Jarrett was confident his style of booking would pack the house in Kentucky as it had in Memphis.

Jarrett took his proposal to Gulas and Welch, who were quick to inform him that Louisville still belonged to Dick the Bruiser. Bruiser's WWA promotion had long since abandoned the town, but Gulas and Welch were not eager to get into a turf war with the volatile promoter.

Nevertheless, Jarrett pressed his bosses on the idea, convinced that he could succeed where the WWA had failed. Welch finally gave Jarrett his blessing to pursue Louisville on one condition: he had to get a television station. Gulas facetiously wished Jarrett well, certain he would fail, but Welch told Jarrett to ignore Gulas and give it a go.

Jerry Jarrett began making weekly treks to the River City where he would pay a visit to all five local television stations. Jarrett's past as a cookware salesman served him well, as he used the same techniques to sell wrestling as he once used to sell pots and pans. Whatever reason the program managers gave Jarrett for saying no, he agreed with them before reminding them that circumstances could sometimes change. In this way Jarrett kept the doors open for future return visits, hoping to eventually transform a no into a yes.

According to Jarrett's biography, he finally got a break at Channel 41, WDRB, where the receptionist informed him a new station manager was beginning the following week. Jarrett was in the parking lot waiting for him when he arrived on day one, asking for the man by name and introducing himself.

His name was John Dorkin, and the initial contact made an impression on the new station manager. He told Jarrett that he needed some time to get his feet wet, but he told the promoter to please stop by a week or so later so they could talk. Jarrett returned to WDRB, and Dorkin gave Jarrett his television deal.

After signing the deal with Channel 41, Jarrett went immediately to Louisville Gardens. In an all or nothing move, he signed a 52 week deal with the Gardens, a huge risk that would make or break his career. Succeed, and he would be a hero. Fail, and he would be finished before he ever got started.

Jarrett began broadcasting Memphis wrestling shows in Louisville several weeks before their first live show. Jarrett allowed himself eight weeks of lead time between the beginning of the TV broadcasts and the first live show at Louisville Gardens. Television was a big part of the success in Memphis, and a lack of television was one big reason the WWA failed in Louisville. Would eight weeks be enough to stir up a fan base?

Jarrett's first show at the Gardens lost money. He lost money the second week and the third week. In week four, he broke even. Four weeks later, eight weeks into his 52 week agreement, he was selling out. The wrestling-hungry fans loved the slam-bang style of Memphis wrestling, and an old Tuesday night tradition was re-born.

Convinced that Louisville would become a steady money maker, Jarrett went forward with his plans to expand into Lexington and Evansville. Jarrett also made his mother Teeny a 25% partner in the Louisville promotion. Teeny would become a fixture in the River City so long as Jerry was running the town.

With Louisville, Lexington, and Evansville making money, Gulas and Welch stepped in to claim their fair share as well. Jarrett was using the Memphis television tapes to build the new markets, and Nick Gulas (under orders from Roy Welch) informed Jarrett they required 50% ownership in the Louisville promotion. Jarrett reluctantly agreed, and his ownership was cut to 25% in the deal.

Gulas and Welch weren't the only ones looking to cash in on the River City revival. Jerry arrived at the Gardens one Tuesday to find Dick the Bruiser and his partner Wilbur Snyder waiting for him. The Indy promoters came on strong, insisting Louisville was still their town. Jarrett refused to give in to their bully act, telling them he had a right to promote in whatever town he chose. Bruiser and Snyder conceded the point but demanded a small percentage of the profits to keep them from promoting in Louisville.

Jarrett took their request to Gulas and Welch, who instructed Jarrett to pay off the Bruiser. Jarrett paid 10% weekly for Bruiser for a number of years, but after a few years, Jarrett stopped sending checks, confident that Bruiser wouldn't do anything about it. He was right.

Jarrett's promotion was officially dubbed Louisville Wrestling Enterprises. Even though Memphis was home, Jarrett considered Louisville to be his town. His television show bounced around between channels 41 and 32 before moving to Channel 3, better known as WAVE 3, in 1979 where it stayed on the air for years.

Much of the success of Memphis and Louisville in the 70s and 80s is directly attributable to Jerry Jarrett's booking. Jerry believed in old fashioned storytelling where good guys were clearly good guys and bad guys were really bad. He knew how to tell a story and create anticipation in his audience so that when the time came for the bad guy to get his, the fans would sell out the building to see the big payoff.

Memphis wrestling was especially known for tag team wrestling and featured some of the greatest tag teams of the era. The Fargos, Jerry and Don, were one of the most dominant tag teams of the 50s and 60s and still one of the top draws when Jarrett opened Louisville. Jackie Fargo was one of the first wrestlers to use tables and chairs in matches and would later be the mentor for the biggest star ever to come out of Memphis, Jerry Lawler.

The Fargos frequently did battle with Jarrett and his tag partner Tojo Yamamoto. Jarrett took a major risk when he turned his mentor babyface, but the fans quickly embraced the long time heel and he became a fan favorite.

Louisville fans had the chance to see a number of tag teams come through the territory, including the Freebirds, the Moondogs, the Midnight Rockers (Shawn Michaels and Marty Janetty), and the Sheepherders (aka the Bushwhackers). But the home grown tag teams were just as popular with the fans. The Rock N Roll Express featuring Ricky Morton and Robert Gibson was born in 1983, the brain child of Jerry Lawler. The Fabulous Ones, Stan Lane and Steve Keirn, were brought together by Lawler and Jarrett. Future OVW founder Danny Davis was a member of both the Nightmares and the Galaxians.

Jarrett was also an innovator when it came to creating anticipation for new talent. When the Fabulous Ones, were brought together, Jarrett created a promotional video set to ZZ Top's "Sharp Dressed Man" to acquaint the fans in each city with their new heroes. The Fabs became an instant hit, especially with the ladies, and Jarrett continued producing videos to promote new talent. Jarrett's backyard became the wilds of Africa when they filmed the promotional videos that introduced Kamala the Ugandan Giant to the world.

Jarrett was also an innovator in the ring. In 1971, he and Don Greene introduced the world to one of the most dangerous gimmick matches of all - the scaffold match. In a scaffold match, a temporary scaffolding is erected or suspended above the ring. Contestants do battle on top of the scaffolding until one or the other is tossed to the ring below. It's a dangerous match with real risk, so dangerous it's never been done in the WWF or WWE, and the very first of its kind took place on August 15, 1971, at Louisville Gardens.

The scaffold used in that first match was only twelve feet above the mat, and Jarrett and Green did not attempt any high risk maneuvers. The match was mostly a lot of pushing and shoving, trying to get the other guy to roll off the scaffold. Later matches would raise the platform higher and higher. Memphis was the only territory to use the scaffold match until 1984, when Mid-South adopted the match for themselves. In 1986 the Road Warriors took on the Midnight Express during the NWA's Starrcade pay-per-view in one of the most famous scaffold matches of all time with a scaffold reportedly 24 feet high. Louisville's Jim Cornette even took a tumble off that scaffold, slipping right through the arms of Ray Traylor (the future Big Boss Man) and twisting his knee in the process.

In just a few short years, Memphis went from just another town on the map to the number one wrestling town in America, and Louisville had a front row seat for what would be the last and greatest if the independent territories. The Memphis wrestlers became the biggest celebrities in both Memphis and Louisville. One night at the Gardens, Jackie Fargo was told he had a huge fan waiting outside the locker room wanting to meet him. Fargo was stunned when he came face to face with his self-proclaimed number one fan, Muhammad Ali.

THE WILD CROWD

Of all the heels who were part of wrestling in Louisville, of all the bad guys who drew blood inside the Gardens, there was one that stood above the rest. One heel drew more blood, used more dirty tactics, and committed more dastardly deeds than any other: the Louisville crowd.

Louisville was the first of the new cities to catch on when Jarrett expanded the Memphis territory. Evansville, Lexington, and many of the small towns took a while to catch on with the boys from down south, but Louisville almost immediately became a money maker. With no Ticketmaster and no box office to call for reserved tickets, fans would line up outside, week after week, in hopes of getting a seat. The line would wrap all the way around Louisville Gardens, and if you didn't get there early enough, you might be left out!

Louisville fans weren't just avid sports lovers. They were demonstrative, sometimes aggressive participants in the weekly shows. The Louisville crowd had a short fuse, and it quickly developed a reputation for being the rowdiest and most dangerous in the territory.

If an object could be thrown into the ring, it was thrown. Popcorn, beer, bottles, even women's beauty products became missiles in the hands of the fans. One of my co-workers recalled a night his mother became so angry, she threw a makeup compact at one of the heels. Bill Dundee still bears a scar from the time he was slashed across the chest by a woman's nail file.

Sometimes throwing things wasn't enough. From time to time a fan would get so incensed, they would actually charge into the ring to take a shot at someone. It's rare to see fans jumping in the ring today, and when it happens, the fan is usually just looking to get on TV. Back in the 70s and 80's, the fans weren't hoping to get on TV. They wanted to hurt someone.

Dirty Dutch Mantell witnessed the wrath of the Louisville crowd first hand. After winning a tag match with partner David Schultz over the native American team of Danny Little Bear and Chief Thundercloud, the victors took the liberty of giving their opponents an extra beat down. The crowd kept their seats until Chuy, the son of one of the two babyfaces, jumped in the ring to save his dad. When Mantell and Schultz tore into poor Chuy, the crowd had enough and stormed the ring.

The angry mob pulled Chuy and the two good guys to safety, but the crowd did not return to their seats. Dutch and his partner found themselves surrounded on all sides as the mob waited, daring them to step out of the ring. With the help of security the two made it to safety of back stage where their opponents were waiting for them, laughing hysterically.

Wrestlers and managers knew they were there for the enjoyment of fans, who paid good money to see them perform, and they knew better than to retaliate when fans became rowdy. That doesn't mean everyone kept their hands to themselves. Bearcat Wright was a former boxer and wrestler working as a manager in the 70s. On June 24, 1975 an irate fan decided to get a piece of Bearcat for himself. After taking a couple of shots from the fan, Bearcat dropped the man with a left and a right. The man dropped to the floor, and Bearcat followed up with a kick to the head with his cowboy boots.

Another fan tried to attack Wright after the incident, and fans began to surround the ring. The referee called for a quick disqualification, and several wrestlers came out of the locker room, ostensibly to get a piece of the heels but actually to protect them and help get them out of harm's way.

As medics attended to the wounded fan, who lay on the ground convulsing in pain, Teeny Jarrett raced over to young photographer Jim Cornette and asked if he got any photos of the incident.

"Yes, ma'am," said Cornette. "But I only got three."

"Get them to me as soon as you can," she said. "We're going to have a law suit." Bearcat was not charged in the incident, but it would be several weeks before he would show his face in Louisville Gardens again.

Earlier that year on March 11, Bill Dundee had a run in with a fan outside the ring. After seeing Dundee tossed over the top rope onto the concrete floor, a fan jumped the barrier and took a swing at Dundee. Dundee retaliated with several real punches of his own before police drug the fan out of the arena. Several months later, after Dundee turned babyface, a fight broke out between two fans at ringside when one of them voiced his objection to the new babyface. Dundee sat on the ropes and cheered the fans on as police made their way to ringside and escorted the brawlers from the Gardens.

On April 22 of that same year, another melee broke out during a tag match between Rocket Monroe and Randy Tyler vs. Jerry Jarrett and George Gulas. Just as Jarrett was about to win the match, a wrestler named John Gray hit the ring and knocked out Jarrett with a chain. After Monroe pinned Jarrett, a fan crossed the barrier and attacked Gray. No sooner was the fan subdued by police, another fan attacked Gray. As Gray assaulted the man with his chain, Tojo Yamamoto raced out of the locker room and chased Gray back to the relative safety of the ring, where the babyfaces and heels did battle. When the heels finally tried to escape to the locker room, a third fan attacked, this time with a knife. Police struggled to restore order as fans showered the ring with cups and other garbage.

Danny Davis had his own incursion with a fan during his early days when he managed the Blonde Bombers. "Wayne (Farris) and Larry (Latham) were holding the babyface for me while I beat him with this steel bar. Suddenly I turn around, and here comes a fan into the ring. So I turned around and laid him out with the steel.

"It was a different time then," recalls Davis with a smile.

The Louisville police took an active role protecting the wrestlers from the fans. Heels were escorted by a group of four policemen to and from the ring. "The cops were heels too," says Davis. "If a fan got out of hand, they'd cuff them and take them into custody. Then they'd give the heels five minutes each with them. Like I said, it was a different time."

The police were not the only protection afforded to the wrestlers. Pat Malone, who three decades earlier wrestled in Louisville as the Green Shadow, kept watch over the dressing room door every Tuesday night. He was not only one of the toughest men in the ring, but one of the most fearless outside the ring, having also served as a trainer for Ginger the wrestling bear. His days in the ring were long gone by the time Memphis started coming to town, but even in his 80's, he was a formidable defense for the wrestlers. Between an angry scowl, cauliflower ears, the knife in his pocket, and the pistol in his car, no one - NO ONE - dared try to breach the locker room while Pat Malone was on duty.

Jim Cornette recalls a story about Pat Malone that proves his toughness was genuine. One night someone dared to challenge Malone and stabbed the old grappler with a knife. Ignoring the wound in his side, Malone chased the man down in the parking lot and pinned him to the pavement. Police arrived on the scene just in time. Malone had a knife in his hand and was about to cut his assailant's head off.

The hot tempered crowd at the Gardens kept the wrestlers and the police on their toes, but the weekly visits to the Garden had an interesting impact on crime outside the building. During the 70s and 80's, the Louisville police noticed a trend. The rate of domestic calls to the blue-collar Portland neighborhood in West Louisville dropped to almost nothing every Tuesday from 7 PM to 11 PM - when a significant portion of the Portland neighborhood was downtown watching wrestling at the Gardens.

Not everyone remembers Louisville as a dangerous town. Bobby Fulton, who wrestled in the territory during the early 80's, remembers the Louisville fans as extremely passionate. From the first time he walked into Louisville Gardens, he was impressed by how much the people loved wrestling. Fulton never suffered the wrath of the Louisville fans himself, but he did suffer more abuse at the hands of fans, including a broken arm, while wrestling elsewhere in Kentucky.

The Louisville police assigned to work the shows wore riot helmets every week up until the early 80's, when the heat started to die down. The mellowing of the Louisville crowd was a welcome development in the locker room, but for a few, the relief was short lived. Just as the Louisville crowd became more tame, Jim Cornette found himself bound for the Mid-South territory, a region that made the Louisville crowd on its worst night look like a Kindergarten class.

TEENY

Jerry Jarrett ran the Memphis territory. He also wrote the TV programs, booked the shows, and performed in many of them. There were only so many hats he could wear, and the responsibility of managing the road shows was more than he could handle. So Jerry Jarrett turned to the person he trusted most to run Louisville, Evansville, and the other stops in the territory: his mother.

For nearly twenty years, Teeny made sure the northern portion of the Memphis territory ran smoothly and on time. Tuesday morning, she would hit the road with a driver (she never drove herself). She went straight to the Louisville TV station to pick up the previous week's tape and drop off the new one. From there she went on to the Gardens to oversee the set up at the arena. After the show, the crew would tear down, eat dinner, and drive home to Nashville that night.

Wednesday morning she'd be on the road again, this time bound for Evansville. As in Louisville, she would first stop by the TV station and then head to the arena. After the Evansville shows, Teeny would drive back to Louisville and spent the night with the Cornettes - Thelma and her son Jim. Thelma and Teeny became close friends after Thelma began bringing young Jim to the arena to take photos. Thursday would find Teeny in Lexington or another small town in Kentucky and Indiana, and Saturday nights she was selling tickets in Nashville.

Teeny was responsible for everything in Louisville, Evansville, and other points north. She placed the ads in the paper. She printed the tickets and oversaw the ticket sales. She kept the books, supervised the concessions and souvenirs, and handled the press. All of the building contracts were in her name, as were all the TV contracts. Jerry Jarrett may have considered Louisville "his town," but it was his mother that kept "his town" running smoothly for so many years.

Professional wrestling was no longer covered as a legitimate sport by the early 70s. At least once a year, one of the local Louisville TV stations would show up to do a story, usually a negative one emphasizing how "fake" professional wrestling was. After a few such stories aired during her tenure, Teeny put a stop to it. Louisville's Channel 32 showed up one night, and Teeny refused to let them in the building. The news reporter tried to appease her, telling her it would be good publicity. "I have a house of 5000 people inside," she told the reporter. "I don't need your help selling tickets!"

It took a strong personality to manage the chaos and egos on the road 52 weeks a year for nearly two decades, but Teeny was more than up to the task. When Teeny appeared at the door leading to the locker room and shouted "BILL DUNDEE!!!" or any other name, the boys knew she meant business.

Teeny had the full respect of the locker room, and more than a few wrestlers who crossed her felt the wrath "the pinch." If Teeny needed to get your attention, she'd pinch your cheeks together in her hands like a small child, look you in the eye, and set you straight.

The Fabulous Ones, Stan Lane and Steve Keirn, were just two of the many wrestlers to feel her wrath. One evening in Evansville the pair was scheduled to compete in the main event, but just before show time, their match was moved up second to last. Either someone failed to inform the Fabulous Ones, or the pair simply neglected to keep track of what was going on, because when their music began to play, the tag team was nowhere to be found.

As their song was winding down, Teeny stormed out of the arena and headed into the parking lot, where she found Lane and Keirn in a van with two girls. Teeny crashed the party, screaming at the boys to pull themselves together and hit the ring immediately.

As she walked back into the arena, she turned to one of the other wrestlers and sighed. "They turned my parking lot into a whorehouse!"

The Freebirds came into the territory as one of the hottest acts in the country, but their stay was cut short after only a few weeks. Teeny has very strict rules regarding the wrestlers and their interactions with female fans. All of the wrestlers went behind her back and did what they wanted, but the Freebirds rubbed her nose in it. When the Freebirds refuse to behave, it was Teeny who kicked them out of Memphis.

The one person who locked horns with Teeny more than any other was the athletic commissioner of the state of Kentucky, Fred Lampson. The athletic commissioner was a political appointment, and Lampson was the very embodiment of a political appointee who had no business in his particular office. He knew nothing about boxing, wrestling, or any of the fight sports, and his ignorance was the usual cause of conflicts with Teeny.

The crew arrived one Tuesday planning to put on a twenty man battle royal. Lampson had no idea what a battle royal was, but when it was explained that contestants in a battle royal are eliminated by being thrown over the top rope, Lampson refused to let the match go on. Tossing your opponent over the rope is an immediate disqualification, Lampson said, and if that were to happen, there would be nineteen winners and one loser.

On another occasion, Lampson fined wrestler Jonathan Boyd for punching out an official during a tag match with the Sheepherders. The blow to the official was a planned spot, part of the story that night, but Lampson insisted the fine be paid or Boyd would not be permitted to wrestle in the state of Kentucky. Boyd was scheduled to compete in a "loser leaves town" match the following week with the Sheepherders. The ads had already gone out promoting the match, and Jerry Jarrett had no choice but to pay Boyd's fine.

Teeny finally had enough with Lampson one night in 1982. On this particular night, Lampson informed Teeny that too many people were using the ring mic. In his mind, wrestlers were there to compete, not talk. Lampson insisted the only person to be allowed to use the PA mic was the announcer.

Unfortunately for Lampson, the Iron Sheik was in the building that night. The microphone was an integral part of the Sheik's performance. The Sheik took the mic before his match to trash the USA and remind everyone that Iran was number one. The Iron Sheik knew nothing of Teeny's battles with Lampson, nor did he care, so when he arrived in the ring, he went straight for the mic.

Jim Cornette was on the mic that night, filling in for the regular announcer. Cornette tried his best to keep the Sheik from taking the mic, but the legendary heel would not be denied. Cornette staged a hopeless tug of war with the Sheik for the microphone, pleading with him to let it go. "The commissioner is here tonight!" Cornette shouted.

The Iron Sheik ripped the mic from Cornette's hands - accidentally turning the mic on in the process - and responded, "F--- the commissioner!!"

Lampson raced down the aisle fuming, ready to pull the plug on the Sheik. Instead he ran straight into Teeny Jarrett, who caught his face in "the pinch."

"Fred Lampson," she said, staring into his wide eyes, "You worry about collecting the taxes, and I'll worry about running the show!" Lampson got the message. He was not seen in the Gardens for about six months following the incident.

Ian Rotten, who later founded Louisville promotion IWA Mid-South, had a run-in with Teeny after insulting a female fan. "I had called one of the regulars in the crowd a whore," he says. "After the match, I headed up the aisle, and there was Teeny, motioning me over. She didn't put me in the pinch, but she grabbed my ear and pulled it down. 'Mr. Rotten,' she said, "We do not call our female fans sluts, whores, prostitutes, or bitches."'

Teeny could be the boss when she had to, but most of the time she was, in the words of Bobby Fulton, a true Southern lady. Miss Christine, as he remembers her, was a sweet woman who treated everyone with respect. She clipped and brought coupons for the boys who were struggling to make ends meet, and dispensed old fashioned advice that stuck with many of the boys. Fulton still remembers the advice Teeny gave him on choosing a girl. "Find a girl who is happy just having a hamburger with you."

Teeny's kindness and generosity were not limited to the talent. She became acquainted with many of the regulars in the Memphis territory, and formed a special bond with many of those fans. One regular at the Evansville show, a farmer, would bring produce to the arena every week in exchange for his ticket. The following morning back in Louisville, the Cornettes awoke to the sound of Teeny snapping peas down in the guest bedroom.

Without question, Jerry Jarrett was the mastermind who breathed life into the Memphis territory, but Louisville never would have been what it was without Teeny Jarrett. From selling shoes and wrestling tickets to becoming the road manager of one of the country's hottest territories, Teeny is a true American success story.

Perhaps nothing captures the specialness of this woman like my first meeting with Jim Cornette. We were sitting in his Fortress of Solitude, surrounded by posters, photos, memorabilia, and yes, fuzzy tennis rackets, when I asked Jim about Teeny. He got up, walked to a small end table, and picked up a Christmas card. It was the last Christmas card he received from Teeny before she passed away, and like all the glitzy memorabilia in the room, it had a special place of honor.

A BOY AND HIS CAMERA

Right about the time Jerry Jarrett invaded Louisville, a young man born and raised in the River City happened to catch Dick the Bruiser's Indianapolis wrestling show on television. The boy was hooked, and he immediately found out when he could catch wrestling on local Louisville television. This was Jim Cornette's introduction to Memphis wrestling and the business that would become his life.

Unable to drive himself to the matches, twelve year old Jim Cornette began attending matches with his mother Thelma in 1974. He soon combined his passion for the sport with a second passion, photography. He began bringing his camera to the matches and snapping photos of the wrestlers en route to the ring and in action.

Jim's mother Thelma upgraded his camera, and with every passing week, Jim's photography improved. Not only did the camera take better photos, Jim's growing understanding of wrestling psychology aided him in taking better action shots. Jim showed some of the photos to Teeny Jarrett, who was impressed with the young man's talent. Teeny had taken a liking to Jimmy, and she and Thelma grew to be close friends. Jim wrote down all the results from the matches he saw at Louisville Gardens and elsewhere in a spiral notebook. On July 1, 1975, Teeny introduced Jim to her son Jerry Jarrett.

Jim's passion and talent were not welcomed by all at first. When Dennis Condrey noticed the teenager snapping photos during a tag match, he screamed at him, "Stay in your seat!" Condrey then threw Wayne Petty out of the ring in the direction of Cornette. Little did either know that eight years later, Cornette would become Condrey's manager.

Jim began selling photos of the wrestlers to Teeny and to some of the wrestlers, who would in turn sell those

153

photos at the merchandise table. It was a win-win for Cornette and the wrestlers.

Before Cornette became involved, only a handful of wrestlers were selling photos. The ones that did sell pictures were selling cheaply made black and white copies. It didn't take long for the wrestlers to see value in the work of the young photographer. Better quality photos meant higher prices and more importantly, bigger sales numbers. Cornette soon found himself in the photography business, taking photos for all the boys and even handling the printing. A handful of black and white photos gave way to a table covered in full color photos that drew a mob of fans - mostly young girls - every week.

It's no exaggeration to say that young Jimmy Cornette revolutionized merchandising for the Memphis promotion. The photos boosted the profits for the promoters and the wrestlers, who got a piece of whatever merchandise had their name or face on it. The Louisville weekly sales averaged between $800-1200 a week, most of that money made from $1 and $3 photos and 50 cent programs. At the height of their popularity, the Fabulous Ones, Stan Lane and Steve Keirn, were splitting $4000-5000 a week on merchandise sales alone.

For those of you who are running the numbers in your head, trying to figure out how two guys could consistently make $5000 a week selling $1-$3 photos in the same towns, I give you the first hand memories of a female fan who was twelve years old when the Fabs were at their peak.

"I loved the Fabulous Ones. I begged my dad every week to let me get their pictures. I'd say, 'Please dad, please let me get one so I can get autographs!' I already had all their pictures on my wall at home, but I didn't care. I wanted more. I loved them!"

The heels were not able to cash in at the same clip as the babyfaces. Heels, by definition, didn't sign autographs, and while the heels had their fans, they were few and far between. That said, even the most hated heel could make a few dollars with a little reverse psychology. "I don't want any of you morons out there to go to my table, buy my photo, and rip it up!"

As with any industry, a well-paid wrestler is a happy wrestler, and Jarrett had no trouble drawing in new stars eager to see a boost in their take home. Other promoters began to see what they were doing in Memphis and followed their lead, most notably Vince McMahon, Jr., who took merchandising to the next level in the mid 80's.

Cornette's photography made its way into the hands of several national publications as well, thanks to the old Louisville veteran Pat Malone. Malone was friends with the publisher of *Wrestling News* and sent in a number of young Jim's photos for publication. Most of these early photos were incorrectly credited to Pat Malone, whom Cornette is sure never took a photo in his life. Nevertheless, Cornette was thrilled seeing his work in a national publication at the tender age of fifteen.

As Jim continued to take photos of the wrestlers, he learned more than just how to take a good picture. He learned the psychology of wrestling. He developed a feel for the action in the ring. He knew when the high spots and big moments were coming. He knew when the babyface was poised to make his comeback. He knew how stories were told through the in-ring action. Jim's desire was to take better, more action packed photos, but the education he received through the lens of the camera was invaluable preparation for the career that lay ahead of him.

When Jerry Jarrett split from Nick Gulas in the late 1970s, Jerry Lawler took over the responsibility of producing the weekly *Action Ringside* programs. Lawler, who is an exceptionally good artist, filled the programs with original sketches and hand written copy, but he turned to Jim Cornette to provide the photo coverage week after week. In time Cornette would become a contributing writer and ultimately the main writer for the program.

Action Ringside led to another publishing venture, *Championship Wrestling Magazine*. The magazine was a much more in-depth look at the personalities and feuds taking place in the territory, and each issue was packed with photos and articles written by Cornette.

Many of the articles and interviews he wrote were complete fabrications, with questions, answers, and quotes completely made up by the teenage writer, but since this was not a national publication, they did not have to be the real deal. After so much time hanging around the wrestlers and fabricating quotes for the weekly programs, Jim had a solid grasp of the way every wrestler in the territory spoke. No one ever took issue with the words Jim put in their mouths.

By the time Jim was twenty, he was attending over 150 live events a year. He was running a successful photography business, publishing his own magazine, selling merchandise, taking photos of every show, and even ring announcing. Jim Cornette might very well have become the successor to Bill Apter, the next great voice in wrestling publications. But fate, and Jerry Jarrett, had other ideas.

The idea to use Jim Cornette as a manager occurred to Jerry Jarrett during a lunch. Jarrett sat a table away from Cornette, who was talking with some of the wrestlers in his natural, rapid-fire pattern. Jarrett liked Cornette and related to him a great deal as the son of a single mother, but that day, Cornette's mouth was getting on his nerves. Jarrett had visions of popping the young man in his big mouth. He knew then that Cornette was generating the kind of heat that heels dream of drawing from a crowd. Jarrett asked Cornette if he wanted to become an on-screen manager. Jim simply replied, "When do I start?"

The idea for Jim's ringside persona came from real life and his close relationship with his mother. Jarrett envisioned Cornette as a spoiled mama's boy who would use his family fortune to break into the wrestling business. When Jim arrived in Memphis for his first TV taping, he asked Jarrett for direction on what he should say. "Jimmy, just be yourself," Jarrett told him. "I'm sure all these fans want to know what a wonderful mother you have."

An article announcing Jim Cornette's new career path appeared in the weekly program on September 6, 1982. The writer of the article expressed doubt about Cornette's ability to be a successful manager and questioned why the nice young man would want to do such a thing. The writer, of course, was Jim Cornette, who was setting the stage for his emergence as a heel.

Jim knew he would have no trouble drawing heat from the crowd in Memphis, where he was an unknown face. What he didn't expect was the heat he received in Louisville and other towns that knew him and his mom. As much as Memphis hated this upstart crashing into their world, the towns that knew Jim really hated him for being a jerk when he had such a sweet mother.

After ten years of observing the wild, passionate Louisville crowd through the lens of the camera, Jim experienced their wrath first hand. He learned the ropes on the job, working alongside Crusher Broomfield (aka the One Man Gang), Jesse Barr, Exotic Adrian Street, and the Galaxians. Jim even acted as a partner and stand-in for Jimmy Hart for a short time before his big break came.

"I left Louisville just as the crowds were really starting to mellow," recalls Cornette. "Then I moved to Louisiana and Mid-South, where the crowds were ten times worse than Louisville ever was!"

In a major talent trade with Jerry Jarrett, Cowboy Bill Watts chose Cornette to be the manager of a new tag team in his Mid-South territory. Memphis stars Dennis Condrey and Bobby Eaton were brought together to form Cornette's clients, the Midnight Express. Watts matched the Midnight Express with the babyface team the Rock &

Roll Express, and in 1984, the tag teams helped Mid-South shatter all box office records.

Success in Mid-South led Cornette and the Midnight Express to World Class Championship Wrestling in Dallas. Success in Dallas led them to Jim Crockett Promotions, where they became even bigger stars appearing on World Championship Wrestling on Superstation TBS. Cornette won the Pro Wrestling Illustrated's Manager of the Year Award in 1985, and in the fall of 1986, Cornette and the Midnight Express took part in the infamous scaffold match with the Road Warriors.

In the early 1990s, Cornette went into business for himself. WCW and WWF were both struggling, and Cornette saw the opportunity to revive territorial wrestling. In 1992 he opened Smokey Mountain Wrestling, a promotion based out of Knoxville, Tennessee. The promotion was small, keeping a roster of no more than sixteen wrestlers at any given time, but the list of talent that passed through SMW is a who's who of 90s superstars. Smokey Mountain was a critical success, and tapes of SMW shows are a much sought after item by wrestling diehards. But the promotion fell on hard times financially, and after four years, they called it quits.

Before the promotion went under, Smokey Mountain opened the door for Cornette and his new tag team, the Heavenly Bodies, to make their mark in the WWF. Cornette's first appearance in WWF TV is on YouTube, and it's a textbook example of an established talent passing his heat on to a new star. With no music and no fanfare, Cornette makes his way to the ring to a smattering of boos. As Vince McMahon wonders aloud who this individual might be, color commentator Bobby "The Brain" Heenan throws down his headset, races into the ring, and embraces the man from Louisville - a man who, by his own admission, "stole" much of his gimmick from The Brain himself. Heenan's embrace is all the reason the WWF crowd needs to unleash a thunderstorm of boos as Cornette takes the mic and announces that he and Smokey Mountain tag team the Heavenly Bodies were ready to invade the WWF.

Cornette would manage a number of wrestlers during his WWF stint, most notably the great Yokozuna. He would also become a member of the WWF's creative team, a job he both loved and loathed. The boy with the camera had risen from ringside at Louisville Gardens to the top promotion in the country, but before the decade was over, Cornette would return home to open the next chapter of his career and Louisville wrestling history.

GARDEN MEMORIES

One of the reasons Memphis held on as long as it did after the WWF conquered the world was the frugalness of Jerry Jarrett. The Memphis territory was a great place for a wrestler to make a good income, but Jerry Jarrett was a man who knew the value of a dollar. If Jerry saw a chance to save a buck, he took it.

One of the biggest money savers Jerry Jarrett found was conserving video tapes. Many territory managers recorded their shows on new video tapes week in and week out, creating a huge library of tapes. Promoters that held on to their tapes were able to exploit them once the home video market and DVD came into vogue. Some were even able to cash in by selling their video libraries to the WWE for use in home video releases and their various television outlets.

Had Jarrett known that video tapes would one day be a gold mine, he might have spent the money to buy new tapes every week. Instead, Jarrett recycled his tapes constantly, recording new shows over old ones for his various television affiliates. Much of the footage that survived the Memphis era is second hand, recorded by fans when the shows aired.

A few months of wrestling were filmed in Louisville exclusively for the Louisville television station, but most of the shows were taped exclusively in Memphis. Fans would catch the action from Memphis on TV and see the story line continue when the wrestlers came to town on Tuesday. The Memphis crew would put on essentially the same show at every stop on their route, so fans who made the Wednesday trip to Evansville would see the same matches and finishes they saw at the Gardens Tuesday.

The continuity between the weekly television shows and the weekly house shows was important to maintain kayfabe and help the audience suspend disbelief, no matter how ludicrous the stories became. But as with any live theatrical performance, live wrestling delivered memories that could not and would not be repeated.

Many such moments were recorded by fans like Jim Cornette, who kept a notebook of results from the shows he attended. On February 4, 1975, during a Southern Heavyweight Title match between Ron Fuller and Jerry Lawler, a man in the crowd suffered a heart attack. The victim was carried out of the Gardens by police and EMT's as the match continued. Lawler lost the match, but would see brighter days ahead. The same could not be said for the fan, who died on the scene.

On May 27 that same year, The Sheik, owner of the Detroit territory, made a rare appearance in Louisville wrestling against Crazy Luke Graham. The Sheik's character was a rich wild man from Syria who never spoke English and loved to inflict pain on his opponents. When the match against Graham ended with a disqualification, the Sheik attacked referee John Randolph, ripping off his shirt and chasing him out of the ring.

Some of the best memories occurred when wrestlers were able to draw the fans into a story line that might go on for weeks, where good guys fight the long but difficult good fight against evil. Such was the case with the legendary Bob Armstrong, who arrived in the summer of 1975 for a feud with Southern Heavyweight Champion the Mongolian Stomper. With manager Bearcat Wright at his side, the Mongolian Stomper managed to thwart Armstrong's efforts to take away the title belt week in and week out. Their first match ended in a disqualification. The second match ended in controversy; Armstrong got the pin, but the referee, groggy from being hit during the match, handed the belt back to the Stomper. The match was ruled a no contest, and the fans attacked the heels as they made their escape.

In the third match Al Greene stood in for Bearcat Wright, who allegedly had struck a Louisville policeman the week before. The match ended with another brawl, and the official held up the title once more. This led to a no time limit, no disqualification match the following week, when the Mongolian Stomper would use a loaded boot to knock out his opponent and reclaim the title.

Match number five proved to be one of the most violent and bloody matches in Louisville history. The "double juicer" ended with both men being counted out. The ring and ring apron were soaked in blood, and the crowd was in a frenzy as the match boiled to its conclusion.

The arch rivals met a week later, with Robert Fuller in Armstrong's corner and Bill Dundee in the Stomper's corner. After that match ended in a disqualification, the four men squared off in a tag match in which Armstrong pinned Dundee. Finally, on October 7, Bob Armstrong defeated the Stomper clean and won the title.

Armstrong and the Mongolian Stomper would meet one more time the following week in a "Loser Leaves Town" match. Armstrong won again, and the Stomper moved on from Memphis, leaving fans with incredible memories of a hard fought rivalry.

One performer who benefited greatly from a story that took off in Louisville was Jimmy Hart. Hart was high school friend of Lawler's and the former lead singer of The Gentry's, who sold a million records with their single "Keep On Dancing." Known to wrestling fans as "The Mouth of the South" and to Memphis fans as "The Wimp," Hart became a heel manager who spent much of his Memphis career searching for the perfect client to put babyface Jerry Lawler in his place.

Hart began his career as an ally of Lawler, but after Lawler legitimately broke his leg in a pick-up football game, Jarrett needed someone to step up and carry the show until Lawler could return. Jarrett received the bad news on a Monday. He didn't sleep that night, and when he arrived in Louisville, he was on a caffeine high. He also had a plan.

Jarrett decided he would transform Jimmy Hart from a sidekick to a leading man. With Jerry Lawler out of action, Jimmy Hart would strike out on his own as a manager and form a stable of heel wrestlers.

Jimmy Hart's transformation began in Louisville. That night when announcer Lance Russell interviewed Hart in the ring, Russell asked about the status of the injured Jerry Lawler. Hart drew inspiration from Louisville's greatest sporting tradition, the Kentucky Derby, for his answer.

"Lance," said Hart, "If you have a horse entered in the Kentucky Derby and the horse breaks his leg, what do you do?"

"I don't know, Jimmy," said Russell, "But I'm sure you do."

"Well, Lance, you shoot the horse in the head and get another horse to ride in the Derby!" Hart went on to introduce his new client, the new King of Memphis, Paul Ellering, who came to the ring complete with cape and crown.

The exchange did not sit well with Lawler. Lawler didn't mind seeing his old friend elevated, and he didn't mind Ellering taking on the King of Memphis moniker, but he took exception to the "shoot him in the head" line. After a long recovery, Lawler returned to the ring and entered a feud with Hart. On another Tuesday night in Louisville, Lawler took a hard swing at Hart, breaking his old friend's jaw - a moment captured on film by Jim Cornette. To this day, Hart insists Lawler broke his jaw on purpose, while Lawler insists it was an accident.

Louisville was the sight of another feud involving Lawler, one the people of Louisville took personally. One of the biggest names in Louisville radio history was Coyote Calhoun. In the 1980s Calhoun became the number one afternoon DJ in Louisville on WAMZ. He helped WAMZ win the coveted Academy of Country Music Radio Station of the Year Award in 1986 and won multiple awards himself as an on-air personality and a program director. He even lent his name to a popular country music establishment in downtown Louisville, Coyote's.

Before he became a country legend, Coyote was a loose cannon on WAKY 790 AM, the town's top 40 station. In the fall of 1976 Coyote began to call out Jerry Lawler, and it wasn't long before Lawler seized the opportunity to yell back. Lawler would call in to trade barbs on the air with the young DJ, and a year after the feud began, Calhoun issued a challenge to the King. The King was eager to get his hands on Calhoun, who agreed to do the match if he could use his "Bohemian Alligator Holt." Lawler agreed, and a match was scheduled for November 28, 1976.

The show was a sellout, but as fate would have it, the show had to be canceled due to a snowstorm and icy conditions on the roads south of Louisville. Fans were told to keep their tickets, and the promotion managed to re-book and re-schedule everyone for the following week. Thus the Lawler-Calhoun match became the first show to sell out the Louisville Gardens twice - a feat OVW would duplicate more than two decades later.

Fans were very high on seeing what would happen when Lawler faced Calhoun, and they got their money's worth. Calhoun, who was six feet tall and weighed barely 130 pounds, came to the ring with a bag of lollipops, saying Lawler was the biggest sucker in the world. Lawler felt like a sucker when he saw the man who came to the ring with Calhoun, a 250 pound giant wearing green trunks, a green mask, and a green shirt with white letters that bore his name: "Bohemian Alligator Holt."

Lawler was fuming, but after all the buildup and the canceled show the week before, the fans were not about to let him back out. For fifteen minutes, Bohemian Alligator Holt bounced Lawler around the ring to the delight of the sold out crowd, and the fans went wild for Holt and Coyote.

But Coyote's vanity got the best of him when he tagged into the match. Lawler picked Coyote up in an airplane spin and dropped the DJ to the mat, pinning him in only fifteen seconds.

Coyote's loss to Lawler didn't give the fans the victory they wanted, but in the wrestling business, wins and losses are never as important as money. A feud like Calhoun vs. Lawler doesn't come around often, but when it does, there are no real losers - at least not backstage.

Lawler would have an even greater celebrity feud a few years later with comedian Andy Kaufman. A lifelong wrestling fan, Kaufman's story has been told in the movie *Man on the Moon* and the excellent documentary *I'm From Hollywood*. They battled on Memphis TV and throughout the Memphis territory. Kaufman even visited Louisville, where a sold out, blood thirsty crowd hoped to see the actor get what was coming to him.

Lawler and Kaufman made a ton of money from their feud, but this was the rare case where even the money was secondary. They were so secretive about their feud and their friendship, the truth did not fully come to light until the release of *Man on the Moon*. Even some in the Memphis crew were unsure if the feud was kayfabe. But while all of Memphis, Louisville, and the wrestling world waited for the King of Memphis to give the jerk from Hollywood his comeuppance, Lawler and Kaufman were hiding in the shadows, laughing at their success, and planning their next stunt.

THE MIDGET WHO BEAT THE GIANT

The city of Memphis has two kings. There's Elvis, and then there's Jerry.

Jerry Lawler's biggest dream growing up was to be an artist, but as fate would have it, his artistic talent led him to his true calling. Jerry began sketching pictures of the Memphis stars and submitting them to the local TV station. He was soon trading pictures for wrestling lessons, and under the tutelage of Jackie Fargo, he slowly made his way into the ranks of Memphis wrestling.

At the peak of his popularity, Jerry was every bit the king of Memphis that Elvis was. His face was everywhere, in storefronts, on billboards, and on television commercials. He even recorded a few singles which sold well, at least in the Memphis market. By the late 1970s Jerry was the face of Memphis wrestling appearing in the main event all across the territory.

But as big as Jerry was in Memphis, he found it nearly impossible to break through on the national scene. Just as every rock star dreams of making it on the cover of *Rolling Stone* magazine, Jerry Lawler dreamt of making the cover of a national publication. In the 1970s the premiere publications were *Wrestling Superstars* and *Pro Wrestling Illustrated*, and Jerry Lawler was determined he would grace the cover of one of the two.

Lawler's popularity earned him a number of write ups in the wrestling magazines. One of the most notable was a feature about an empty arena match he had with the legendary Terry Funk at the Mid-South Coliseum in Memphis, where the two of them met with no official, no fans, and no rules in the empty building. Lawler made sure the footage of the match made its way into the hands of his good friend and pro wrestling journalist Bill Apter.

The empty arena match earned Lawler and Funk a nice spread in the magazine, but no cover. The magazine did its best sales in the New York, Atlanta, and mid-Atlantic regions. As interesting and unique as the story was, the editor didn't think a Memphis cover would sell magazines.

Lawler needed something big, or someone big, to help him get his magazine cover. When he finally made the cover of *Wrestling Superstars*, he did it in Louisville, and he did it with the biggest star in all of professional wrestling.

There was no star bigger, physically, than Andre the Giant. Born Andre Roussimoff in Grenoble, France, Andre began his wrestling career at age 17, bouncing from promotion to promotion under a number of different monikers. It wasn't until he reached New York and became the pride of Vince McMahon Sr.'s WWWF that he reached his greatest fame as Andre the Giant.

Like all wrestlers, Andre traveled frequently from territory to territory, never working the same territory for too long a period of time so that his name didn't go stale. But unlike most, Andre was not a free agent. Vince McMahon, Sr., was highly protective of the Giant, and he could only be booked with the blessing of McMahon, Sr.

Andre wrestled some singles matches, but more often than not appeared in Battle Royals. Andre never lost a match, nor a Battle Royal, no matter how steep the challenge or how big the challengers. That was part of the deal in booking Andre; if you booked Andre, Andre had to win.

In 1977 Jerry Jarrett booked Andre for a run in Memphis, which meant the Eighth Wonder of the World would also appear in Louisville. Looking to take advantage of the opportunity to make yet another bid at the elusive magazine cover, Lawler invited a photographer friend to take photos at the Louisville show. The match produced some terrific photos that Lawler sent to Bill Apter in New York.

Apter loved what he saw. He asked Lawler for permission to use the photos and to title the story however he chose. He also specifically asked permission to refer to Lawler as a "midget" in the story. Lawler was so thrilled with finally getting his dream shot, he agreed, and in short order, Jerry Lawler was on the cover of *Wrestling Superstars*.

Lawler's dream put him and Jerry Jarrett in a heap of hot water.

A few months later, at the NWA convention, Vince McMahon Sr. took to the podium with a copy of the magazine in hand, McMahon was furious with the story and especially the headline: "The Night a 'Midget' Defeated Andre the Giant."

Andre didn't lose to anyone. That was the deal, and as far as Vince, Sr., was concerned, this was a serious problem. Magazines like *Wrestling Superstars* were a threat to the territory system that once kept wrestlers and their story lines isolated by geography. Wrestling journalism meant anyone could read about any match anywhere. Andre was one of the single greatest attractions in professional wrestling - his attraction, to be specific. Andre was undefeated, and that undefeated streak had to be honored by all.

McMahon's face turned red as he screamed at his fellow promoters while Lawler and Jerry Jarrett sunk deeper and deeper into their seats. To add insult to injury, Terry Funk, there representing his father's Texas territory, spoke up.

"Well, who was the little bastard who beat Andre the Giant, Vince?"

"Jerry Lawler, that's who it was," said Vince, as Jerry sank even further into his seat.

Funk knew darn well who the "midget" was, as did everyone else in the room.

It was Jerry Jarrett who booked Andre to lose by count out that night in Louisville. Jarrett knew the rules when it came to booking Andre, and he assumed that a disqualification would not be against the rules. Jarrett discussed the finish with Andre, and Andre not only agreed to it, he felt it would make a good set up for a return match later on. He may have been booked as a monster in the ring, but he was a true professional in and out of that same ring.

A month after McMahon's blow up at the NWA retraction, Apter published a make-up article entitled "Why Andre the Giant is Wrestling's Only Undefeated Superstar." The loss was swept under the rug, along with every other loss Andre had suffered or would suffer prior to Wrestlemania III, when Hulk Hogan became the "first" to body slam and pin the giant.

Luckily for Memphis and Louisville wrestling fans, McMahon eventually forgave the two Jerrys and allowed Andre to return. With attendance dwindling in early 1983, Jarrett needed to inject some excitement into the promotion. McMahon agreed to send Andre in to fight alongside Lawler and Stagger Lee (a masked Koko B. Ware) in Lawler's on-going feud with Jimmy Hart and the Hart Family.

Andre returned to Louisville a few more times before his career was out, both with Championship Wrestling and the WWF. Dean Hill recalled a time he got to see Andre in person. Following his post-match shower, Hill witnessed the 7 foot 5 giant walk over to where Jim Duggan and another wrestler were sitting talking. Andre pulled two chairs together, set one butt cheek on each chair, and joined in the conversation nonchalantly as a pool of shower water collected beneath his feet.

Andre cast a long shadow over the wrestling world wherever he went. He was a dominating presence inside the ring, and an unforgettable presence outside the arena. He loved to entertain people, whether he was tossing foes over the top rope or putting on one of his astonishing feats of drinking. Rip Rogers had a front seat for one such drinking adventure when Andre killed a case of beer in Rip's car.

Andre was truly one of a kind, as a talent and as an individual. And yes, he even left his mark in the River City.

THE SPLIT

By 1977, Memphis was the hottest territory in the country. While many long standing promotions were scaling back and shutting down, the Memphis crew saw sold out crowds all over the territory. The television ratings were phenomenal, and Louisville fans packed the Garden every Tuesday night.

Jerry Lawler was now the sole king of Memphis and beyond. Early in the decade, Louisville police contacted Teeny Jarrett asking that her son and his tag partner Tojo no longer go shopping downtown due to the disruption their presence tended to cause.

Likewise, the police had trouble containing the crowds at Winner Furniture, one of the first regular sponsors to sign on to the wrestling broadcast. When word leaked out that some of the wrestling stars would be in the store shooting ads, police had a hard time holding back the crowds.

Jerry Jarrett was making good money for himself and the Gulas/Welch partnership, but Nick Gulas was about to make a decision that would cost him dearly.

Wrestling has always been a family business of sorts, from the Harts in Calgary to the Von Erichs in Texas, from the Gagnes in Minnesota to someone named McMahon in New York. Like many promoters, when Gulas thought about the future, he thought about his son George.

When Nick Gulas looked at his son George, he saw a future star. He was clearly looking through a father's eyes because the young grappler had zero wrestling ability, zero wrestling physique, and zero personality. The elder Gulas, who controlled the southern end of the territory, pushed his son as a babyface from the get go, putting him over the top heels in the southern half of the territory.

It didn't take long for business to drop off in the South. The fans wanted no part of George Gulas, and attendance plummeted across the territory. Payoffs for the wrestlers were bad, even worse than they usually were with Nick Gulas. Guys working the southern end of the promotion begged Jerry Jarrett to bring them up to the Memphis circuit.

Nick was sharp enough to know a change was necessary, but not sharp enough to see the change needed was finding his son a new line of work. He called Jerry Jarrett into his office and gave him a choice: either Jarrett would take over the South, or Jarrett would send a few of his wrestlers to Birmingham in exchange for a few of Nick's men - one of whom had to be George.

Jerry Jarrett wasn't blinded by a father's love. He knew George Gulas was poison, and he knew his houses would decline as swiftly as the houses in the South. He refused either option. Gulas informed Jarrett he didn't have the option of saying no. Gulas owned the business, and Jarrett worked for him.

This was news to Jarrett, who recalled signing a contract that gave him part ownership in the territory, but a close inspection of the contract drawn up by Nick Gulas's attorney revealed that Jarrett owned nothing. Jarrett was furious. He collected his things from his office and went to see Nick Gulas.

Jarrett told Gulas that a wrestling promotion was in the mind, not an office. The only thing he was leaving by walking out were a few wrestling rings and some belts. He would buy those, and he would make Nick Gulas regret this decision for the rest of his life.

After consulting with an attorney and his wife, Jerry Jarrett began putting his own territory together. Jarrett and Gulas were soon on the phone with the Memphis talent, both promoters begging the stars to choose their side. A few of the old guard, including Jackie Fargo and Jarrett's mentor Tojo Yamamoto, agreed to stay with Gulas, but

Jarrett grabbed the promotion's number one star in Jerry Lawler along with Bill Dundee, Rocky Johnson, Dutch Mantell and many others who wanted nothing to do with Gulas.

"Jarrett had been one of the boys and understood what a wrestler goes through," said Bill Dundee of his decision to leave Gulas. "On top of that, he treated the talent right. I would not have worked for Nick under any situation and if Jarrett would have not opened his own company, I would have headed back to Australia."

Jarrett's most important maneuver involved television. The television contracts in Louisville, Lexington, and Evansville were in his and Teeny's names, so switching to the new promotion would be no trouble. Memphis, on the other hand, proved to be a challenge. Lance Russell was the television announcer for wrestling and the program director at Channel 13. Russell initially committed to going with Jarrett when he opened his promotion, but the deal fell through when Channel 13 informed Jarrett that the contracts were in the name of Mid-South Wrestling.

Despite the contract situation, Russell was a friend of Jarrett's and a fan of wrestling. As Jarrett began discussions with Channel 3 and later Channel 5 in Memphis, he asked Russell what he was making at the station. Russell told him, and he also told Jarrett he would be willing to make a lateral move so long as his combined income from television and wrestling remained the same.

By the time he sat down with Channel 5, he had an offer they could not refuse. Channel 5 would get wrestling. Jarrett would hire Lance Russell away from Channel 13. Jarrett would also get Channel 5 a meeting with Dave Brown, Channel 13's weatherman. Brown also happened to be Russell's co-announcer and had just been voted Memphis's most popular TV personality. In effect, Channel 5 would gain the top rated programming in the city and gut their arch-rival's news staff in the process. When the deal was sealed, Channel 5 general manager Mori Greiner told Jarrett, "Remind me never to get on your bad side, Jerry."

The Continental Wrestling Association (CWA) was soon on the air and on the road. Channel 5 had the number one program in Memphis, and the fans were quick to switch their allegiance at the box office. For the Louisville fans, the change was hardly noticeable. They still had wrestling on the same station and enjoyed the same familiar faces every Tuesday at the Gardens, where the contract was also in Jarrett's name and not Mid-South.

The Louisville fans gained one new benefit from Jarrett's coup. Until the split, Louisville fans had to make do with the weekly programs printed for the Memphis show. One of Jarrett's innovations was to create a new publication specifically for the Louisville fans. *Action Ringside* featured interviews with the wrestlers, photographs suitable for autographing (some by teen photographer and future legend Jim Cornette), and art work by Jerry Lawler.

Gulas did not give up the North without a fight. He tried to get Jarrett blackballed at the annual NWA convention that year, but the play backfired. Jarrett had a number of powerful friends in the NWA, including Florida promoter Eddie Graham, while Gulas soon found he had very few friends among the promoters he had cheated and scammed over the years.

Gulas ran a number of shows at the Coliseum in Memphis. He managed to get his own promotion back in the air in Louisville for a short time at WHAS 11, and he booked a number of shows in Louisville, attempting to out-do Jarrett by booking the Commonwealth Convention Center. He brought in Lou Thesz and the Sheik to try and draw the numbers Jarrett once did. It was not enough. With his health failing and his business floundering, Gulas eventually gave up the battle and ceded Memphis, Louisville, and the rest of the northern territory to Jarrett.

THE OUTLAWS

The definition of an outlaw wrestling territory is a promotion that sets up shop in an established territory and takes fans and revenue away from the established promoter. Outlaw territories have been a part of the wrestling business from the early days, and their existence was one of the key motivators behind the founding of the National Wrestling Alliance. If an outlaw set up shop in a member's backyard, the other NWA members would come to the aid of their fellow NWA promoter, lending them top talent and other assistance in an effort to stamp out the outlaw.

If we use this strict definition to define an outlaw territory, the ICW - or International Championship Wrestling - was not an outlaw territory. The ICW ran shows across the Bluegrass, including weekly shows in their home base of Lexington - but the ICW never posed a serious threat to Memphis. Ever. As a matter of fact, despite all the noise ICW generated, Memphis never even acknowledged the existence of ICW until it was, as a business, dead and buried.

ICW may not have been the outlaw it pretended to be, but ICW still left a mark that few regional promotions did. ICW began in 1978 when Angelo Poffo decided to go into business for himself. Poffo was a long time hand in the wrestling business, a journeyman who won titles and did good business in the NWA, AWA, and WWA. Poffo was also a World War II veteran, having served his country in the Navy. He loved playing chess, and in 1945 he set a new world record for sit-ups.

Poffo's brightest days were behind him as a performer when ICW opened its doors, but the Illinois native had something other than self-promotion in mind. Poffo's sons, Lanny and Randy, were both promising young newcomers just getting their feet wet in the business. ICW would be their launch pad to stardom.

Lanny, the younger son, was born in Calgary, Alberta, Canada in 1959. He was billed at 6'2" and went under the name Leaping Lanny Poffo. Lanny began wrestling as a teenager in the early 1970s. He also enjoyed writing poetry, a hobby that would become part of his character when he moved up to the WWF in the 1980s.

Lanny's older brother was the unquestioned superstar of the promotion, but he almost took a completely different path than his father and brother. At the age of 18, Randy Poffo was drafted by the St. Louis Cardinals and began playing minor league baseball right out of high school. He dabbled in wrestling during the off-seasons, but when his baseball career ended in 1974, he turned to wrestling full time.

Randy Poffo began working for Georgia Championship Wrestling as "The Spider," a character modeled on Spider-Man. Years later Poffo would portray Spider-Man's in-ring comic book nemesis Bonesaw McGraw. It was Ole Anderson who gave Poffo the name he would use throughout his wrestling career. Poffo, said Anderson, was not a name fitting for a man who "wrestled like a savage." With those words, Randy Savage was born.

Randy and Lanny followed their Dad to Lexington when ICW opened. They started out working the armories and high schools in the area, but the Poffos had dreams of giving Jerry Jarrett and his crew a run for their money.

On March 13, 1979, the ICW crew invaded the WTVQ television studio in Lexington. "They taped the first ten shows in one day," recalls Rip Rogers, who got his start in wrestling working for the Poffos and was one of the partners in ICW. "I wanted to travel. I wanted to go to different territories, work new styles. Randy convinced me to stay and work for his Dad, but I still got away to Portland a few times during those years."

From the very beginning, ICW targeted Memphis Wrestling. Angelo employed fellow wrestler Bob Roop to be the voice of ICW. Roop took the mic at show after show, week after week, boasting to the ICW faithful that the best talent in Kentucky was with Lexington. Roop implored the fans to write or call the Memphis office, demanding that they accept the challenge of ICW's bright young stars.

"Call Jerry Jarrett!" Roop urged the fans. "Tell him you want to see Lanny Poffo vs. Bill Dundee! Tell him you want to see the King Jerry Lawler versus the Macho Man! Tell him to give the people the matches they really want to see."

The Memphis crew never answered the challenges, either privately or in the ring. According to Bill Dundee's biography, the Lexington crew was seen as a bunch of misfits who had burned their bridges in other promotions. Drugs were rampant in Lexington, and the Memphis workers didn't want anything to do with them.

That didn't stop ICW form shooting for the moon with match ups and story lines. They even held a wedding in Rupp Arena. Savage's manager Steve Cooper said the vows to his third wife in the ring while the fans threw boos instead of rice at the heel and his bride. Unlike WWF/WWE weddings there were no run-ins, altercations, or snakes in a box when the gifts were opened.

While the talent of the Poffo brothers was hard to deny, Jerry Jarrett simply didn't see the ICW as worthy of his time. ICW was never mentioned in house shows or on television. Jarrett's silence only added more fuel to Bob Roop's tiny fire.

"They won't answer us because they're afraid of us!" said Roop. "Jerry Lawler knows he doesn't stand a chance against Randy Savage!"

In truth many in the Memphis promotion were nervous about the possibility of a real altercation taking place in Lexington. One night about twenty of the ICW wrestlers bought tickets to a Memphis show in Rupp Arena. Rumor had it the ICW wrestlers were going to rush the ring and attack Dundee, but that evening they stayed put, drank beer, and never made good on the threat.

The situation came to a head a short while later when Dundee was attacked in the parking lot outside a gym in Nashville. In Dundee's version of events, Dundee was blind-sided by Savage, who approached him with a few other ICW wrestlers in the parking lot intending to waylay him. Dundee managed to get to the handgun in his trunk, ending the matter and sending Savage packing. According to Jim Cornette, Dundee came out of the incident with a broken jaw and was unable to compete for a time. Like most wrestling stories, this is one of those stories where the whole truth may never be known. The incident was reported to the police, but rather than risk exposing the business, both sides later agreed to drop the matter.

While Memphis enjoyed one of its greatest years in 1982, a year that saw Lawler feud not only with Dutch Mantell but Andy Kaufman, ICW was on its last legs. By 1983 the Lexington promotion had run its course. ICW was never able to tap into Memphis's following, and the Poffos decided to close shop.

ICW would not be the end for the Poffo brothers. Savage asked a mutual acquaintance to contact Jerry Jarrett and ask if there was any animosity that would prevent him from getting a job in Memphis. Jarrett assured Randy through the intermediary that there was no hostility at all. ICW never posed any real threat to Jarrett's territory, so Jarrett had no reason to hold a grudge. Soon as Savage got the okay, he contacted Jarrett personally.

Jarrett invited Savage to join the CWA, opening the door for the Savage-Lawler feud to finally happen. Dundee had moved on to Mid-South Wrestling by the time the Poffos came on board, so he never had to work with the people who attacked him. Dundee would later bury the hatchet with both Poffo brothers and work with both men in later years. When asked about the incident by Dundee's son Jamie, Savage gave a very short explanation. "Shhh, kid, lot of bad drugs back then; lot of bad drugs."

Those who wrestled with Randy discovered a man who was as professional and dedicated to his craft as any. They also found him to be the same guy off camera as he was on. He was larger than life and always able to draw a crowd. Rip Rogers, who traveled with Randy during his stint in Memphis, would plead with Randy to keep his mouth shut while they ate in restaurants so they could get back on the road quickly. Randy would sit and eat in silence, but inevitably, as soon as the meal was over, Randy would open his mouth. "Oh yeah, that was good!" Two hours later they'd still be in the restaurant, with Randy signing autographs and taking pictures with his fans.

Rogers saw Savage get himself into even bigger trouble in a Waffle House one holiday night. "It was Thanksgiving or Christmas," Rogers recalls. "This guy comes in with his new bride and wants the whole place to congratulate them on just getting married. Randy was hopped up on pills and shouted out, "Who f---ing cares?'"

The groom decided to pick a fight with Randy, and Randy was more than willing to oblige. Randy grabbed a knife from the table, escalating the fight and giving the manager cause to call the police. Randy refused to surrender when the police arrived. The police brandished their night sticks, but Randy snatched them out of the officers' hands.

"That's when they sent in Beau the police dog," says Rogers. "Randy didn't quit at first, but Beau took a big bite out of his leg. He still had the scars from it years later." Savage finally surrendered. As Rogers puts it, "Beau the police dog wouldn't put him over."

Savage was destined to rise to the top, and Memphis was his final stop on the way. Within a few short years, the WWF talent raid was on, with Vince McMahon cherry picking the top talent from territories all across the country. Lured by the big money and fame of the WWF, most wrestlers packed their bags and left town without notice. To his credit, Savage insisted he give and fulfill two weeks notice with Jerry Jarrett before he left town.

Savage's final match took place in Lexington, a loser leaves town match against Lawler. Despite being Savage's "hometown," the Lexington crowd was largely behind Lawler that night. The King got the pin, and Savage packed his bags for New York.

Randy Savage took the WWF by storm, drawing instant heat from the fans and big bucks for his employer. A "bidding war" broke out among the heel managers for Savage, including Classy Freddie Blassie, Bobby Heenan, the Grand Wizard, and Captain Lou Albano. Savage gave them all a pass and chose an unknown to be his manager - Kentucky native Elizabeth Hulette, Savage's real life wife, better known to her fans as the First Lady of Wrestling, Miss Elizabeth.

Savage had a Hall of Fame career in the WWF and WCW. His brother enjoyed a brief stint in the WWF as Leaping Lanny Poffo and then as The Genius, but he never achieved the same level of stardom as his brother.

Miss Elizabeth, who divorced Randy in 1992, died of a drug overdose in 2003. Angelo Poffo died at age 84 in 2010, and in 2011, his son Randy died of a heart attack while driving in Seminole, Florida with his new wife. They may not have been true outlaws, the Poffos cast a long shadow over Louisville and the WWE, where Randy Savage remains the biggest name yet to be admitted into their Hall of Fame.

"SEE YOU AT RINGSIDE"

The majority of the men and women who reached the hallowed halls of Louisville Gardens got there after logging thousands of miles, hours, and body slams in pursuit of wrestling greatness. One man who (literally) towers above most reached the top via a different route: on the backs of the chairs inside the Gardens.

Dean Hill was already a veteran of the Louisville police force when he was assigned to work the Gardens as part of the escort that would lead the heels to and from the ring. Hill was a wrestling fan, and he enjoyed working the shows at the Gardens. The idea of actually working in the industry never even occurred to him. Hill would tell you that his entry into the business was a matter of being in the right place at the right time. His baritone voice and pitch perfect delivery would make him the voice of Louisville wrestling for years to come, but it was his own athletic skill and balance that brought him to the attention of Teeny Jarrett.

The incident occurred during a match between Jerry Lawler and Bill Dundee. The match spilled out of the ring, and the competitors began making their way into the upper level of the Gardens. The seats inside Louisville Gardens were arranged in a horseshoe shape. Fans were seated on either side of the horseshoe, while the bottom section was roped off. Hill noticed a group of teens jumping the barriers into the restricted seats to race around and get close to the action.

The last thing a promoter wants is to see fans hurt during an altercation in the crowd. Hill leapt into action, literally, by racing up the restricted seats. Teeny Jarrett couldn't believe her eyes when she saw the nearly six and a half foot tall policeman running up the backs of the seats on his way to intercept the potential troublemakers, and she made sure to get Hill's name before the end of the night.

Teeny took a liking to Hill, and in the coming weeks and months, the two would chat more and more frequently during their Tuesday night visits. Hill continued to fulfill his duties working security while Teeny kept an eye on him, looking for an opportunity to utilize him in some form.

At the time, the CWA had a regular announcer working their Louisville shows. On the rare occasions when he was unavailable, Al Antee, the manager of the Gardens, would fill in. Once again, being in the right place at the right time opened a door of opportunity. Teeny Jarrett approached Hill and asked if he would fill in as the ring announcer. Hill accepted her invitation.

"They handed me a microphone and some money," Hill recalls about that night. Hill wasn't expecting to get paid for the extra duty, but he certainly didn't mind. When Teeny asked him to come back and fill in the following week, he was more than happy to say yes again.

Hill made a point to watch as much wrestling as he could that week, studying the delivery of legendary announcers like Gordon Solie and Mean Gene Okerland. Hill practiced his own delivery, dropping his voice a little deeper and adapting some of what he heard from Solie and Okerland. "The French Angel" Frank Morrell became a mentor to the rookie announcer, along with Jeff Jarrett, Jerry Jarrett, and Jerry Lawler. It wasn't long after that Teeny asked Hill to become the regular Tuesday night announcer.

A few months into his new assignment, Hill went to the annual discount sale at Sam Meyers, a Louisville formal wear rental shop, and purchased a few tuxedos. Hill was rapidly becoming a fixture in the Tuesday night scene, and before long he found himself moving into a new venue, television.

The CWA taped their weekly shows in Memphis, and the shows would air in Louisville the following week.

Hill was asked to do a weekly spot for the Louisville show, previewing the matches that would take place "This Tuesday in Louisville Gardens!" Hill worked with producer Randy West on these promo spots, and he credits West with giving him the phrase that would become his trademark: "See you at ringside!"

Hill's importance to the Louisville wrestling scene became most evident during a time when he took a brief leave of absence. When Jerry Lawler became embroiled in one of his many legal issues, Lawler's attorney advised him it might not be wise to have a police officer on the payroll. Hill had to step down from his announcing position, and veteran official Joe Wheeler stepped in.

The crowd hated the change. Wheeler was greeted week in and week out with chants of, "We want Dean!" Wheeler was no happier with the situation than the crowd, and one night, in the middle of a "We want Dean!" chant, Wheeler fired back, "I want Dean too!" The crowd was thrilled when Hill returned to his post in the ring, but no one was more thrilled than Wheeler.

Despite his size and athletic prowess, Hill had no desire to get in the ring himself. He occasionally found himself knocked to the floor when the action spilled outside the ring, but Hill was happy to keep his seat beside the ring bell - outside the ring itself.

That said, Hill did let the powers that be coax him into the ring for one match, a tag match with Handsome Jimmy Valiant. Hill had a score to settle with one of the heels, and it was Valiant who offered to help him get his revenge. With no training, no rehearsal, and no preparation, Valiant talked Hill through the brief match that saw the announcer and his ally get the victory.

After leaving the ring, Hill passed by where Luke and Butch, the Sheepherders, were sitting watching the action. "First time?" one of the two asked Hill.

"Yes," he replied.

"Not bad for a talker," said the Sheepherder. Hill took the comment as the high praise it was intended to be.

When the CWA folded, Hill was left with nothing to do on Tuesday nights like the rest of the workers. But Hill's years beside a ring were far from over. When Danny Davis opened Ohio Valley Wrestling, he knew that television would be a key component to his training program. Dean Hill would not only resume his duties as ringside announcer to add a new one - on air commentary.

BEAUTY

On May 31, 2013 a Reddit user with the screen name Xombie Christ posted this message: "I was a professional wrestler from 1985-2000. Since then over 40 of my wrestling friends have died. AMA."

For the uninitiated, "AMA" is Reddit-speak for "ask me anything."

Within minutes, wily Reddit users were on Facebook and other sites, trying to verify the authenticity and identity of the poster who claimed to be Terry Garvin - not the late Terry Garvin of the WWF, but Terrence "Beauty" Garvin, aka Terry Simms, who wrestled for multiple territories in the 80's and 90s. In truth Xombie Christ was not Terry Garvin. Xombie Christ was Terry's step-son's screen name, and it was Terry's step-son at the keyboard. But the Shepherdsville, KY native was sitting right beside his step-son, ready and waiting to be asked anything.

"It was my step-son Casey's idea," says Terry, recalling that night. "He's a much faster typer than I am. And I never would have done it if I had known his screen name was Xombie Christ!"

Simms grew up watching Memphis wrestling on WAVE 3 like many Louisville fans in the 1970s, but he didn't set out to be a wrestler. He was married at 17 and divorced with two kids by 22, "The biggest regret in my life," he admits. Simms packed his bags and moved south to Nashville, where he began a very successful career as a hair dresser. His clientele included Marie Osmond, Reba McEntyre, Roseanne Cash, and John Schneider, and he was making a very good living.

Then Simms met one of his long time heroes, Bill Dundee. Next thing he knew, Simms was a member of the first class to train at Dundee's wrestling school.

After training, Simms split time between hairdressing and wrestling. He hooked up with Dale Mann, who ran a promotion out of Jamestown, Kentucky near Lake Cumberland. Mann's promotion was a nod to the carny origins of the sport, featuring midgets and women as regular performers. He had a building with a ring and apartments upstairs where most of his crew lived when not traveling.

Simms began talking with his training classmate Mark Guleen about forming a tag team, and the pair drew inspiration for their new alliance from a Disney film just released - *Beauty and the Beast*. "I was a hairdresser," Simms says, "So naturally I'd be Beauty. All we had to do was turn Mark into a beast."

Simms and Guleen pitched the concept to Bill Dundee and Jerry Jarrett, who loved it. Dundee and Jarrett decided to change Terry's ring name to Terrence Garvin. Simms resembled wrestler Jimmy Garvin, and the name was a nod to the flamboyant character once portrayed by Terry Garvin.

Jarrett decided to introduce his new tag team through a series of videos, just as he had done with the Fabulous Ones and Kamala the Ugandan Giant. Five shorts were filmed at Bill Dundee's house that would introduce fans to the odd pairing of Beauty and the Beast. "I fixed Mark's hair up to make him look more beast-like," says Simms. "We had him in a tuxedo with the sleeves ripped off. He was in Bill's backyard lifting these huge weights while I sat in a hot tub sipping Dom Perignon. The whole thing was set to the tune 'As Time Goes By' by Liberace."

The promos had the desired effect on the Memphis fans. Beauty and the Beast had heat the moment they took the ring. They wrestled on a pink mat, because Beauty refused to wrestle on a dirty mat where Jerry Lawler and Bill Dundee had rolled around. "Heaven knows what women those two have slept with!" Beauty quipped in his defense.

The pair started feuding with Jeff Jarrett, who brought in a number of tag partners to try and take down the newcomers. Double J's feud culminated with the pair when he partnered with Bill Dundee. Beauty scored a shocking victory at a house show when he kissed Dundee on the lips and rolled him up for the pin. The finish aired on Memphis TV, and the heat on Beauty and the Beast swelled to a fever pitch.

Dundee decided he needed a partner as unpredictable and dangerous as Beauty if he wanted to get revenge. He found that partner in Adrian Street.

"People thought I was wild," says Simms, "But Adrian? Adrian Street made me look like Arnold Schwarzenegger."

Beauty and the Beast were all set for a hot summer program with Dundee and Street, but then plans changed. It was at this time that Jerry Jarrett entered a deal with the Von Erichs and World Class Championship Wrestling (WCCW) in Dallas, Texas. The Von Erich patriarch Fritz had retired and handed the reins of WCCW to his sons, but in the year and a half since the transition, business had plummeted. The Von Erichs needed help, and they turned to Jarrett to bail them out.

Memphis and Dallas began sharing talent. Eric Embry came up from Dallas to work a program with Jeff Jarrett, and he fell in love with the Beauty and the Beast tag team. He asked Jarrett to send the two to Dallas, and to Dundee's dismay, Jarrett agreed.

Beauty and the Beast won the tag belts shortly after arriving in Dallas, but in spite of all their success together, the powers that be were discussing changes. Simms and Guleen were both still fairly green, but Guleen's inexperience was a bit more noticeable than Simms'.

What's more, while Guleen's Beast gimmick had worked well in Memphis and Louisville, it was a harder sell in Dallas. "The Texas fans were used to watching the Freebirds and Von Erichs beat the hell out of each other," says Simms. "Mark just didn't compare to what the fans were used to."

"Mark wasn't very beast-like for a beast," recalls Jim Cornette. "He was big and hairy, but that was really it."

The bookers in Dallas began using Terry as a single, leaving Mark out of the picture. It was then that Terry and Mark decided they were ready to move on.

"I got a call from the original Terry Garvin about that time," says Simms. "He and Pat Patterson were booking for the WWF, and they loved our gimmick. But they wanted to give me a new partner too. They didn't think Mark was 'beast' enough to be the Beast, and they wanted to replace him. We had some conversations, but nothing came of it."

Simms and Guleen left Dallas for Continental Championship Wrestling in Alabama, where they reunited with their mentor Bill Dundee. But no sooner did they arrive in Alabama when Dundee left to return to Memphis. Simms recommended Robert Fuller as a new booker to Continental owner David Woods, and under Fuller, Simms got his first singles run in a feud with Adrian Street.

"We were pretty much given free rein," said Simms. "We had a lot of good talent at that time, and it was a solid little promotion."

Simms continued to wrestle throughout the nineties, most notably for the Global Wrestling Federation in Dallas. By the turn of the century he had retired and moved home to Kentucky, where some of his biggest memories were made.

"I was doing a singles match with Lawler in Louisville," Simms says. "Jerry came across the ring and told me to get on the mic. He wanted me to point at a girl in a wheelchair and say, 'That's what happens when you let cousins get married.' I told Frank Morrell, the referee, I didn't want to do it. This was my hometown, and I couldn't say something like that. Lawler knew we could come back the next week and draw more money, so when he insisted, I did it. Man, you would not believe the heat with that crowd. They were hot!"

Simms had no idea the heat his comment would create. The owners of the Louisville Gardens contacted Teeny Jarrett about Simms' comments after the incident. It was Teeny's name on the lease at the Gardens, and the owners made their displeasure about Simms' comment known. On Saturday of that same week, Simms was called into Teeny Jarrett's office at the Nashville venue. Simms knew he was in trouble.

"How are you?" Teeny asked.

"I'm fine," said Simms. "A little nervous."

Teeny told Terry that she thought he was a good wrestler with a world of potential and a lot of ability. Simms smiled thinking he might actually be okay.

"But if you ever do what you did in Louisville again," said Teeny, "I will fire you."

Simms was also present for one of the most memorable backstage incidents to ever take place at the Gardens - a race between Randy Hales and referee Frank Morrell. While waiting for bell time one Tuesday evening, Hales began harassing Morrell about being slow. Morrell, who was older but still athletic, took exception to Hales' ribbing and insisted he could out run the younger man.

Once talk of a race began, there was no turning back. With Simms, Guleen, Dundee, and others egging them on, the two agreed to have a race.

The backstage area of the Gardens ran the full width of the building. Hales and Morrell lined up at one end and set a finish line ten feet from the wall on the other end. When the race began, both men took off, running for their lives. "Randy's arms were flailing, Frank was huffing and puffing, and they were neck and neck the whole way."

As they neared the finish, Morrell suddenly realized he was not going to be able to stop. He shot right past the finish line, put his arm up, and smashed his head and arm into the wall, knocking himself out.

The boys in the back raced to Frank's aid, asking if he was okay. "Yeah," said Frank, "But I think my wrist is broken."

They called EMS, and Frank went to the hospital, leaving the boys without a referee for the night. Luckily, they had a part-time referee on hand, but he was without a shirt. "I believe they took the shirt off Frank's back before he went to the hospital," says Simms with a laugh.

That Saturday at the weekly TV taping the entire crew got a tongue lashing from Jerry Jarrett, reminding them they were to do a job, not kill each other backstage. Years later, those who were there continue to share the story about the night Frank Morrell smashed into the backstage wall at the Gardens.

Simms is retired now, enjoying life in Kentucky with his family. He loves to discuss old stories and old times, but unlike many former wrestlers, there's not a trace of bitterness or negativity to his stories. True, he has seen a number of his closest friends pass away, but Simms, a born again Christian, prefers to focus on the positive. He visits fan conventions and wrestling reunions when he can, he gives interviews when asked, and he is always happy to hear from his fans.

Terry's AMA is still on online. It became one of the top 100 threads on Reddit, and as of March 2014 it was still ranked in the top 100. And yes, if you happen to meet him, you are welcome to ask him anything.

FULL CIRCLE

Wrestling fans under 25 (and those who never watched anything other than WWF/WCW in their younger years) know Dutch Mantell as the portly, xenophobic Zeb Colter. Their first exposure to the man came when he became the mouthpiece for Jack Swagger in early 2013. In his prime, Dutch Mantell was one of the top stars in Memphis, a multi-time heavyweight champion who could hold his own in the ring against any and all comers as a heel or a babyface.

Jim Cornette remembers Dutch Mantell as the only guy who, if he wanted, could get his hands on Cornette any time he wanted. "I was young and quick, and once those big guys were gassed, I could out run just about anyone. Not Dutch. If Dutch wanted to get his hands on me, there was nothing I could do to stop him."

Dutch Mantell holds another unique distinction in the history of professional wrestlers. He and Jeff Jarrett are enshrined in the Smithsonian Institution, thanks to a wrestling match held in Louisville's modern day opera house, the Kentucky Center for the Arts.

The wrestling match was not on a card with other wrestling matches, but the finale of an evening of percussion presented by the Lonesome Pine Specials. Begun in 1986 by Kentucky Center programming director Richard Van Kleeck, The Lonesome Pine Specials featured performances by an incredibly diverse range of musicians. Guests of the Lonesome Pine Specials over the years included Junior Wells, Lyle Lovett, Bela Fleck and the Flecktones, Buddy Guy, Los Lobos, and Emmylou Harris.

By the late 1980s the Lonesome Pine Specials were broadcast on more than 130 PBS stations and Channel 4 in England. In 1990 Van Kleeck contacted Jerry Jarrett about supplying a ring, two wrestlers, and a referee for a very special performance. The Lonesome Pine Specials had gathered a number of artists for an evening of percussion only performances entitled, "Masters of Percussion."

The finale of the event would be a composition by Wichita State University music professor Walter Mays, performed by the Wichita State percussion ensemble. The title of the piece: "War Games for Extended Percussion and Two Wrestlers." The money Van Kleeck offered was good, and Jarrett offered up his two best men: his son Jeff, and Dutch Mantell.

This was not the first performance of Mays's experimental piece, nor was it the first to feature a Louisville mainstay in the ring. In 1987 Rip Rogers was working Kansas City for Bob Geigel when he and Bart Bratton were booked for a performance at the University of Nebraska in Lincoln with Mays and his ensemble. "It was a wrestling audience that night, and they didn't know what to make of it, but they cheered and booed us anyway," Rogers remembers.

Mantell recalls his experience with "War Games" as a bizarre affair, even by wrestling standards. The atmosphere when he and Jarrett arrived felt like a pay-per-view, with television crews hustling all over the building preparing to tape the performance. Each performer took their turn rehearsing their piece. Jarrett and Mantell were given the rundown on their "piece" as well. They would have exactly twelve minutes for their match. The match could not end early or go long. They had to end in exactly twelve minutes. "Piece of cake," Mantell foolishly thought to himself.

Mantell's wife was on hand for the event as well, and they spent most of the day in the green room, partaking of the food and speaking with the other performers. Despite the fact that few of the musicians had ever witnessed a wrestling match, they were genuinely fascinated by the wrestlers and eager to see how their work would fit in with the piece. Mantell and Jarrett were wondering the exact same thing. Somewhere around 10 PM, Jarrett and Mantell were escorted to their places beneath the stage, and the performance commenced.

The "War Games" performance is on YouTube, and it is a fascinating and entertaining performance to watch. The piece begins with the percussion ensemble alone on stage, playing on traditional instruments like the timpani, chimes, and piano along with "extended" percussion items like hammers, pistols, and a jackhammer.

A few minutes into the performance, a platform rose into view. Surrounded by smoke, the wrestling ring emerged from below. The Lonesome Pine crowd - made up of modern music enthusiasts rather than rasslin' fans - welcomed the wrestlers with a huge ovation. The referee checked both men for foreign objects, called for the bell, and the match began.

The "piece of cake" Mantell and Jarrett expected turned out to be much harder than they anticipated. The percussion was incredibly loud and distracting, and Mantell and Jarrett felt as if they were giving a one hour Broadway (wrestler speak for a match that goes the full time limit). Both men were exhausted half way through, the day spent eating in the green room taking its toll as they pressed on.

Despite their weariness, both Jarrett and Mantell gave a game performance, with Mantell drawing true heel heat from the black tie crowd. Mantell pulled hair, used the ropes for leverage, and sought every unfair advantage he could gain as he dismantled Jarrett for most of the twelve minutes. He paused several times to play to the crowd, eliciting boos from the high society art lovers in the audience.

As the music drew to its climax, so did the battle between good and evil. Mantell climbed out of the ring and grabbed both the bass drum and bass drum player, bringing both into the ring. Mantell takes out the bass drummer and tries to use his instrument on Jarrett, but just at the magic moment, Jarrett gets the roll up and the pin, bringing the crowd to its feet and War Games to a dramatic finish.

However awkward the performance was for two men who had done the same thing thousands of times, it was well worth it. War Games was far more than just a wrestling match accompanied by percussion, or vice versa. It was interactive musical theater, with the audience contributing to the "music" of the piece by their cheers and boos.

What's more, War Games proved to be Jeff Jarrett and Dutch Mantell's entry into the most prestigious museum in America, the Smithsonian. In 1993 Mantell and Jarrett received letters from Richard Van Kleeck informing them that the Lonesome Pine series - including their episode - had been added to their permanent collection. The War Games performance received special recognition as one of the ten best segments from the entire run of the series

The episode proved to be a ratings winner for PBS and aired numerous times after its initial screening. "Masters of Percussion" also screened at the prestigious Golden Rose International Video Festival in Montreaux, Switzerland.

Strange as it seems, Mantell and Jarrett's night at the opera proved to be a fitting moment. More than 100 years prior to that night, the first professional wrestlers to visit Louisville squared off on the bare stage of the original opera house, the first Buckingham Theater. Mantell, Jarrett, and the Wichita State percussionists made their mark on the world of music that evening, but as memorable as the occasion was, I wouldn't hold my breath that you'll ever see a wrestling match follow a performance by the Kentucky Opera.

END OF THE ROAD

Dean Hill had come a long way in just a few years working Tuesday nights at the Gardens, from security officer to ring announcer to television promos. One day the Memphis television folks came to him with a new offer: they wanted him to take a seat at the announcer's table on the Memphis broadcast. The money and the schedule was perfect, so Hill accepted the officer.

But Dean Hill's climb to the announcer's table was not meant to be in Memphis. The day he drove down for his first television taping was the day the promotion died. He arrived to find the studio locked. The parking lot was filled with wrestlers, somber looks on their faces, each wondering if his days in the ring had come to an end.

It was inevitable. The creation of two super promotions, WWF and WCW, meant the old days of the territories was over. Wrestling was national, even global. And when Memphis lost its promotion, so did Louisville.

That Memphis had survived as long as it did was a tribute to the relationship between Jerry Jarrett and Vince McMahon. When Vince began building WWF into a global empire, he ruthlessly raided the top promotions in the country, luring their best talent away with the promise of bigger paychecks and bigger exposure. Vince wasn't concerned with keeping good relations with the NWA members because, as far as he was concerned, their time was past. A new day was dawning, and when the ball got rolling, nothing could stop the Rock 'n' Wrestling juggernaut.

But as the promotions began dying off one by one, Vince realized he was killing the goose that laid the golden egg. The regional territories had, in a way, served as the testing ground for the talent that helped him expand the WWF. The list of wrestlers who had come through Memphis (and Louisville) looks like a who's who of the

WWF royalty: Hulk Hogan, the Undertaker, Kane, Stone Cold Steve Austin, Kamala the Ugandan Giant, the Honkey Tonk Man, and so on.

Memphis hung on in part due to Jarrett's genius for booking and the passion of the fans in the territory. The territory even grew when the Von Erichs came calling, asking Jarrett to bail out their dying World Class Championship Wrestling. WCCW merged with Championship Wrestling to become the United States Wrestling Association (USWA), the name it would carry until the promotion shut its doors.

The merger did not go over with the talent, who now had to add a weekly trek to Dallas to their travel schedules, but what choice did they have? Memphis was the only territory still making money, and unless Vince McMahon or Ted Turner called, their only chance to keep working.

When business at the WWF took a dip in the early 90s, Vince contacted Jarrett to ask for assistance with booking and programming. Jarrett accepted and began splitting his time between Memphis and New York. Vince was very gracious with Jarrett and did his best to keep Jarrett happy, even flying him home on his personal jet so Jarrett wouldn't miss his son's football games.

The two promotions also began to share talent, with Kerry Von Erich and Jeff Jarrett getting a chance to prove themselves in the national spotlight. Vince also began using Jerry Lawler on WWF television where he began his legendary feud with Bret Hart. Glenn Jacobs, who traveled the territory only briefly, had his first national exposure as Lawler's personal dentist, Dr. Isaac Yankem. He shook off that identity and an even less fortunate one as "fake Diesel" to become the Undertaker's brother Kane.

Vince sent some of his marquee stars to USWA to help them keep the show running. Vince even appeared on USWA television himself, where he became the USWA champion and developed the evil "Mr.

McMahon" persona. McMahon also used Memphis as a proving ground, sending developmental talent to the territory to work on their craft. One of the standouts from this first developmental territory was a former University of Miami football player going by the name Flex Kavana. He was already somewhat familiar with Memphis and Louisville, having traveled a bit when his father, Rocky Johnson, was part of the promotion. When Dean Hill first met Krash, he predicted that the young man would be WWF champion within five years. Krash beat that prediction by two years when he became known as The Rock.

When Jerry Jarrett's employment with the WWF came to an end, he was ready for a change in his life. Jarrett was burned out on the wrestling business and made a deal to sell out to Lawler and a business partner Lawler had brought on board. Both of the Jerry's tell their side of the story in their autobiographies, and there's a lot of finger pointing regarding what happened next. The end result, however, is simply a matter of history. Memphis shut its doors, and the territory folded.

The era of WWF Attitude and the Monday Night Wars were just beginning, bringing unprecedented exposure, popularity, and money to professional wrestling. The WWF would make a number of trims to town, and Louisville even played host to three pay-per-views , but Louisville had lost a beloved Tuesday night tradition.

Many of the wrestlers in the Memphis parking lot turned to Hill. They asked what his plans were, and if he might become their salvation and open his own. Hill would play a key role in the future of Louisville wrestling, but it was another man who would step out of the shadows to become "The Wizard," the man behind the curtain who revived a Louisville tradition and made possible a new golden era of wrestling in the River City.

ONLY ON PAY-PER-VIEW

No memoir of Louisville's wrestling history would be complete without mentioning the federation that ended the era of territories like the USWA. Under the leadership of Vince McMahon, Jr., The World Wrestling Federation, now known as World Wrestling Entertainment, began signing away the top stars in every territory across the country in the early 1980s. The WWF offered national exposure and merchandising payouts that the small territories could not match. Despite the best efforts of regional promoters - which were meager at best - the WWF ultimately nationalized professional wrestling and as a result killed the old territory system.

Louisville has long been a stop on the WWF/ WWE's tour schedule, making appearances at Louisville Gardens, Freedom Hall, Broadbent Arena, and the Yum! Center. Only three pay-per-views have ever taken place in Louisville, but each one of those shows has a number of important distinctions in wrestling history.

In Your House 6: Rage in a Cage

Louisville's first time in the pay-per-view spotlight was one of the early In Your House shows on February 18, 1996, at Louisville Gardens. As the final pay-per-view prior to Wrestlemania XII, much of the action served to build up the year's biggest show.

Razor Ramon defeated the heel 1-2-3 Kid in the first match. Hunter Hearst Helmsley, still in his pre-DX days, defeated Duke the Dumpster Droese. Yokozuna won his match over The British Bulldog Davey Boy Smith by disqualification after Louisville legend Jim Cornette got his man disqualified. Cornette returned to the ring for the fourth contest, a number one contender's match for the WWF championship.

In the main event, WWF champion Bret Hart took on Diesel in a steel cage. The match ended with a victory by Hart, but the action was far from over. Following his defeat, Diesel found himself drug into the depths of Hell, as the Undertaker rose up through the ring to pull him beneath.

Strangely, the Undertaker reappeared after the cameras stopped rolling to win a match by count out over Goldust. Three other dark matches took place that night. Jake the Snake Roberts got a win over Tatanka. The Godwins took down the Bodydonnas with Sunny at ringside. Ahmed Johnson defeated an up and comer named Isaac Yankem. Yankem would join Jerry the King Lawler in a feud with Hart that summer and then spend a few months as the "fake Diesel" before going on to his greatest fame with a third character.

Michael's victory that night is significant because one month later he would use his number one contender's status to take on Bret Hart in their legendary Wrestlemania Iron Man Match. It was not the last time Hart would defend his title and lose it two months later to Michaels. Nor was it the more infamous occurrence of the two.

In Your House 6 is a tricky show to track down because it was not released on video in the US using the In Your House name. The US release was re-titled was "Spring Explosion '96." The Goldust/Undertaker match is included on the video.

Ground Zero: In Your House

The WWF returned to Louisville Gardens for the seventeenth installment of the In Your House series on September 7, 1997. It was the first of the series to make "In Your House" the subtitle of the show, signifying a changing in the way the WWF would brand its pay-per-views. It was also the first in the series to clock in at three hours, and it was jammed full of action.

The opening match at Louisville Gardens that night pitted Brian Pillman against Goldust. A unique wager was on the line in this match, as it had been revealed that Pillman was the (kayfabe) father of Goldust and Marlena's son. If Pillman had lost, he would have quit the WWF forever. Pillman won, and for the victory, he won the services of Marlena for 30 days.

Pillman fans know this night as the last time Pillman would appear on a WWF pay-per-view. A month later the WWF traveled to Bloomington, Minnesota for their next pay-per-view, Badd Blood. When Pillman failed to arrive by 7 PM, Jim Cornette phoned the hotel where Pillman was staying. The front desk told Cornette that the maids had found Pillman dead in his hotel room earlier that day. An undiagnosed heart condition took his life at age 35.

Brian Christopher, who spent a good deal of time in Louisville wrestling for the USWA before his move to the WWF, defeated Scott Putski in the second match. Brian's real life father, Jerry Lawler, joined him in the ring to celebrate after the match.

The third match was a triple threat featuring Savio Vega, Faarooq, and Crush, representing their various factions at the time. Vega claimed a victory by pinning Crush. This was followed by a high octane midget match in which 83 pound Max Mini defeated 101 pound El Torito. Mario Mejia Jimenez, the man beneath the mask of El Torito, previously wrestled for WWF for a short time as Mini-Vader. He returned to the WWE in 2013 making appearances with the tag team Los Matadores.

Prior to the fifth match, a four-way tag team match for the tag team titles, Sgt. Slaughter and Jim Ross came to the ring to require Dude Love (Mick Foley) and Stone Cold Steve Austin to forfeit the belts, due to an injury to Austin. Austin tossed his belt at Slaughter's feet and hit

Ross with a stunner, taking the announcer off the show for the rest of the evening.

The Headbangers went on to win the belts in a match against the Legion of Doom (aka The Road Warriors), Owen Hart and the British Bulldog, and the Godwinns. The victory came with a small assist from Austin, who hit Owen Hart with a stunner behind the official's back to let Mosh get the pin.

The sixth match saw Bret Hart defeat the Patriot to retain his WWF championship. Hart was a heel at the time, playing the part of a proud Canadian who was down on all things American. It would be the final successful title defense for Bret Hart in the WWF. Two months later, Hart lost the title to Shawn Michaels in a controversial match at Survivor Series. Long time and diehard fans know what happened in November of 1997 as the Montreal Screwjob - and the dawn of the Attitude Era.

The main event at Ground Zero was a non-title match between Shawn Michaels and the Undertaker. Michaels and the Undertaker had a number of legendary battles over the years, including a Wrestlemania XXV match that Ricky Steamboat declared to be the best Wrestlemania match of all time and Shawn Michaels' retirement match at Wrestlemania XXVI. But on September 7, 1997, Michaels and the Undertaker had their first in-ring confrontation at Louisville Gardens.

Judgment Day 2000

By the year 2000, the McMahon-Helmsley Era was in full swing, on May 21, Judgment Day came to Louisville. A red hot Louisville crowd welcomed the WWF to Freedom Hall for the first pay-per-view following Wrestlemania 2000, where Triple H outlasted Mick Foley, the Big Show, and the Rock for the WWF title. WWF chairman Vince McMahon made amends with his formerly estranged daughter and son-in-law Stephanie and Triple H and turned against his former ally the Rock, setting up an iron man match between the Rock and the champ to be officiated by Shawn Michaels.

The show opened with a six man tag match pitting Too Cool and Rikishi against Kurt Angle and Edge and Christian. The heel took to the ring to mock the city and the state, with Christian calling the city "Lewis-ville" and the trio offering a variation on the five-second pose called the jug band complete with buck teeth crossed eyes. Too Cool and Rikishi would get the last laugh, winning the match, and Kurt Angle would suffer the stink face.

A triple threat match for the European championship followed the opener with Dean Malenko, Perry Saturn, and Eddie Guererro facing one another. Eddie just happened to have Chyna in his corner, and she proved to be the difference in his victory. Likewise, Shane McMahon had help in his No Holds Barred match against the Big Show. Test, Albert, and Bull Buchannon got in on the action in a match that ended with Show taking a cinderblock to the head.

Chris Benoit and Chris Jericho were next in a spectacular submission match for the Intercontinental Championship. While Benoit's name has been demonized since his death, there's no denying the chemistry these two had in the ring. Benoit took the match and the title when Jericho passed out in the Crippler Crossface.

Throughout the evening, a series of vignettes aired showing Jerry Brisco's attempts to evade having to defend the 24/7 Hardcore Championship. The sketches took viewers all over the back stage and outer parts of Freedom Hall as Brisco put as much space between him and opportunist challengers as possible.

Brisco put in an appearance in the fifth match, a tag match between D-X (represented by X-Pac and the Road Dogg) and the Dudley Boys. Brisco stepped in to defend D-X's valet Tori and was put through a chair for his troubles. D-X took the win thanks to some other dirty dealing.

The night ended with a one hour iron man match between Triple H and the Rock for the World title, with Shawn Michaels as special guest referee. Three years prior, in the same building, Rocky Maivia defeated Hunter Hearst Helmsley for the Intercontinental title nine days before Wrestlemania XIII. The earlier match drew less than 5000 fans, but on this night, the Gardens was sold out to see the superstars who had grown out of those earlier personas.

Michaels called the match down the line, and in true WWF fashion, the match was tied five pins to five heading into finish. With minutes to go, the McMahon-Helmsley minions swarmed the ring to defend Triple H and take shots at the Rock.

Suddenly, a creepy video with three little girls appeared on the Titantron, hailing the return of an ominous figure. Like a shot, the Undertaker rode out for the first time on his bike. 'Taker cleared the ring, but he also took a shot at Triple H. Michaels declared the final fall to Triple H on a disqualification, and the Game retained his title.

Road to Wrestlemania

Louisville has never hosted a Wrestlemania, and given the WWE's current preference for big cities and colossal stadiums, it's unlikely it ever will. But Louisville hosted one of the key moments leading up to Wrestlemania XIX: the contract signing between Vince McMahon and Hulk Hogan.

McMahon and Hogan's feud was built around the question of who created Hulkamania. Was it the superstar who became a household name around the globe, or the promoter who gave him the platform to do so? The nefarious Mr. McMahon was out to prove that he not only created Hulkamania, but he had the power to kill it.

Contract signings in professional wrestling are a lot like weddings in professional wrestling. They never go as planned, and someone usually takes a beating. The contract signing that took place at the end of Smackdown, taped on March 18, 2003, was no exception.

As the show reached its conclusion, "Tutti Frutti" played over the sound system and legendary announcer Mean Gene Okerland made his way down the ramp. Hogan followed with his entrance music to a thunderous ovation that only got louder when the music stopped. The crowd would not quiet down, and it wasn't until Hogan motioned for quiet that Mean Gene was able to move on with the evening's proceedings. A short interview between the two AWA veterans followed, and Hogan's old school line, "Well you know, Mean Gene," got another huge pop.

Mean Gene turned to introduce Mr. McMahon as he made his way down the ramp. Without warning, McMahon attacked Hogan from behind with a chair. After beating the legend several times with the chair, he grabbed a pen off the table and jabbed Hogan in the head repeatedly. With Hogan bleeding profusely, McMahon signed the contract and then smeared some of Hogan's blood on the contract. Hogan recovered just enough to sign the contract and then make his exit.

Pro Wrestling Torch subscriber Matt Riggs commented on just how over Hulk Hogan was with the crowd. Hogan's reception was by far the loudest of the evening, surpassing even former OVW stand out and top babyface Brock Lesnar. Hogan's shirts and red and yellow boas were flying off the merchandise tables and visible throughout the arena.

The Wrestlemania match was a blood-spattered affair low on technical merit but high on drama. Hogan's old rival Rowdy Roddy Piper even put in a cameo, smacking his old nemesis with a lead pipe. In the end Hulk

Hogan and Hulkamania triumphed. Shane McMahon emerged from the back to escort his father out of the building as Hogan and his fans reveled in their victory.

The OVW locker room in the early days.
(Photo courtesy Dean Hill.)

Danny Davis and Dean Hill.
(Photos courtesy of Dean Hill.)

The Prototype, John Cena, with manager Kenny "Starmaker" Bolin.

(Photo courtesy Jason Saint.)

Batista on a return visit to OVW, where he was known as Leviathan.
(Photo courtesy Jason Saint.)

Chris Hero does battle with CM Punk for IWA Mid-South in one
of indy wrestling's most legendary rivalries.

(Photo courtesy Jason Saint.)

CM Punk ready for action in IWA Mid-South.
(Photo courtesy Jason Saint.)

Lisa Marie Varon, best known as Victoria in WWE, at Six Flags for OVW.
(Photo courtesy Jason Saint.)

Beth Phoenix with Aaron "The Idol" Stevens, best known as WWE's Damien Sandow.

(Photos courtesy Jason Saint.)

The Glamazon, Beth Phoenix at OVW.
(Photo courtesy Jason Saint.)

The Miz, Mike Mizanin.
(Photo courtesy Jason Saint.)

Kelly Kelly after her first show at OVW.
(Photo courtesy Jason Saint.)

Scott Sheffield, best known as Ryback in WWE.
(Photo courtesy Jason Saint.)

The Spirit Squad performs for the OVW crowd. That's the future
Dolph Ziggler in the top photo, center.
(Photo courtesy Jason Saint.)

Nick Nemeth, now known as Dolph Ziggler in WWE.
(Photo courtesy Jason Saint.)

Top: Dean Hill and Kenny Bolin at the announcer's desk. Bottom:
Former OVW wrestler Johnny Jeter.

(Photos courtesy of Dean Hill and Jason Saint.)

Cody Rhodes at OVW, where he wrestled as Cody Runnels.
(Photo courtesy Jason Saint.)

Outlaw Ben Wood puts the squeeze on OVW trainer and WWE
star Al Snow.

(Photo courtesy Ben Wood.)

Dean Hill with Brock Lesnar: NCAA champion, WWE champion, UFC champion, and conqueror of the Undertaker's undefeated streak at Wrestlemania.

(Photo courtesy Dean Hill.)

Dean Hill with Louisville's favorite wrestling alumni, John Cena.
(Photo courtesy Dean Hill.)

PART FOUR
TOMORROW'S SUPERSTARS TODAY

Super heavyweights Mark Henry and the Big Show.
(Photo courtesy Jason Saint.)

THE WIZARD

Steve Austin almost quit wrestling. Had he walked out, he never would have made it to ECW, WCW, or the WWF. Austin 3:16 would never have happened, and the Monday Night Wars might have had a very different end.

Austin was burned out. He was learning a lot from Dutch Mantell and the veterans in the Memphis territory, but he felt like he was going nowhere. That's when Danny Davis pulled him aside and told him he couldn't quit.

"It would be the biggest mistake of your life," said Davis. "I don't know how I know this, but something deep inside tells me it would be a mistake."

Austin didn't quit, and the conversation helped set both men on their future course. Austin would become one of the biggest stars in the history of the business, and Davis would become the guiding force behind the next generation of superstars.

Danny Davis grew up a wrestling fan, but unlike most of his peers, when he grew up, he got married, had kids, and started a good career. He was working as a manager for Sterling Stores in Tennessee in the mid 1970s making forty grand a year. That's when his mother called from Jackson, Tennessee with some news.

Danny's mom spotted an ad in the Jackson newspaper about a wrestling tryout at the Jackson Coliseum. Casting caution to the wind, Davis drove 70 miles to Jackson to give it a try.

"When I got there, I saw about two hundred people waiting outside the Coliseum," recalled Davis. "And of those two hundred, I was the smallest guy there."

As so often happens in the wrestling business, Davis was the right guy in the right place at the right time. He was one of a half dozen men singled out by Memphis veteran Buddy Fuller and invited into the Coliseum. After participating in a series of shoot matches with the others, Fuller invited Davis to train with him.

Buddy Fuller had just started a wrestling school in Bolivar, Tennessee, and he made the new recruits an offer they couldn't refuse. If they agreed to live on Fuller's farm and work for him for free, he would train them free of charge.

Davis left the security of his job and the suburban life with his family for an unheated farm house with sixteen other guys. It was the dead of winter, and the day began at 6 am. The men would get up and get dressed for the day before having breakfast at 7 am. By 8 am they were out on the frozen farmland, where they worked without a break until noon. After lunch, prepared by the same local girl who made their breakfast, it was back out into the field.

Finally, when 5 pm hit, the work was done. There was no time for a shower; the boys grabbed their bags and headed to the gym, where Fuller's trainer Terry Sawyer would stretch and hurt them night after night after night. It was all stretching but no in-ring technique, and Davis caught on fast that he wasn't learning the craft he saw on television.

"I've always been a hot head," says Davis, recalling the days of endless stretches. "One day, I finally stood up and yelled, 'I wanna learn that s--- I see on TV!' Well, the trainers took me around back, gave me a short talk, and that was that. It wasn't about training wrestlers. It was paying your dues."

Over the weeks Davis spent on the farm, the class of sixteen began to shrink. Guys who realized they weren't cut out for the life packed their bags and went home. "We were doing duck walks around the gym one night," recalls Davis. "Two guys duck walked out the side door and never came back."

Of the sixteen that started on the farm, only five made it to the end. Only one would go on to a career with any sort of longevity. So it goes in the world of wrestling.

Davis began working as enhancement talent for the Memphis promotion, doing jobs for all the top babyfaces. Despite being enhancement talent, a position that meant losing every night, his work in the ring made him the most hated man in the territory.

"Ron Bass came into Memphis at that time as a babyface," says Davis. "He told Lawler to pair him up with the heel who had the most heat. Lawler told him, 'I know you won't believe this, but the guy with the most heat right now is a jobber!'"

Davis was in the thick of things for some of the biggest stories in Memphis history. As Sgt. Danny Davis, he became the manager for the Blonde Bombers, Wayne Farris and Larry Latham. Davis was in the middle of the action when the Bombers did battle with Bill Dundee and Jerry Lawler in the legendary Tupelo Concession Stand Brawl.

Davis was also ringside as Lawler's manager years later during Lawler's first clash with Andy Kaufman. It was Davis who relayed the messages between Lawler and Kaufman post-match, when Andy refused to get up and insisted on selling his injury.

"Andy wants an ambulance," Davis told Lawler.

"Tell Andy an ambulance costs $500, and I'm not paying for it," said Lawler.

Davis relayed the message and came back to Lawler with another. "Andy said he'll pay for the ambulance."

"I told Lawler to get on the mic and say, 'Instead of calling an ambulance, maybe we should call him a taxi," said Davis, referencing Kaufman's role on the sitcom Taxi. "That almost got me fired for being more clever than the boss, the boss being Lawler."

Memphis was a huge tag team promotion, and Davis partnered with Kenny Wayne to form two teams, the Nightmares and the Galaxians, an odd, video game-inspired gimmick, managed by a very young Jim Cornette. Wayne and Davis won the Southern Tag Team Championship titles on four separate occasions. Davis also won the Southeastern Heavyweight Championship once and the United States Junior Heavyweight Championship five times.

In the early 1990s the road life began to wear on the veteran, and the idea of starting a wrestling school came to mind. Every week, fans came up to the autograph tables and asked Davis where they could go to train to become a wrestler. He saw a need, and he saw Louisville would be an ideal spot. In 1992 Davis found a building in Portland neighborhood and opened Nightmare Inc. Wrestling.

One of the very first students to sign up with Davis was Frank Miller, a Louisville native who grew up attending the Memphis shows at the Gardens. Miller trained with Davis and became one his first students to get a shot at Memphis TV. His first on-air appearance was with his hero Jerry Lawler, who also gave Miller his nickname.

"You look like trailer park trash," Lawler supposedly said. "That's your name. Trailer Park Trash!"

Trash, as he's known to fans and peers, stayed with Davis after Memphis closed shop in the mid 90s. The school relocated to Jeffersonville, Indiana, and in 1997 Davis changed the name to Ohio Valley Wrestling. Trash became OVW's first heavyweight champion in 1997 and helped establish the territory the school would use to train their students. Fellow Memphis veterans Flash Flanigan and Bill Dundee also joined the promotion, helping to break new ground and draw fans of the old Memphis days. Davis also paid tribute to the Memphis era by dubbing the OVW tag team title the Southern Tag Team Championship.

From the beginning, Davis envisioned a school that would train new wrestlers the old fashioned way. Students didn't just watch videos and take bumps in the ring. Davis wanted them to travel, giving them the experience of working a territory. OVW became known throughout the region, and Davis booked as many spot shows as he could.

Davis also knew television had to be a key component to training. Every student who came in to OVW would have their sights set on the WWF, and you couldn't get there without knowing how to wrestle on television. After paying a visit to the Davis Arena to see what his old friend had planned, Dean Hill agreed to become the voice of OVW on television.

Davis also recruited his old friend Rip Rogers to be the head trainer at OVW. After wrestling for ICW and Memphis, Rogers traveled the country and the world, learning different styles of wrestling everywhere he went. When he came to OVW, he brought the knowledge and experience gained from two decades on the road with him.

Rip's training style is coarse and demanding, with no filter whatsoever. You never knew what he was going to say. He cursed and swore constantly in the ring while training his students, who accepted the harsh treatment willingly to learn from him.

"We were at St. Therese's Gym one time," recalls "Crybaby" Chris Alexander. "We found Rip's tape recorder that he used when he was watching our matches to take notes. We decided to hit play to see what he was saying about us. We were shocked to hear the language he used when no one was even listening!"

Davis was training for a new era of wrestling, but his methods were intentionally traditional. "Every student begins the same way," says Davis. "Doesn't matter how many years they've been working, doesn't matter if they were sent down from WWE. They started in the beginner's class and worked their way up. They paid their dues."

Even the Big Show, who had been a main event star for WCW prior to his WWF run, found himself running the ropes and doing fundamentals alongside every other student. "One of the reasons the WWF sent Show to us was to help him lose weight," said Cornette. "He hit those ropes so hard, he bent the posts and had to buy Danny replacements. He also had a barf bucket out back of the Quadrangle. Show was always running out back to puke, so we got him his own bucket and put his name on it!"

The old Davis Arena, located in the Quadrangle in Jeffersonville, was an ideal spot to pay your dues. Now a thriving, redeveloped plaza filled with office space and restaurants, the Quad in the late 1990s was a rundown relic, a former military warehouse dating all the way back to the Civil War.

"There was no bathroom inside," recalls Chris Alexander. "If you had to go, you went outside and relieved yourself on the gravel lot."

That gravel lot would soon become the training ground for some of the biggest names in the modern wrestling era. When a hometown hero returned with a new crop of students, everyone knew they were witnessing the beginning of something big. They just didn't know how big it would be.

HOMECOMING

Jim Cornette hated Connecticut. He hated working in the office at Titan Towers. More than anything, he hated being part of the machine, trapped in the bureaucracy of the promotion that had become not just the only game in town, but in the world. The Louisville native was miserable, and while he didn't want to leave the business, he very much wanted out of Stamford.

Cornette returned for a visit during the Christmas holidays. During a trip to Clarksville Seafood, he ran into Danny Davis, who invited Cornette to have a look at OVW. Cornette was blown away. Davis had a great space. He had a ring and lights. He had camera equipment and more importantly, television distribution. He had not just a training school, but a mini-promotion that was grabbing eyeballs and filling seats.

Davis had built the perfect opportunity for Cornette to escape the office and return to what he loved.

Training was a critical need for WWE. With the territories gone, the company had need for a place to send its developmental talent. At the time, the WWE had Tom Pritchard and Dory Funk, Jr., training students in the same cold warehouse where the company built its elaborate set pieces for the road. OVW had everything the warehouse did not, and then some.

The touring schedule was one of the major selling points for OVW as a training center. Trainees had the opportunity to experience life on the road on a small scale playing high school gyms and national guard armories the same way others had done for nearly a century. Those who couldn't handle the schedule of OVW would never have made it with the WWE's travel schedule, and the travel served to weed out those unfit for the road.

The television programming at OVW was even more important than the touring schedule. Future WWE talent needed to learn not only how to talk on the microphone, but how to wrestle in front of a camera. The WWE production crews cut the arena in half, with all their cameras to one side of the ring. OVW television crews did the same thing at Davis Arena, and their student learned to play to the cameras, keeping their bodies and faces turned toward the camera side of the ring. They learned to tell stories with their bodies and their facial expressions.

When Cornette returned to Stamford, he made his pitch to Jim Ross. Cornette would take a fifty percent pay cut, move back home, and run a WWE developmental training program. Once Ross saw all that OVW had to offer, he agreed it was a great idea. With blessings from on high, Jim Cornette moved home.

OVW was stocked with Danny Davis's students at the time. His nephews Doug Basham and Danny Basham (better known as the Damaja), were his top prospects along with fellow Hoosiers Nick Dinsmore and Rob Conway. All four would eventually earn WWE contracts, but the WWE wasn't just interested in home grown talent. Soon after Cornette arrived, Rico Costantino became the first developmental talent to arrive.

Rico was a former police officer and SWAT team member from Las Vegas who first made a name for himself on the TV show American Gladiators. Rico came up short in his quest to become the grand champion of season one, but his mastery of gladiator Gemini in the Joust event made him a fan favorite.

After a brief stint with the Christian strong man ministry known as The Power Team, Rico decided to give professional wrestling a try. He started his training with the Empire Wrestling Federation in New York. After only twelve matches, he was recruited and signed to a developmental contract and sent to OVW.

Rico became a star at OVW thanks to his athleticism, his sheer strength, and a unique hair style. He was a favorite backstage with OVW management and talent. Rico got his call up to the main roster in 2002, partnering with the tag team Billy and Chuck. After struggling to catch on with the fans, he was released in 2004. He retired from the business in 2005, but after a seven year hiatus decided to give it another go with a Nevada promotion in 2012.

Two more WWE signees arrived from the University of Minnesota. Paired as a tag team, former Golden Gophers Brock Lesnar and Shelton Benjamin became fan favorites. As a tag team, they complimented each other extremely well. Lesnar was terrifying combination of power, strength, and speed while Benjamin combined speed and athleticism with remarkable balance. Fans of WWE will recall Benjamin stealing the show nearly every time he took part in a ladder match during his tenure with the company.

"Brock oozed arrogance," says Danny Davis. "He's the kind of man who looks at himself in the morning and needs a challenge."

Arrogance aside, Lesnar worked as hard as anyone who ever trained under Davis. He often volunteered to drive Davis's truck to the gyms, hauling the ring equipment with him, and he took charge of setting up the ring.

Although Cornette sometimes referred to Lesnar as Block Lesnar - short for Blockhead - Lesnar impressed everyone with his work ethic as much as his raw talent. One former wrestler recalled watching the super heavyweight rehearse what he hoped would be his signature move, the Shooting Star Press. The Shooting Star Press is a move normally reserved for the smaller high fliers, a dangerous maneuver because it involved doing a front flip off the top turnbuckle, landing blind on top of your opponent. Lesnar would take to the empty ring and practice the move over and over and over, flopping to the mat, picking himself up, climbing the corner and doing it again.

Lesnar only got to use the move once, at Wrestlemania XIX in Seattle during his title bout with Kurt Angle. It was supposed to be Lesnar's Wrestlemania moment, an immortal image that would live in Mania lore forever. For whatever reason, Lesnar shorted himself on takeoff and nearly broke his neck. A quick move by Kurt Angle on the mat saved the wrestler's neck and career, and the match ended with an anti-climactic finish.

"To see a man that big do that move was just unreal," says Rip Rogers. "But I always told him, 'You only need to do that move once. You don't need to do it every night.' Snuka didn't jump off the cage every night. He did it one time. That's all you need."

Lesnar missed his chance for an iconic Wrestlemania moment in Seattle, but he made up for it eleven years later. At Wrestlemania XXX, Lesnar stunned the world when he ended the Undertaker's Wrestlemania undefeated streak at 21-1. Lesnar's victory was one of the most shocking moments in Wrestlemania history, but his power and intensity made him was a fitting choice to end the streak.

Lesnar was known for his intensity even at OVW, but there was another side of him that came out at times. "In his early days he had a bad habit of muttering 'm------ f-----' under his breath when he wrestled," says Dean Hill. "I pulled him aside and pointed it out to him. When I told him, he was like, 'Oh my goodness, I'm so sorry!' Very apologetic. To this day, when I see him, I'll sneak up behind him and say, 'What's up, m----- f-----?'"

Hill wasn't the only one to make Lesnar backtrack like a scolded puppy. "The caterers had already set up one night backstage on a show Lesnar wasn't wrestling," says Rip Rogers. "Lesnar was always eating, and he dove right in. I jumped on him and yelled, 'Put the food down! That's not for you!'" It was mostly a rib, but once again, Lesnar apologized and backed away.

Randy Orton had a third generation pedigree when he arrived at OVW. He was born in Lexington, Kentucky, and his first home was not far from that of his future trainer Rip Rogers. "He was mischievous," says Danny Davis. "He never gave me any grief, but he was always up to something. One time he and Rico were messing around at the announcer's desk. Randy blurted out, 'I really don't care what happens, just as long as I get my $750.' Randy didn't realize the mics were hot. I always kept them hot, and I recorded everything. I still have the tape somewhere."

Dave Batista was a Vince McMahon favorite, a big man with huge muscles and a great look, but as Cornette recalls, he was one of the greenest recruits they ever trained. Batista had no experience in the ring or on the mic, and he wasn't the quickest or most serious learner at first. Cornette gave him the name "Leviathan," and made him a monster, a move that allowed Batista to do a lot of hitting, pushing, and shoving without having to actually wrestle.

Leviathan was drawn up out of the waters of the Ohio River by his evil manager Synn (Cornette's now wife Stacy). His ascension from the water was captured on film, and the unholy event took place at a boat dock in Indiana between New Albany and the Horseshoe Casino in Harrison County.

"I couldn't believe they got him to go out in that water," says Chris Alexander, who was on camera that night. "The river was filthy, but Dave went out into the muck and rose from the river as directed."

Cornette's expectations weren't as high for Batista as they were for some of the other talents, but a renewed drive to become a success and a friendship with Triple H helped him rise to the top during his tenure in the WWE.

The WWE signees were not the only new faces following Cornette to Louisville. Established WWE Superstars and WWE personnel, many of whom were former superstars themselves, became regulars at the Davis Arena.

"There were always major stars around rehabbing injuries or helping train guys," recalls former wrestler and trainee Ben Wood. "Bradshaw [JBL], Ron Simmons, and Mark Henry spent a lot of time there. Every couple weeks someone new drop by like Randy Orton, Stevie Richards, Crash and Bob Holly. Dr. Tom and his brother Bruce Pritchard were always coming in to evaluate guys. Terry Taylor, Sgt. Slaughter, and Arn Anderson would stop in to check on progress. These are guys you grew up idolizing now helping you reach your dreams."

Chris Alexander felt a similar rush being around such legendary figures. "I remember being in the back parking lot giving Arn Anderson directions to the hospital. Someone got hurt. I don't remember who, but here comes Arn Anderson and I'm like, 'Sure, I'll give you directions, Arn Anderson!'"

THE PROTOTYPE

Sitting in a coffee shop in Louisville, I asked Dean Hill to take me back to the days when OVW had arguably it's greatest crop of talent ever. OVW was still in Jeffersonville at the time in the Quadrangle on 10th Street. The Quad was in terrible disrepair, a square of crumbling brick buildings in a rundown industrial area. Hill bypassed the front parking lot, reserved for the fans, and drove around back of the arena. As his car slowly rolled over the unpaved drive, he could see them stretching and warming up on the gravel lot.

Brock Lesnar. Rico Costantino. Randy Orton. Shelton Benjamin. Charlie Haas. Leviathan. Nick Dinsmore. Rob Conway. Doug and Danny Basham. Within a few short years, millions of fans would shell out big money to catch a glimpse of these stars as they slowly infiltrated and took over the WWE. In the early 2000s you could see them all for free every Wednesday in Jeffersonville.

While no one on the OVW staff could say for certain just how many of the trainees would truly "make it" at the next level, everyone from Cornette down to the lowest guy on the roster knew one man was destined for greatness: the Prototype, John Cena.

"Within five minutes of meeting John Cena, I knew he was going to be great," said Danny Davis. "Most guys when they came here needed a little babysitting, help finding a place to stay and get acclimated. Cena already had an apartment. He had his act together."

Rip Rogers had a similar assessment when he met Cena prior to a house show on the road. "He was setting up the ring, and he had a smile on his face," said Rogers. "Most guys did their best to duck out of setting up, but Cena worked hard at everything he did."

When Jim Ross signed John Cena to a developmental contract, he went back to Connecticut and told Vince McMahon he had signed his Wrestlemania main event star of the future. Vince McMahon was not so sure. He was not crazy about the green wrestler with the "GI Joe" look, and he even toyed with the idea of cutting him.

Cena had a lot to learn about working a match, but his desire to succeed was unparalleled. Cena worked hard to improve his skills in the ring. He was a true professional who was never late and always willing to do personal appearances in the community. More important, John Cena had something going for him that no wrestling school in the world can teach.

"To me, the one thing you can't teach anyone is charisma," said Danny Davis. "You have charisma, or you don't. John Cena oozes charisma."

Cena was one of the first clients assigned to Kenny Bolin, who ran the heel stable Bolin Services. It's odd to think of Cena as anything but a hero, the ultimate babyface good guy, but Cena excelled at playing the heel. He was one of a number of wrestlers in Bolin's stable, but even when he was just in the ring to back up someone else's push, all eyes were drawn to Cena.

Cena was an eye catcher whether he was running the ropes or just part of the crowd, but he was at his very best when he was on the mic. A natural talker, Cena filled his promos with energy and humor, never stumbling and never missing a beat. He became known for his "backwards promos" Cena would issue a statement or a challenge to an opponent, followed by the catch phrase, "Oh, you didn't get that? Let me rewind it for you!" He would give the line in reverse, reversing his physical actions as well, and then repeat his statement just as before.

Cena was flawless on the mic, one of the rare breed that didn't need a script. He could pull a promo out of thin air that would not only get over with his competitive classmates, but leave them rolling with laughter. A game evolved in their rehearsal sessions that came to be known as "Stump Proto." A student of staff member would give Cena some ridiculous match to sell, and Cena would then cut a three minute promo.

"One time they told him to sell three way dance at Wrestlemania between Mario, Luigi, and a peanut butter cup," recalls Kenny Bolin. "He never stammered, never paused, he just rolled with it. By the time he was done, I wanted to see that peanut butter cup wrestle at Wrestlemania!"

Dean Hill was present for another of these rehearsals, when Cena was told to deliver a promo about his upcoming opponent - a fruit cup. Cena's full personality was on display as he described the fruit cup with its succulent, sweet juices dripping over the sides and what he intended to do with that same fruit cup.

Cena's most outrageous performance came the day he was asked to sell a match where he would tag team with Rocky the flying squirrel. Since John Cena is the WWE's kid-friendly, PG star, I will leave the details of that promo out of this book, but you're welcome to ask Kenny Bolin or any of the other witnesses to this historic promo about Rocky.

"I remember Rocky the flying squirrel," Dean Hill told me, shaking his head.

"All the ladies loved the flying squirrel," said Jim Cornette with a laugh.

Outside of the ring, Cena was a guy who loved to have fun and pull the occasional rib. Shortly after Ric Flair's son David was assigned to OVW, Nick Dinsmore told Flair he needed to ask Cena about his sister. Dinsmore said Cena's sister was an accomplished piano player and that Cena was very proud of his sister.

Flair did was he was told and was shocked when Cena went off. He flew into a rage, throwing a garbage can against the wall.

"My sister has no arms!!!" he screamed.

For the record: John Cena does not have a sister.

Bolin was so impressed with Cena's potential, he made one of his famous unilateral decisions to cut an angle involving none other than Mark Cuban. The billionaire was already owner of the Dallas Mavericks, but he had not yet become a nationally known celebrity. A few months after his OVW cameo, Cuban made his now famous remark that a certain NBA official was not smart enough to be a ref and should be working at a Dairy Queen. Dairy Queen objected to the comment and challenged Cuban to try working as a DQ manager for a day. Cuban not only accepted, he bought Blizzards for every customer to visit the store that day and made himself a household name in the process.

Bolin contacted Cuban by email, and to his surprise, Cuban answered back. Cuban was a huge wrestling fan, and he loved the idea Bolin proposed. The two made arrangements to meet up when the Mavericks traveled to Indianapolis for a game with the Indiana Pacers and make a little OVW history.

On game day Bolin headed north with Cena, his son Chris, and a camera man. "Cena was convinced we were ribbing him," said Chris Bolin. "But when we got there, Cuban took us everywhere. We got to shoot around with the players. We ate dinner with them. It was amazing."

Cuban had agreed to give Bolin a half hour of his time to shoot video, but the energetic entrepreneur spent nearly two hours with them. They took over the Pacers press room and shot a series of vignettes.

The premise of the angle was that Bolin wanted Cuban to invest in Bolin Services with the ultimate goal of taking over the WWE. Unfortunately for Bolin, the Prototype got off on the bad foot when he bumped into Cuban, unaware of who he was, and called him a dork.

When Bolin finally introduces the two, the arrogant Cena switched gears and began kissing up to Cuban. That changed when Cuban turned to Bolin and asked what happened to Leviathan. It was an ad-libbed moment that both surprised and impressed Bolin. Leviathan had never been mentioned in his discussions with Cuban. Cuban had done his homework on OVW and their current roster, and he had come to play.

Cuban and Cena continued to butt heads throughout the promo while Bolin tried to convince both men, "We don't have to like each other. We just have to work together." Cuban and Bolin finally came to an understanding, and the segment ended with the ominous prediction that they would squash the WWE like a bug.

Bolin had told Cornette about his planned angle with Cuban, but Cornette, who was used to Bolin's tall tales, didn't believe a word of it. When Bolin returned home with the footage, Cornette was thrilled to eat his words. It isn't every day you get a billionaire to appear side by side with your prospective wrestling students!

One of Cena's most memorable matches was with a young talent that would become one of his greatest rivals in the ring. Randy Orton received the call up to the main roster before Cena, and when Cornette brought Orton in the ring to congratulate him, the Prototype stormed the ring. Cena ended Orton's OVW career with a loss in a match that foreshadowed they main event showstoppers at the next level.

Another Cena match left a lasting impression on Chris Alexander, who later ran his own promotion in the Portland neighborhood. Former ECW wrestler Nova had just arrived at OVW and was booked to face Cena in his first match. Davis say Alexander before the show and smiled. "You want to see how you get a new babyface over? Watch this."

"Cena had been the top dog for a long time," says Alexander. "He was unstoppable. When you build a top heel as someone whom no one can beat and bring a new guy who is relatively unfamiliar in the territory and you want

243

to get him over, have him take down the heel with his most prized possession." Nova defeated Cena that night and won the OVW fans over in a memorable main event.

Cena made his first appearance on WWE TV when he accepted an open challenge by Kurt Angle. The Prototype took to the ring, lined up eyeball to eyeball with the Olympic hero, and slapped him in the face, making an immediate impression on the live crowd. He lost the match, but afterward, he got a televised handshake backstage from the Undertaker. He was on his way to the top, but he had unfinished business back in Louisville.

Cena lost his final match at OVW to his former in-ring manager Kenny Bolin. He was already working the main roster for the WWE when Bolin cost Cena the title in a match against former ECW star Nova. Cena challenged Bolin to a "Loser Leaves OVW" match, and Cornette appointed fellow Bolin Services member Sean O'Haire as special guest referee. The Prototype took it to Bolin, bashing (in Cornette's words) his "huge jowls" into the turnbuckle, but Bolin would employ misdirection and dirty tricks to send Cena packing.

Cena was not done with OVW. He would put in a number of appearances for the promotion that helped launch his career, even after he reached the top of the WWE. At a house show for WWE in 2012, Cena ended the night by thanking the people of Louisville and reiterating his love for the city that help launched him to superstardom. The feeling is mutual among those who knew him best.

"The day we drove to Indy to meet Mark Cuban," said Chris Bolin, "I asked Cena what his goal was. He told me, 'I want to be the next Don Kernodle!'"

For the 98% scratching their heads, Don Kernodle was an obscure journeyman wrestler in the 1970s. It's safe to say that when John Cena left Louisville, he exceeded his goal.

THE OTHER GUYS

It would be easy to only write about the great ones, the big names who made it from Davis Arena to the main event, but that's not even half the story. For every one man who made it from the Quadrangle in Jeffersonville to the WWE, there were many who never got past the smaller spotlight of the Davis Arena. Ben Wood, who wrestled locally as the Outlaw, Outlaw Ben Wood, and the Prophet, made the journey from New York City to Louisville in hopes of scoring a WWE contract. A hard worker with a great look, Ben's first stint with OVW ended badly due to some backstage issues and personal demons. Wood took a step back, got himself together, and gave wrestling another try, working with smaller promotions throughout Kentucky, Indiana, and Tennessee.

By the time Wood returned to OVW, the WWE had moved their developmental operation to Florida, but WWE personnel still kept a close eye on the OVW scene. Things went much better the second time around, and after a weeklong wrestling camp with Harley Race in Michigan, he got his dream shot, a tryout at WWE Smackdown. The tryout went well, and Wood was certain a WWE developmental contract was in his grasp. A week later, on October 9, 2009, Wood agreed to wrestle one more match at OVW to put over the new TV champion.

"I was two minutes into a match on top of the world and suddenly something went very wrong," Wood recalls. "Catching my opponent off the ropes I snapped my knee in half tearing my patella tendon. My career was over after two failed surgeries."

In spite of his tragic end, Ben Wood looks back on his wrestling days with fondness and gratitude. He came closer to achieving his WWE dream than most of the students who walked through the doors of OVW, but even the students who never even sniffed the coveted WWE developmental contract played a role in the development of OVW and the WWE talent within.

"Crybaby" Chris Alexander was one of those local guys always loved wrestling and thought he would give it a try. Born Jason Alexander Lindsey, Alexander spent his high school days in New Albany playing rock 'n' roll and marching with the school band. His fellow band mates, many of whom never knew about his wrestling obsession, were surprised in their post high school years to learn the long haired trumpet player had not gone on to musical stardom, but the squared circle.

Alexander's heroes growing up included Shawn Michaels and Ric Flair. His preference for these flamboyant personalities came through in his wild wardrobe and his elaborate entrance. With his blond hair unfurled over his colorful, flowing robe, Chris Alexander took his time entering the arena and the ring, basking in the boos and hatred of the crowd that longed to see him get his butt kicked. His win-loss record clearly shows the crowd got their way more often than not, but in pro wrestling, wins and losses are secondary to putting on a great show.

Alexander put on a great show, from the moment his music hit to the moment he limped back through the curtain. While on the road at a high school that allowed the wrestlers a bird's eye view of the ring out of view of the public, Cornette would send the troops out to watch Alexander make his entrance, hoping some of them would learn something about showmanship from the overachiever.

Much of the blame for Alexander's low wins total can be attributed to his status as one of the go-to guys for first matches. When a new wrestler was ready for their first match before a crowd or the cameras, Alexander got the nod. It was his job to carry them through, get the butterflies out, and put them over by taking the fall.

Alexander recalls stepping into the ring with a future WWE champion for the latter's first televised match.

The bell rang, the future star moved in, locked eyes with Alexander, and whispered, "What do I do???"

Perhaps the most heartbreaking story is that of Matt Cappotelli. Cappotelli first became known to wrestling fans on the WWE's reality show, *Tough Enough*. Cappotelli was a co-winner with John Hennigan, who became known as John Morrison at both OVW and in the WWE. The two started out as a tag team at OVW. Hennigan was later teamed with Joey Mercury and Melina to form the team MNM, while Cappotelli teamed up with Johnny Jeter. After a split with Jeter, Cappotelli became the OVW champion.

Cappotelli's future was looking bright. He was brought up for a few tryout matches with the Miz on the road before two leg injuries set him back. Then tragedy struck. After suffering what appeared to be a concussion in a match against Chris Cage, Cappotelli was sent to the hospital. Shortly after doctors diagnosed Cappotelli with brain cancer.

As he left to do battle with a much different opponent, Matt Cappotelli bid a tearful farewell to the OVW fans. His peers surrounded the ring, and the entire arena chanted his name as he relinquished his title belt to Danny Davis.

Jason Saint, an OVW fan who now works for a number of indie promotions as a manager, wrote about Cappotelli's departure in his blog. "Anyone who met Matt Cappotelli met someone who had truly reached a golden standard of life. A man of faith, Matt was the kind of guy who you could talk to for a few minutes and walk away feeling empowered. He had a strength in his stance that made him unmatched. Someone you could trust, love, and believe in." Cappotelli beat cancer and now runs a Christian T-shirt company.

Two Southern Indiana natives who started in the beginner's class made it all the way to the WWE. Rob Conway was a New Albany native who made it to the WWE for a brief time. A stand out athlete during his years at New Albany High School, Conway spotted the school while driving through Jeffersonville and thought he'd give it a go. He had a brief run on WWE TV as a member of the French group La Resistance, when he laid claim to being the only Louisville native to ever win the WWE Tag Team Championship. He went on to become successful indy wrestler and a two time NWA champion.

Nick Dinsmore was also a Hoosier, a Providence High School graduate from Jeffersonville. Nick was as solid an in-ring worker as Davis and Rogers had ever seen, but the WWE wanted nothing to do with him because of a perceived lack of character.

"I suggested the U-Gene character to him," says Rip Rogers. "I said to him, 'What if you played this character who emulated all his favorite wrestlers?' I planted the seed, but Nick really created the character."

U-Gene was a unique character in the history of the WWE and professional wrestling. The mentally challenged character could copy any other wrestler's moves. Dinsmore also studied some of the fans who came to the Davis arena to pick up other mannerisms to fit the character. It was a fine line to walk, but he made U-Gene a fan favorite during his short stint in the big time.

Dinsmore later returned to run the beginner's class for OVW. Dinsmore's aptitude for teaching emerged quickly, and it didn't take long for the WWE to make another call. Dinsmore became a WWE Developmental Trainer in the fall of 2013.

"They have their own way of doing things," says Danny Davis of the modern WWE training methods, "But they took Nick to be one of their trainers. Maybe they realized they do need a little bit of that old school style down there."

Kenny will never forget the day he got "smart" to the business of wrestling. As a wrestling fan growing up in the 1970s, Kenny lived for Tuesdays at the Gardens and the monthly wrestling magazines. Whenever a new issue came out, he flipped right to the rankings page, and if Jerry Lawler was not at least in the top ten, he flew into a rage.

"Kenny," said his friend Jim, "You know those rankings are bull----, right?"

Kenny was taken aback. "They are?"

"Yes!" said Jim.

"How do you know?" asked Kenny.

"I found out when I started sending them my pictures. I would send the results with the photos, but every time they would make up their own stories to go with the pictures."

Kenny couldn't believe it. "It's made up?"

Thanks to his friend Jim Cornette, Kenny Bolin learned the secret of the wrestling business. But like his good friend, the truth did not diminish his passion. The teens were hooked, and both were destined for a life in the wrestling business. In an online podcast, Cornette boasted that as kids, Kenny did a great Lawler impression while he did a perfect Jimmy Valiant impression.

"He was a terrible Jimmy Valiant," laughs Bolin, recalling the old days. "He did a lot of good impressions. He did a great Dusty Rhodes. But he was an awful Jimmy Valiant."

Even early on, the two men had a feel for the business. "Can you imagine if one day, a guy were to suplex someone from the second rope?" Kenny once asked Jimmy.

"I'll go one better," said Jimmy. "What if someone suplexed a guy from the top rope?"

"No way," said Kenny. "It'll never happen!"

"Or what if someone really went nuts and brought a chainsaw into the ring?" said Jimmy.

It was an intriguing thought, but both agreed a bad idea. "Where would you go the following week? How do you follow up a chainsaw?" Twenty years before the rise of ECW, Kenny Bolin and Jim Cornette had already predicted the course that would be its downfall.

At age nineteen, Bolin had a brush with a true wrestling legend completely by accident. In the summer of 1979 he traveled to Virginia where he met his real father for the first time. Kenny's dad knew his son was a wrestling fan, so as a special treat, he took him to the Norfolk Spoke, home to the ABA's Virginia Squires and "Dr. J" Julius Erving, to see Ric Flair competing for Jim Crockett's Mid-Atlantic Championship wrestling.

Bolin and his father sat in the third row from ringside. Kenny brought along a scrapbook of photos given to him by Jim Cornette. The book contained mostly photos of Bolin's favorite star, Jerry Lawler, and that caught the eye of an elderly fan sitting next to Kenny.

"Is that Jerry Lawler?" the old man asked.

"Yes," said Kenny.

"I wrestled him a few times," said the old man.

Up until this point, Kenny hadn't really looked at the man seated next to him. When he did look, he was star-struck.

"You're Lou Thesz," he stammered.

"Yes I am," said Thesz.

"What are you doing down here?" said Kenny.

"I'm a fan just like you," said Thesz. "I enjoy sitting with the fans."

When Jim Cornette left town, following his dream to Mid-South, WCCW, Smokey Mountain, and the WWF, Bolin remained in Louisville, waiting for his own opportunity to enter the business. "Jimmy always wanted me to make it on my own rather than him help me. I preferred to sit back and wait for that opportunity come to me," Bolin says with a wink.

Kenny's big break happened thanks to a chance encounter with Nick Gulas at a Service Merchandise in Nashville. After introducing himself and dropping a few names – specifically Lawler and Cornette – Bolin was offered a chance to audition to be an on-air announcer. He was less than thrilled when his audition turned out to be interviewing the infamous George Gulas, but Kenny did a good enough job to get himself hired on.

Kenny worked off and on as an announcer and as a manager for a number of promotions while working a number of other jobs on the side, first in Nashville and then in Louisville. When Cornette decided to make his return to Louisville, the first person he called was Kenny Bolin.

"I was announcing and managing for OVW, but I was also managing for Ian Rotten at IWA Mid-South at the time," said Bolin, who served as the manager for a number of long time Louisville mainstays. "This was during the NWO days, and I would enter with the NWO music. One night I came out, and there were these four boys from UK wearing KWO T-shirts. I was so excited! I had never had a Kenny Bolin shirt, and here these boys had made their own."

On closer inspection, the T-shirts were actually UK shirts purchased from the UK bookstore. "The shirts said, 'Kentucky World Order,' but the boys had taken black tape and covered up 'tucky.' Within a few months there were about thirty of them, my own cheering section."

Bolin was surprised that the WWF actually signed off on OVW as its developmental territory. "Ian had the better building," he said. "He was working out of an old K-Mart. He had his own logo on the side and everything.

"Ian had bigger names. He drew bigger houses. Danny was running out of a dumpy old warehouse in

Indiana. I told Jimmy he'd never get the WWF to put their name on that place, but he did."

It wasn't hard to convince Bolin to leave IWA. Ian Rotten was a hardcore wrestling guy with roots in ECW. He regularly brought in ECW originals, and he packed the house every week. But Bolin was tired of barbed wire, fluorescent light tubes, rings of fire, and rings surrounded by piranhas. He was also tired of people pestering him to cut himself and bleed in the ring.

Kenny had a plum job waiting for him at OVW. In addition to his managing duties, Kenny served as the advertising salesman. Kenny sold the ads that lined the barrier wall in the arena, television ads, and later seating rights for the Louisville Gardens show. A sponsor's table beside Stone Cold Steve Austin's autograph table sold for $10,000, and Kenny got 30% of everything he made.

The ad sales helped Kenny make a living, but it was the managing that made him a star. Cornette explained his plan when he arrived in Louisville. "We're going to get rid of all these old timers around you. We're going to give you young talent. Your job is going to be to make these guys and get them to the WWF."

"Jimmy, these people know me and they know my clients," said Kenny. "How are you going to do this?"

Cornette smiled. "You'll see."

Cornette unleashed his plan at his first TV taping. After stepping into the ring to announce that he was now co-managing OVW as a WWF territory, Kenny Bolin left the announcer's desk to manage one of his clients in a match. Before the match even began, Cornette picked up the microphone again.

"Kenny, I've got some good news," said Jim. "You don't have to worry about announcing any more. This is now my chair."

Bolin was livid in his reaction, but Cornette was not done. "And another thing. Those men you manage are property of OVW. They belong to us. You're fired!"

Bolin blew up. For weeks, he had been telling the fans of OVW how much he despised his old friend. He even accused him of being the man responsible for the infamous Montreal Screw Job. His vitriol fell on deaf ears, and the fans cheered as they saw the hated manager escorted from the building.

"If you want to come back," said Cornette, "Go out and sign your own clients. Maybe then, we'll let you back in the building."

Bolin took a few weeks off from television. As planned, he returned in a series of video vignettes. Bolin was starting his own management business, and he was coming back with his own roster of talent.

The original idea, proposed by Jim Cornette, was to call Bolin's operation Bolin Management, or BM. Cornette found the idea of calling Bolin's business "BM" hilarious, and he told Bolin to get a briefcase made with the logo on the side. Bolin wasn't thrilled, but he was prepared to go forward with the idea. That was before he told his brother what they were planning.

"Kenny, the people don't want to chant 'BM' at you," he said. "They want to chant, 'BS.' Why can't you use BS?"

Kenny's brother Timmy John never had a head for the business of wrestling, but Kenny knew his brother was on to something. Without consulting Cornette, Bolin Management became Bolin Services.

When Kenny showed up at OVW with a briefcase bearing the "BS" logo, Cornette was confused. "I thought we agreed on BM," he said. Kenny explained the conversation with his brother, and Cornette nodded. "I like it. Let's go with it."

"Cornette later tried to take credit," said Bolin. "Much as I hate to admit it, it was Timmy John's idea."

Cornette's plan was to make Kenny the constant in what would be an ever-changing territory. Knowing the WWF could call up talent at any time, Cornette made Bolin

Services the focal point of the OVW fans' ire. The names and faces under Bolin Services could change week to week, but the fans would remain engaged due to their hatred of Bolin.

Cornette trusted his top prospects to Bolin, and very quickly, that trust paid off. Bolin Services became the launch pad for a slew of wrestlers to jump to the WWE including John Cena, Rico Costantino, Mark Henry, Sean O'Haire, Nick Dinsmore, Rob Conway, and Orlando Jordan. Jim Ross had originally told Cornette he wanted OVW to produce two good stars a year, but two jumped to twenty in a hurry, due in part to Kenny's skill for selling new talent.

Bolin was on a hot streak, but Cornette was sure it wouldn't last. After a number of call ups, Bolin was given Lance Cade and Mark Jindrak. "No way either of those two will see a day in the WWE," said Cornette. Yet in spite of the odds, both Cade and Jindrak were called up and given a shot at the big time.

Shortly after Cade and Jindrak left, Cornette gave Bolin a new nickname - Starmaker. During a TV taping, Cornette called Bolin into the ring to give him his due.

"Well if it isn't the old Starmaker," Cornette said in greeting.

Bolin laid right into his old friend. "You told me Cade and Jindrak would never make it to the WWE! I told you I'd get them to the WWE, and you looked at me like I had a smoking turd in my mouth!"

Bolin Services continued to make stars after Cornette's departure. Bolin also rented rooms to some of the OVW talent. The arrangement benefited the cash-starved wrestlers, but it also benefited Bolin, who made a nice profit renting rooms in a home he didn't even own. Bolin has always been shrewd when it comes to money, and his penchant for bartering is legendary not just in the wrestling community, but all over Louisville.

When he was finally ready to call it quits as a manager, Bolin handed the reins down to the Prince, his son Chris. Chris had long been a fixture at Davis Arena, and he and his friends had long established their power to make and break stars from the stands. Sitting middle center of the Arena, Chris and his crew could get the entire crowd to cheer and boo talent almost at will. When Cornette disputed their power to put stars over, Chris took it as a challenge. The following week, the group refused to give any kind of reaction for one of OVW's lead babyfaces. To Cornette's surprise, the entire crowd went along with the Prince, and the babyface entered to deafening silence.

Chris Bolin holds the unique distinction of being not just the only second generation manager in wrestling history, but the only third generation manager. It's a distinction he earned thanks to a canceled flight and Jerry Lawler. Lawler was in town for one of the summer shows at Six Flags. When his flight was canceled the following day, he called Bolin. Lawler wanted to come back, and he wanted Kenny's mother to be his manager.

"The fans loved watching your mother cheer against you last night," said Lawler. "What would you think if she came out as my manager?"

It was an intriguing idea. It was also technically illegal. The state of Kentucky required anyone who manages wrestlers to have a wrestling license, and Ma Bolin certainly didn't have one. But Bolin knew that neither Danny Davis or Jim Cornette would be at the show that evening. That left only one obstacle.

"Jerry, it's my mother's Bingo night," said Kenny.

"Can you call her and ask her anyway?" asked the King.

Bolin called his mother, and as expected, his mother objected. "It's Bingo night."

Bolin had to beg. "Mom, I can't call Jerry Lawler and tell him you won't do it. Please do this for me."

Ma Bolin sighed. "Okay, but I may bring some of the girls with me."

"That's just fine, Mom," said Bolin.

Jerry Lawler put Ma Bolin over like a WWE Legend. With Bolin and his client in the ring, Jerry came out on a mic and told the crowd, "The woman Kenny Bolin had thrown out of here last night, the woman he got evicted because he refused to pay her mortgage, his own mother was here. Kentucky Kingdom admitted her to the park, and she was coming to the ring as his guest."

Ma Bolin got the biggest pop of the night as she walked the aisle and took her seat beside the ring. The match came to a fever pitch climax when Lawler tied Bolin up in the ropes and brought his mother over to him.

"Slap him!" said Lawler. "Slap him for every evil thing he ever did in his life!"

Ma Bolin hesitated. For a moment Kenny feared that his mom would ruin the angle and deny the fans what they wanted. Lawler kept insisting, and Ma Bolin finally gave Kenny a weak slap.

"Hit him again!" Lawler shouted. Dean Hill leapt into the fray and joined in. "Come on, Ma Bolin, slap him!"

Ma Bolin finally gave her baby boy the slapping he deserved, but in the end, Bolin came out the winner. Lawler hit him with the illegal pile driver and was disqualified. That victory, coupled with Bolin's victory over John Cena in his "Loser Leaves Town" match, means Bolin has career victories over an NWA champion, a CWA champion, an AWA champion, a WWF/E champion, and a World Heavyweight Champion.

Kenny Bolin finally retired from OVW in 2012. His son Chris followed him two months later to pursue his college education. Many heroes and heels came up in Louisville wrestling, and the majority of them left town for the big shows and big money. Kenny Bolin is proud to say he gave 19 years of his life to Louisville exclusively. Love him or hate him, he fulfilled every goal set before him at OVW and lived up to his nickname, Starmaker.

Kenny and his black Bolin Services vehicle can often be spotted around town at one of his favorite restaurants, from Clarksville Seafood to Golden Corral, where they don't close the buffet until Kenny says they can close the buffet.

And no... I am not exaggerating when I say that.

Cornette knew that the old days were gone, and kayfabe was a thing of the past. Still, he saw value in teaching new talent to follow kayfabe. He wanted his wrestlers to be real, to look real, to make it real.

Chris Alexander recalls an incident that took place in the ring one night. During an otherwise ordinary match, an altercation took place between the two wrestlers. Watching from backstage, everyone could see that the two guys were no longer working, but really trying to hurt each other. The match ended, and the two men had to be restrained from one another.

The dispute carried over into the locker room. The two men still wanted a piece of each other, and Cornette did his best to break up the fight while a stunned locker room looked on. The wrestlers were finally separated, and the show went on.

Sometime later, the bystanders in the locker room learned what Cornette and the two men in the ring knew - it was all a work. The fight in the ring, the fight in the locker room, it was all staged at Jim Cornette's direction.

Cornette's message came through loud and clear: "The way you felt when that was going on is the way that audience needs to feel, every time you step in the ring!"

Cornette had his rules that he expected talent to abide by, and when talent got out of line, he didn't care if you were a local or a WWE prospect, he brought the hammer down. When those WWE prospects would call, Ross would give Cornette his full backing. "If you can't follow their rules, that tells me you can't follow our rules either," said Ross to many a recruit.

Cornette's old school ways extended far beyond the ring. No one was allowed to talk business outside of the locker room, especially not with people outside the business. Good guys dressed with good guys. Bad guys with bad guys. Heels and babyfaces were not allowed to be seen together in public.

"We were in a small town," says Cornette. "If you're threatening to kill somebody on TV Saturday night and they see you eating at McDonalds with the guy, it ruins the illusion." Those who thought Cornette was bluffing soon learned Cornette meant business when he said, "We will find you, catch you, and fine you."

John Rodman, who worked for a short time as a manager for students in the amateur's class, recalls a kayfabe moment that found him in a Steak and Shake. "Kenny Bolin walked in with Rico Costantino. Rico sat beside me. Kenny sat across from me. Kenny leaned across the table and whispered, 'There are some wrestling fans in here. Follow my lead.'"

Bolin sat back and spoke up loudly. "What's this I hear about you telling people you're a better manager than me? Do you know who I am? Do you know what I've done?" Rodman played along, stammering and apologizing to the veteran manager while Rico reached over and drank his soda.

It wasn't uncommon for the trainees at OVW to bristle under Cornette's rules. If an OVW student had problems, Cornette would simply kick them out. Things were a little more complicated when it came to WWE talent, especially the big names. So long as Jim Ross was in charge of talent, however, Cornette knew he had full authority to dish out whatever discipline he wanted.

"If a student called and complained to Ross, Ross would remind them they were in our house and had to abide by our rules," said Cornette. "And if they couldn't play by OVW rules, that said to Ross they couldn't play by WWE rules either."

Mark Henry was one of the few to challenge Cornette's authority. Henry was assigned to work the Kentucky State Fair with Kenny Bolin, promoting OVW and soliciting bookings for the promotion. The fair tales place in August, and it was a typical, blazingly hot day. Henry was not keen to complete his assignment.

"How long we here today, Bolin?" he asked.

"I would say from 9 to 9," Bolin responded.

Henry shook his head. "I get ten grand for an appearance. I'll stay until eleven."

"Look," said Bolin, trying to be diplomatic, "We can take turns taking breaks. You take a break for an hour, then I'll take one."

Henry shook his head again. "Ain't doing it, Bolin."

Kenny called Cornette and explained the situation. Cornette was furious. As far as he was concerned, Henry was there to learn the business like everyone else. He was also making six figures, and Cornette saw no harm in him doing a twelve hour promotional shift.

"Here's what you do," said Cornette. "You go over there and tell Mark Henry he's fired. Tell him you're firing him. It's coming from you."

This was not what Bolin had in mind. "You serious?"

"Yes!" said Cornette. "Tell him to pack his bags and go home!"

Bolin didn't want to do it, but he did as he was told. "Cornette told me to fire you."

Henry was in disbelief. His bravado was gone. "What do I do?"

"I guess pack your things and go back to Texas," said Bolin.

"What's the WWE gonna go?" he asked.

"I don't know," said Bolin. "When they hear what happened, they'll probably fire you too."

Henry left the Fair, and Bolin worked the day alone, the consequences of the day's events sinking in as he did. Henry was advertised all over Kentucky in the coming weeks doing battle with the Big Show. People had already bought tickets to see Mark Henry, and he knew the fans would not be pleased with the change.

A few days later, Bolin called Cornette to discuss the matter. Cornette was still seething, but he knew Bolin was right. "Do this," Cornette said. "Call him, tell him that you would be willing to let him come back if he plays ball. He does appearances for free. He shows up early. If he screws up again, he's done."

Bolin hung up and called Mark Henry. He explained the terms and told Mark to think about it. "If you decide you want to come back, be at the arena Friday."

Henry thought about it for a second. "I'll be there Tuesday."

"That's tomorrow, Mark," said Kenny. "You don't have to decide right away."

"I messed up," said Henry. "I'll be there tomorrow. Thank you for what you're doing for me."

Henry was a changed man after being fired. He was not only one of the most humble wrestlers on the roster, but also one of the nicest.

Another wrestler who fought the law was Henry's OVW rival, the Big Show. Like Henry, Show was not interested in doing unpaid promotional appearances, even after seeing what happened with Mark Henry. When Bolin pressed the Big Show on an appearance at Louisville Motor Speedway, Show cussed him out. Bolin called Cornette. Cornette called Jim Ross. Jim Ross called the Big Show.

As far as Ross was concerned, Bolin's orders were as good as anyone from WWE. Cornette worked for WWE, Bolin worked for Cornette, and if Bolin wanted him to do an appearance, he better do it. Ross told Show to apologize to Bolin and do the appearance. What's more, Ross told Show he had to do any other appearances OVW assigned him. If he was late even one minute for an appearance, Ross would fine him $2500.

Show apologized, but only half-heartedly. Word of the half-hearted apology got back to Cornette, and Cornette gave orders to Bolin. "Book him at every gas station in town. Book him to show up and hand out tickets to the next Gardens show. Book him two hours at a time, fifteen minutes apart!"

Bolin booked Show up and down Preston Highway, signing autographs and handing out tickets. Show was furious with Bolin, but he did as he was asked and made every appearance booked.

Cornette wasn't done with the pair. He then ordered Show to spend three days in Indianapolis at the Indiana State Fair with Bolin. Show had to pay for his hotel room and Bolin's. He also had to pay all meals for both of them.

Bolin was no more pleased with the orders than Show, and the ride to Indianapolis in Show's Cadillac Escalade was silent and tense. Around mile marker 40, Show turned to ask if Cornette was serious.

"Yes, he's serious," said Bolin.

"Was it your idea?" asked Show. "Me paying for you?"

"No, it wasn't," said Bolin. "But you did bring this on yourself."

Show nodded his agreement.

"Tell you what," said Bolin. "What if I were to show you how to use your celebrity to cover my room. Would you like that?"

"Yes I would," said Show.

"What if I were to get your room covered too?"

"Even better," said Show.

"And what if I showed you how to get your meals taken care of as well?"

"Hell yes!" said Show, all ears.

Bolin picked up his phone and called the hotel. "You have a reservation for a Paul Wight. You may or may not know this, but Paul Wight is actually the Big Show from wrestling. We're coming up to do some charity appearances, and we were wondering if you might be willing to take care of us if he signs some autographs and take some pictures?"

The hotel staff was more than happy to accommodate Show and Bolin. Big Show did some photos and autographs, and the hotel tab was waived. The same thing happened when Bolin called ahead for meals. Once again, Show traded some photos and autographs with the restaurant staff in exchange for two free meals. By the end of the trip, Show had softened to Bolin, and the two became good friends.

Both Show and Henry were model citizens by the time they left town. In fact Henry and Show made significant contributions to the new Davis Arena. Mark Henry bought three large fans to cool the unconditioned arena area during shows and training sessions, and the two super heavyweights went in together to buy an air conditioning unit for the wrestlers' dressing area.

"A lot of the guys saw coming here as a demotion," says Rip Rogers. "They felt like it was beneath them. They resented being here. By the second month, you couldn't chase them away. They learned so much being here. Paul and Mark both credit their time here with making them a success in the WWE."

A little old school discipline probably didn't hurt them either!

THE BIG STAGE

Most of the shows put on by OVW took place in smaller venues like the Davis Arena, but on several occasions, Davis and Cornette gave their students a chance to experience a thrill they once cherished when they booked shows at the venerable Louisville Gardens. The Gardens shows gave OVW's up and coming talent a chance to showcase their skills on a bigger stage with veteran WWE talents. It also gave WWE personnel a chance to evaluate the young stars in the ring with more the established stars. And yes, just like the old territory days, a bigger venue with bigger names meant a bigger box office.

The Rockin' Rumble, held during the summer of 2000, was the first show to incorporate big names from the WWE roster, with Kane and Mick Foley appearing alongside the OVW superstars. In the fall of 2000, the WWE and OVW decided to give rising star Batista, still known as Synn's disciple Leviathan, a chance to shine by booking him against the Big Show.

Chris Alexander was at ringside for most of the matches that evening. Alexander often wrestled the first match on the card, an important slot for getting the crowd engaged and fired up. As soon as the job was done (pun intended), he'd retire to the back, slip into a crew uniform, and return to ring side with a video camera in hand.

Usually, Alexander didn't mind becoming the anonymous camera man, but on the night of The Rockin' Rumble, he had to watch a dream pass him by. The evening ended with the heel locker room storming the ring to get a choke slam from Kane, a brain buster from OVW star Damaja, or a brush with the infamous Mr. Socko. Alexander watched the scene unfold with sadness; it was his one missed opportunity to take a real choke slam from the one and only Kane.

Cornette remembers that evening for a different reason. He, Tom Pritchard, and Synn, were the last three to take the ring. Pritchard and Cornette took their medicine from Kane and Damaja, leaving Synn to get Mick Foley Mr. Socko. When you're watching on television and Mr. Socko goes on a rampage, you don't stop to realize what a dirty, disgusting thing that is. Socko spends the time up until his appearance down Mick Foley's pants, and on a busy night, Socko gets inserted in a number of mouths. So after taking a gummy, wet mouthful of Mr. Socko, Synn rolled out of the ring on top of Pritchard and Cornette screaming, "I'm going to throw up on Bruce!!"

Night of the Demon was another huge night at the Gardens. In addition to the main event that saw Leviathan score a victory over the Big Show, fans were treated to a heavyweight championship bout in which Rob Conway defeated Nick Dinsmore. Randy Orton, Mark Henry, and Brock Lesnar also appeared on the blockbuster card.

After playing host to Kane, Mick Foley, and the Big Show, Cornette knew he had to go even bigger for his next show. The date was set for December of 2000, and Cornette set his sights on the number one star in the promotion. On a Monday night, he called Bruce Pritchard's cell phone.

"Is Stone Cold anywhere near you?" Cornette asked.

"He's sitting at a table near me," answered Ross.

"Ask him if he'll come to Louisville for $25,000 in a paper bag and all the beer he can drink."

Stone Cold accepted; he also accepted a check in lieu of the cash. So, too, did Kane, Chris Benoit, the Hardy Boys, and Lita. The WWE talents would appear on a blockbuster card that also featured the Big Show, Mark Henry, Randy Orton, the Minnesota Stretching Crew (tag partners and former Golden Gophers Brock Lesnar and Shelton Benjamin), Nick Dinsmore, Rico Costantino, and

Leviathan. Christmas Chaos was a quick sell out, and Louisville fans prepared themselves for a holiday treat.

Then Mother Nature struck. Louisville was hit with a huge snow storm on the day of the show. The WWE talent was not able to fly in for the show, and the event had to be canceled.

Jim Cornette has never been one to accept defeat easily. Rather than give up on the Christmas show, he rescheduled Christmas Chaos for January 31, 2001. Tickets went on sale, and Christmas Chaos became the second show in the history of Louisville Gardens to sell out twice.

OVW's final show in the Gardens took place on June 28, 2001. Appropriately named the Last Dance, the main event marked the return of a WWE Superstar who made the trek from Memphis to Louisville numerous times on his way to the top - the Undertaker. Paired with his kayfabe brother Kane, the Brothers of Destruction defeated Diamond Dallas Page and Leviathan via disqualification.

Fans who attended the last dance also saw the Minnesota Stretching Crew defeat Perry Saturn and Dean Malenko. OVW champion and Louisville main stay Flash Flanigan defended his title against Chris Jericho, and the Big Show and Mark Henry won a tag match against Bolin Services' Jack Black and the Prototype, John Cena.

A year later, OVW took a page from the old Heywood Allen playbook and moved outdoors, holding their first ever event at Six Flags Kentucky Kingdom. The theme park, located on the grounds of the Kentucky Fair and Exposition Center, began as a local operation in the 1990s but traced its roots back nearly a hundred years to the old Fontaine Ferry Park. It was a bold experiment, and once again, the WWE delivered a big name main event, allowing OVW's David Flair to tag with his father, Ric Flair. The Flairs defeated the Prototype and former WCW tag champion Sean O'Haire, and a new Louisville tradition was born.

Six Flags Kentucky Kingdom hosted a number of concerts and events in their outdoor amphitheater, but none were as successful as the shows put on by OVW. The Summer Sizzler Series began in earnest during the summer of 2002 and ran four years.

As with the Louisville Gardens shows, the Six Flags events gave WWE and OVW management a chance to evaluate up and coming Superstars side by side with the WWE talent. OVW hopefuls had a chance to test their skills against the likes of Jerry Lawler, the Hurricane, Christian, Benoit, the APA, Scott Steiner, Mark Henry, Booker T, Chris Jericho, Kane, Al Snow, Rey Mysterio, the Dudley Boys, and Big Show. In the summer of 2006, the legendary Dusty Rhodes tagged up with his son Cody to take on KC James and Idol Stevens.

Six Flags also became a venue for former OVW stars who made the big time to return to their roots. Fans who remembered Shelton Benjamin and Charlie Haas from their OVW days had a chance to see them return as the WWE's World's Greatest Tag Team. Nick Dinsmore returned as Eugene. John Cena and Randy Orton returned as... John Cena and Randy Orton.

Six Flags became a spotlight for future WWE stars to shine as well. Idol Stevens had a series of matches with established star John Cena. In 2013 Stevens would cash in the Money in the Bank briefcase on World Champion John Cena under his new persona, Damien Sandow. Future divas and women's champions Mickie James and Beth Phoenix traded victories with one another as they waited for their chance to shine on the WWE stage. Jillian Hall, Nattie Neidhart, the Miz, and CM Punk also entertained the fans at Six Flags.

The fans and the superstars made a lot of memories at Six Flags. Roni Jonah, who worked as a wrestler and the Miz's valet at OVW, recalls the night she received a sweaty kiss on the lips from the Big Show.

"The Miz was getting his ass handed to him, so I got on the apron to try and distract The Big Show so The Miz could pull some kind of shenanigans. The Big Show grabbed my head, and his hands were the size of my head, it was crazy, and kiss me. Of course, I pretended like I hated it, but it was definitely one of my more memorable experiences."

For Dean Hill, nothing could ever top July 7, 2007. The day began with fans waiting in line through a light drizzle for the chance to get an autograph from two Louisville legends - Jerry Lawler and John Cena. As the day rolled on, and bell time approached, the rain came down heavier and heavier. Despite the bad conditions, it was standing room only by the time the divas made their way to the ring for the opening match.

Beth Phoenix won the opener, a Divas Scramble Match, with a pin on Nattie Neidhart. TJ Dalton and Jamin Olivencia faced the new Hart Foundation in the second match as the rain grew worse and worse. Visibility was decreasing by the minute, and fans kept moving closer and closer to the ring just to see what was going on. Despite the conditions, no one left the amphitheater. They were there to see the triumphant return of the Prototype.

Cena made his entrance in a downpour, escorted to the ring by members of the Armed Forces and riding atop a Humvee. The crowd went berserk for the champion, who battled through the rain with OVW's Shawn Spears. When Cena hit the Attitude Adjustment, Shawn Spears literally splashed down on the mat. The referee counted three, and the match was over.

The champ left the ring. The rain continued to pour, but no one left their seats. The fans stayed to see the Hall of Famer Jerry Lawler face KC James in a no disqualification match. It was a sloppy bout, with plenty of slipping and sliding, that ended with Lawler's signature pile driver. Lawler took out Kenny Bolin and the rest of James's entourage, and the show finally came to an end.

As special as it was to see Cena's return, it was the reception the fans gave Lawler that stood out in Dean Hill's mind. Few, if any, of the fans at Six Flags saw Lawler compete at the Gardens in his prime. Many of them were not even born when he was doing battle with Bill Dundee and Dutch Mantell. But the fans proved that Jerry was still the King by staying to give the Hall of Famer the same love and respect they gave John Cena.

Cornette was thrilled to be back in his hometown. He reveled in being the booker for OVW, and he enjoyed imparting his experience and wisdom on the OVW trainees. Cornette was now hundreds of miles away from Titan Towers, but the politics and headaches of WWE corporate were still very much present.

OVW proved to be a far greater success than anyone imagined. Instead of two good superstars a year, WWE was calling up wrestlers by the dozen, churning out new stars every month. However, the WWE paid no attention to the story lines or booking happening in Louisville, creating havoc for Cornette.

Cornette hated the WWE's complete lack of concern and interest in what was going on with OVW. When the WWE wanted to call talent up, they did so suddenly and without any regard for what the current OVW booking looked like. Cornette's strategy of using Bolin and Synn as the focal point of his heel factions helped to soften the blow when talent was called up to the big leagues, but Cornette was old school and would have preferred to give his wrestlers a proper sendoff, such as the traditional "loser leaves town" match that would wrap up the out-going star's career and give a much needed boost to one of the rising stars left behind.

Orton's call up was the last straw for Cornette. The WWE had called Orton up to the main roster, but Cornette had a verbal agreement with John Laurinitis, the director of talent relations, to use him at Six Flags over the summer. The TV and print ads were already done and out when Cornette got a phone call from Tommy Dreamer. Laurinitis had failed to tell Orton about the booking; Orton would be on vacation and miss the Six Flags shows.

To make matters worse, the WWE routinely ignored Cornette and Davis's advice when choosing what talent to call up. "If I gave the WWE a list of 25 names," Cornette recalls, "of who is most ready to move up, without fail they'd take 21, 23, 24, and 25. And the only reason they wouldn't take 22 is because he was injured."

Cornette did enjoy a good working relationship with Jim Ross while he was the director of talent relations, but things changed when Ross stepped down. When Laurinitis took over as head of talent relations, the support Cornette enjoyed from corporate vanished. Ross always had Cornette's back in matters of discipline regarding WWE signees, but Laurinitis refused to back Cornette. Laurinitis did not take OVW seriously as a territorial promotion, and under his command, keeping the developmental talent in line became more and more difficult.

The WWE also became more demanding in terms of what they wanted done on OVW TV. Cornette would receive calls on Wednesday, the day of the show, with instructions to use certain talent or not use other talent completely irrespective of what Cornette and Danny Davis had promoted.

One week, Cornette had to tell corporate that he could not use a certain performer who had shingles. "He's contagious, he has Shingles, we had to send him home."

The voice on the other end paused and then asked, "Could he do a promo?"

There was no love between Cornette and Laurinitis, and the more agitated Cornette became with WWE's talent and creative teams, the more Laurinitis wanted a reason to replace Cornette. After Cornette exchanged words with Tough Enough alumni Linda Miles, Laurinitis flew to Louisville to suspend Cornette for a few weeks.

Laurinitis sent former ECW mastermind Paul Heyman to OVW while Cornette was under suspension. Some saw this as Laurinitis's attempt to drive Cornette out, but according to Cornette, Laurinitis was also trying to get Heyman to quit by "demoting" him to Louisville. While Heyman and Cornette rarely saw eye to eye, they made a solid effort to work together when Cornette returned from suspension. Laurinitis would have to look elsewhere for a reason to get rid of Cornette, and he finally got that reason thanks to the Boogeyman.

The Boogeyman was a creation forced upon Cornette and OVW by the WWE, a character created for former Tough Enough hopeful Marty Wright. Wright was a charismatic performer well suited for the role of a monster who would appear out of nowhere, stalk his opponents, and squash them. Wearing face paint and antlers, dressed in a garish costume, and carrying a smoking voodoo stick, the character was a throwback to the 80's style of cartoonish wrestling characters, a complete contrast to the "Ruthless Aggression" motif the WWE held at the time. Cornette didn't like the idea, but as with many things that had to do with the WWE, he had no choice but to go along.

The Boogeyman was scheduled to make his first appearance in the summer of 2005. The Boogeyman would appear during a match, squash everyone in the ring, and then make his exit through the side exit door between the fan seating and the babyface entrance. To further sell the idea of the Boogeyman as an intimidating, frightening character, he put a number of OVW trainees in the audience by the exit. When the Boogeyman made his way to the exit door, their role was to scatter and run in terror, giving him a clear path.

The Boogeyman did his part, rising from beneath the ring and squashing the wrestlers inside. He proceeded to cut a great promo, introducing himself and his character, that was slightly marred by the fact that the antlers on his head kept falling off.   When he had his say, the Boogeyman made his way toward the exit. The OVW students in the audience played their part as well. The students and a woman holding a baby who happened to be sitting close by all got up and scattered as the Boogeyman approached - all except for one. When the wrestlers cleared out of the Boogeyman's way, Cornette saw one guy, one round-faced trainee still sitting in his chair, laughing at what he saw. The Boogeyman shook the railing, trying to intimidate the man. Cornette stood up at the announcer's table shouting, "Get out of the way! He's dangerous!" The student shook his head and laughed.

"I was screaming so hard, I actually s—- myself," recalls Cornette. "I never ate the day of a show, and by the time we went to air, I had had a dozen Sierra Mists. My stomach was nothing but liquid, and when I started screaming, I lost control."

Cornette was furious with the laughing student. When they went to commercial break in the taping, he stormed into the locker room, demanding to know who had refused to sell out for the Boogeyman. When he learned that it was in fact a student - one who only arrived a few weeks prior - he called the man up in front of the entire roster. With the Boogeyman at his side seething with rage, Cornette had words with his student.

"Why didn't you run from the Boogeyman?" demanded Cornette.

The student shrugged and giggled. "Nobody told me I should run from the Boogeyman."

Cornette screamed, "Look at this m--- f---! He's got a painted face, he's wearing antlers, came from out of the ring, he had a voodoo stick, and twenty people around you ran screaming. And you say no one told you? Did I tell you I was going to do this?"

Cornette proceeded to slap the student repeatedly in the face. He challenged the man to a fight, daring him to step into the parking lot and take him on while slapping him a few more times. Finally, Cornette tossed him out of the building and the TV taping went on.

Cornette thought nothing of the incident, and the entire OVW roster, many of which are now part of the current WWE roster, were all on Cornette's side. Cornette saw his action as a gesture of mercy. Cornette knew that if the Boogeyman got his hands on the much smaller student, he would have wrung his neck.

It was all the opportunity John Laurinitis needed. Laurinitis got wind of the slapping incident and called Cornette, telling him he could not treat students that way. Cornette quickly countered that the student in question - Anthony Carelli of Ontario, Canada - was not WWE talent, but a regular OVW student paying for the privilege of being stretched week in and week out by Rip Rogers and his crew. Cornette was right, he wasn't the WWE's concern, but within a matter of weeks, Cornette was out the door.

It came as little surprise when Cornette got his walking papers, and it actually came as a relief. He was finally free of the headache that is WWE corporate and ready to move on to new ventures.

The WWE assigned former ECW promoter Paul Heyman to take Cornette's place. That fall, Heyman sent Carelli out to the ring as Boris Alexiev, a Russian character specializing in stiff moves and submissions. He received his WWE developmental contract in 2006, and in 2007 he made his debut during an episode of Smackdown filmed in Milan, Italy with a new name - Santino Marella. The "Milan Miracle" would win the Intercontinental Championship that night from Umaga and go on to become the resident clown prince of the WWE.

The Boogeyman was future endeavored (WWE-speak for "let go") in 2009 and now works on the indie circuit, still using a Boogeyman-type gimmick from time to time.

"THERE ARE NO RULES!"

In 1979 in an act of desperation to stave off dropping ticket sales, the Memphis wrestling promotion staged one of the most legendary battles in the history of professional wrestling. After losing the majority of the heels in his territory thanks to a roster split, Jerry Jarrett threw together a tag team match pitting champs Bill Dundee and Jerry Lawler against the relatively obscure pairing of Larry Latham and Wayne Farris, the Blonde Bombers, and their manager. The match ended with the heels cheating to win and the babyfaces chasing the heels toward the concessions area. Lawler gave orders to cut the cameras and end the TV taping right after the match ended, but to turn the cameras back on and continue with commentary thirty seconds later.

The Tupelo Concession Stand Brawl, as it came to be known, proved to be one of the wildest and most violent fights caught on tape to that point. Memphis saw an immediate boost in ticket sales, and provided inspiration for a new movement in wrestling. Under the direction of Paul Heyman, Eastern Championship Wrestling became Extreme Championship Wrestling in 1994 and took the violence of Tupelo even further. ECW in turn became the inspiration for dozens of backyard and extreme fighting leagues, including a Southern Indiana promotion known as IWA Mid-South.

The mastermind behind IWA was Ian Rotten, a man every bit as controversial as the aforementioned Heyman. Rotten grew up in the WWWF city of Baltimore, but he spent his summers in Florida, where he fell in love with the hard-nosed, violent world of Florida Championship Wrestling.

"Most guys I knew in Baltimore were WWF guys," Ian says, "My heroes were guys like Dusty Rhodes, guys

275

who didn't fit the mold but knew how to put butts in the seats."

Ian's passion for wrestling grew thanks to a friend whose parents had satellite TV. "I'd go over to his house at 8 AM, and I wouldn't go home until 4 AM, after the Hawaiian wrestling show went off the air. We watched everything - Continental, Jim Crockett's show, Portland, WCCW. I watched every style of wrestling and fell in love with them all."

The promotion opened its doors in 1996, when Memphis was on its last legs and the territories had all but died out. Rotten saw an opportunity and opened his doors to any and all displaced talent who had the heart and the passion to be a part of something new.

A big part of that something new was the extreme wrestling style Rotten had embraced during his time in Japan and with ECW. Rotten brought in hardcore superstars like Mad Man Pondo, Ox Harley, Tracy Smothers, and Bull Pain to introduce the hardcore style to Louisville.

"There were barbed wire matches, death matches, no DQ matches, piranhas around the ring matches, fans bring the weapons matches," remembers Kenny Bolin, who worked as a manager for IWA prior to his OVW run.

IWA became known for matches held under IWA rules. "IWA rules say, there are no rules," the ring announcer gleefully announced to the fans. "If you see the action coming your way, get your stuff and get out of the way!" IWA matches could and did spill out of the ring, into the seats, and out of the arenas. They were unpredictable, and they frequently became graphic and bloody.

Contrary to popular belief, IWA was never all about blood and violence. IWA shows area true reflection of their founder, who has a deep love for all forms of professional wrestling. You'll see traditional matches, hardcore matches, three way matches, four way matches, battle royals, tag matches, and everything in between.

IWA also prides itself on giving female wrestlers the spotlight. Women's matches are not only included in the cards, they are given equal time and hype. Women's matches are not just "bathroom breaks." They are action-packed, hardcore, and sometimes just as bloody as the men's.

During the first few years, Rotten booked shows in Louisville, Lexington, New Albany, and other cities, but he set up a home base in a former Kmart store on Dixie Highway. Devoted fans helped to fund the renovation of the building, and IWA was soon performing to packed out houses on a weekly basis.

IWA ran strong for two years in the Kmart building, but then the same Kentucky Athletic Commission that once bedeviled Heywood Allen and Teeny Jarrett went after Rotten. After a television spot aired highlighting the blood and violence at IWA Mid-South, Rotten was called to testify in Frankfort and explain himself. Rotten was not shy about voicing his opinions and defended his promotion vigorously, but the athletic commission refused to listen and took away his license. IWA and Ian Rotten were banned from Kentucky, and the promoter and the promotion had to vacate the Kmart building. They were down, but they would not be out of business for very long.

In 2000 IWA Mid-South resumed operations across the river in Indiana. Unlike Kentucky, Indiana does not regulate professional wrestling because it defines pro wrestling as performance art. Much of the credit for Indiana's relaxed stance on pro wrestling goes to Dick the Bruiser who, like Rotten, occasionally liked to draw a little blood in the ring.

"I was called to testify in Indianapolis once," said Rotten. "I told them flat out, your own court cases state pro wrestling is entertainment, not a sport. If I want to stab a guy with a fork in a wrestling match, that's between me and him. Not you. It's art."

IWA set up shop in Charlestown, Indiana in a warehouse that became known as the House of Hardcore. This time around, Rotten expanded IWA's offerings beyond the extreme and began featuring young, technical wrestlers hungry for their big break.

Investing in young talent is one of the things Rotten prides himself on the most. "A lot of promoters won't give young guys and ladies a chance to develop," he says. "They wait until they've hit a certain level, and then they'll bring them in. I always thought heart and passion were more important than talent. You can teach talent. You can't teach heart."

The childhood Dusty Rhodes fan prides himself especially on discovering talent that doesn't fit the classic wrestling stereotypes. Rather than looking for a certain size or physique, Rotten looks for diamonds in the rough with the desire to succeed. IWA offers young athletes a chance to learn the business the old fashioned way, through hard, hard work. "If you only take established stars, you can have some great matches. But if you never take chances on someone, you'll never get a chance to see someone grow."

Rotten continues to take chances on guys no one else would. Some of the names that passed through IWA became national stars: CM Punk, Colt Cabana, Chris Hero, Cesaro, Daniel Bryan, Seth Rollins, Dean Ambrose, Luke Harper, and Sami Zayn. Rotten also seized the opportunity to bring in stars like Rey Mysterio and Eddie Guerrero when they were between the big promotions. Guerrero even won the IWA championship in a three way match with Mysterio and a very young CM Punk, who more than held his own against the seasoned vets.

Punk became a draw very quickly when he arrived in IWA. His foul-mouthed tirades and "I'm better than you" straight edge attitude made him public enemy number one. Fans packed the house any time Punk was scheduled to appear, eager to see someone put the arrogant champion put in his place.

Perhaps the biggest match in IWA history, and one of the biggest indie matches in the last twenty years, took place at the House of Hardcore on February 9, 2002. CM Punk and Chris Hero had been battling over Punk's championship belt for weeks, and the rivalry came to a head in a winner take all tables and ladders match. What happened that night is a match no one in attendance would ever forget. Punk and Hero battled all over the building, climbing into the rafters, taking a double back body drop off the second floor through a table, beating the Hell out of each other for 43 minutes.

When the match finally ended in a victory for Punk, the fans showed their awe and appreciation by carrying Punk and Hero from the ring on their shoulders. The usually abrasive Punk thanked the fans for their support, reminding them that it was because of the fans that Punk and Hero and others like them put their bodies on the line every night.

Sadly for IWA, the tables and ladders match was not just the finale of a great rivalry, but the House of Hardcore. A dispute with the landlord forced IWA to relocate to Clarksville. Within a year, IWA was forced to leave that building, known as the IWA Arena, following another landlord dispute.

Rotten may have lost a lot of buildings, but he always found a new one when he needed it. He found venues in both Indiana and Illinois to keep the show going, and he continued to draw in new talent looking for a chance to break out just like his more famous counterparts at OVW.

"Someone once said to me that I have more than my share of enemies," says Rotten. "I told them that's because I've run more than my share of shows."

Ian's track record with landlords may be spotty, but his talented roster and his reputation as a stellar booker kept the company going. After the tables and ladders match, Punk vs. Hero evolved into something very special at IWA Mid-South and across the country. As word of the match spread, they became the star indie attraction all across the country. They met several more times before Punk departed for OVW and then WWE, including a 60 minute draw and a 93 minute two out of three falls battle. Videos of their matches are highly sought after by indie wrestling fans and well worth the investment, if you love watching two young stars bring the very best out of one another.

IWA also created two shows that have become a tradition for fans and wrestlers alike, the annual King of the Death Match Tournament and the Ted Petty Invitational. The King of the Death Match is just what the name implies, an all-out bloody affair featuring four rounds of hardcore action to crown a new King of the Death Match.

A colorful list of wrestlers has competed in the King of the Death Match Tournament, and the matches held during the tournament are equally colorful: Fans Bring the Weapons, Glass and Sandpaper Taipei Death Match, Barbed Wire Corners and Light Tubes, Texas Bull Rope, Stairway to Hell, Unlucky 13 Staple Gun Death Match, Cactus Caribbean Spider Webs Death Match, Barefoot Thumbtacks Match, and even a Curt Henning Drunken Tai Pei Death Match. For a time, the King of the Death Match Tournament stretched over a weekend and ran in conjunction with two other tournaments, the Queen of the Death Match Tournament and the Double Death Tag Team Tournament, and the matches featured in those two tournaments were equally bizarre and bloody.

The Ted Petty Invitational, by contrast, is a showcase for technical wrestlers. Created as the Sweet Science Sixteen in 2000 by Ian Rotten, the show was renamed to honor Rotten's late friend and fellow wrestler Ted Petty in 2002. After three rounds of action, the event culminates in a 3-way battle for the title. The Invitational is an internationally acclaimed tournament, and the list of alumni and winners is distinguished, including the likes of Chris Hero, Colt Cabana, CM Punk, Cesaro, Daniel Bryan, Sami Zayn, A. J. Styles, Christopher Daniels, and Samoa Joe.

IWA Mid-South is easily the most controversial promotion in Louisville wrestling history. The promotion has its fans and detractors, as does its founder and chief architect, Ian Rotten, and together the two have also had more lives than some cities have had promotions, period. In 2007 IWA shut down following what was billed as Ian Rotten's retirement match. The promotion resumed operations again in 2008, and Ian came out of retirement on March 1 at the promotion's 500th show. In 2009 IWA announced it was "scaling back" to do smaller, lower budget shows. Then in 2011, they announced they were closing down for good.

That was not the end for IWA Mid-South, nor for Ian Rotten. Two years later, the phoenix once again rose from the ashes, and IWA Mid-South resumed operations once more. Many familiar faces returned, inside the ring and out, joined by a new generation of talent and fans eager to play a part in the next chapter of the controversial but legendary promotion.

Time will tell how long this latest run will last, but so long as there's breath in Ian Rotten's lungs, you can be sure the show will go on, somewhere, sometime, some place. There will be no rules in that place, and if the action comes your way, well... you know the drill.

THE SECOND WAVE

With Jim Cornette no longer in charge, Paul Heyman was now the man at OVW. One of the most divisive and controversial figures in the history of wrestling, Heyman is regarded as a booking genius by some and a complete con man by others. The truth is probably somewhere in the middle.

"There was a time in my life I would have walked through a wall on fire for Paul," recalls Ian Rotten. "I'd have taken a bullet for him. That's the kind of influence a leader like Paul has on people."

Heyman's impact on professional wrestling is undeniable. Heyman took a tiny independent promotion called Eastern Championship Wrestling and transformed it into the game changing Extreme Championship Wrestling. He helped to jumpstart the careers of Mick Foley, Chris Jericho, Steve Austin, and Eddie Guererro. After ECW folded he moved on to WWE, where he turned Brock Lesnar into an overnight main event star. He followed that with a hugely successful run as the booker for WWE Smackdown. Fans still remember the top notch main events week in and week out featuring Kurt Angle, Chris Benoit, Edge, Rey Mysterio, and the Guerreros.

Heyman brought his own style to OVW, and the results were, at times, mixed. "One of the ideas I had way back was to put students in the audience," remembers Kenny Bolin. "The students knew what would happen in the show, and we had them cheer and boo to kind of get the fans into the game. When Heyman arrived, he moved all the students down to the front row center. You could tell there was something up watching on TV when you had a dozen guys leaning over the barrier wall and pounding on it. It took seats away from some longtime fans, and it kind of turned the crowd off for a while."

Not everyone was as turned off by Heyman. One student who loved Heyman was Roni Jonah, a Canadian born wrestler turned actress/film producer who moved to Louisville to train at OVW. Roni was in the amateur class when Heyman arrived, and one of her best friends was Seth Skyfire, a former OVW main eventer whose star had fallen in recent months.

"Seth was no longer getting time on the show because he wasn't under contract with WWE, and Paul came down to showcase those guys."

Roni wanted to make sure Seth got noticed by the new boss. She sat with her friends dead center in the audience and held signs calling out for Seth. Heyman noticed, and when he put Skyfire back on TV, he was impressed with what he saw. Heyman was equally impressed by the determined young woman in the crowd. "One night, he told him to go out to the ring and kiss 'his girlfriend' in the audience. Seth said, 'But, she isn't my girlfriend.' Paul said, 'She is now.'"

Seth did as he was told, but the kiss was weaker than Heyman wanted. When Heyman called him out on the weak kiss, Mike "The Miz" Mizanin chimed in: "She can be my girlfriend."

Heyman now had a great angle, and Roni had her first chance to make a splash on television. She credits Heyman not only for the opportunity, but bringing out the best in her.

"Seth was having a hair vs. hair match and he was going to use this opportunity to get me out of the audience," says Roni. "Paul, as you know, is one of the best most inspiring speech givers there is. Whatever people think of him as a person, it doesn't negate the fact that that guy can speak. He wanted me to cry, like someone has died, when Seth got his hair cut off. He said, in his passionate Paul voice, this was my opportunity. I needed to nail this spot and I would be on TV. And, of course, I did. I cried my eyes out. I had to be removed from the building. And being that Seth was the darling of OVW, the fans ate it up. Then, of course, I turned on Seth and went with The Miz."

And so it goes, in the soap opera world of wrestling relationships.

Perhaps the most important achievement Heyman had at OVW was going to bat for one of the most rebellious pupils ever to set foot in Davis Arena, CM Punk. The Chicago native and IWA Mid-South veteran was not as naturally gifted as many of his classmates, but his work rate was only exceeded by his attitude - and his mouth.

Early in his OVW career, WWE Hall of Famer Tony Atlas came in to visit the students. Atlas was a long time veteran used to commanding respect, but when Atlas told Punk to stop wrapping his forearms in tape (a ritual he carried into the WWE), Punk fought back. A verbal joust followed, with Atlas screaming in Punk's face and Punk screaming right back.

The exchange with a respected veteran of the WWE didn't sit well with corporate, but it generated a great deal of Internet buzz when the Majors Brothers, who would later morph into Curt Hawkins and Zack Rider, tweeted about the incident.

"Rider and Hawkins acted like they were right there with Punk," recalls Punk fan Chris Bolin. "The truth is they were scared as the rest of them. Punk stood up to Atlas on his own.

He was waiting for some of the other students to back him up," says Jim Cornette. "Punk thought he was as big as Atlas. He wasn't. Not then. But that attitude is a big part of why he went as far as he did."

It would not be Punk's last brush with the authority during his time at OVW. During a charity fundraiser at a bowling alley, Punk caught the ire of Kenny Bolin when he threw the manager's briefcase down one of the lanes.

"Punk refused to go get it," Bolin recalls. "Then the manager got on the intercom and said, 'We know who threw the briefcase. Please retrieve it, or you will be banned from the building.' He walked up that alley like a scolded puppy and brought back my briefcase."

Punk had his run-ins with other talent at OVW, but he got along well with the men who mattered most, Danny Davis and Rip Rogers. He also had Heyman as his most vocal cheerleader, and Heyman made sure he got a shot at the next level. By the time Punk left OVW, he was one of only six wrestlers to win the world title, television title, and tag title during his reign, and only the second of those six to move up to the WWE. The other - Aaron "The Idol" Stevens, better known to WWE fans as Damien Sandow.

Like John Cena before him, WWE did not see a future star in CM Punk, but Heyman stuck his neck out for Punk, convinced that the rebellious indie star had a bright future. If Heyman did nothing else in Louisville, most fans would agree shepherding CM Punk to the top was enough.

Al Snow, an ECW and WWE veteran who served as a trainer on WWE's *Tough Enough* TV series, came to OVW as a trainer and later became the booker. During Al Snow's tenure, OVW had arguably as strong a roster than they did under Jim Cornette. Cody Rhodes (then known as Cody Runnels) arrived in Louisville, following in the footsteps of his father Dusty Rhodes and brother Dustin (Goldust), making a name for himself as a talented work horse. Idol Stevens, a long time OVW favorite, took his next steps toward the big time under Al Snow and eventually made the WWE roster a Damien Sandow. Other future stars who worked for Snow included The Miz, the Major Brothers, John Morrison, and Wade Barrett.

The women's division during Snow's tenure was equally strong and arguably the best in OVW's history. Melina, Mickie James, Beth Phoenix, Rocha (Rosa Mendes), and Jillian Hall all made the leap to the WWE, while Serena, Gail Kim, and ODB became building blocks for the TNA Knockouts division.

One of the oddest things to come out of OVW during the post-Cornette era was a faction known as the Spirit Squad. Comprised of developmental wrestlers Ken Doane, Nick Nemeth, Mike Mondo, Johnny Jeter, and Nick Mitchell, the Spirit Squad was a male cheerleader gimmick that managed to get a brief run with the WWE. The idea as not their own, and none of the five really wanted to do it, but when the opportunity to jump to the WWE arose, they embraced their inner cheerleader.

After some training with a local cheerleading squad to perfect their moves, the Spirit Squad arrived at Titan Towers with one chance to impress Vince McMahon. They went into a cheerleading routine right in the chairman's office. McMahon loved the act, and the Spirit Squad found themselves in a feud with one of the biggest factions in wrestling history, Degeneration-X.

During their WWE run, the Spirit Squad captured the WWE tag titles. Invoking the Freebird Rule, the Spirit Squad took turns defending the title using different combinations of two. When the gimmick ran its course it was Degeneration-X that put the nail on the proverbial coffin. Triple H and Shawn Michaels defeated the cheerleaders and packed them in a shipping crate addressed to Ohio Valley Wrestling. Only Nick Nemeth would make it long term in the WWE after changing his name to Dolph Ziggler and becoming one of the hardest workers in the business.

The WWE trainees became part of the community when they came to Louisville. They were regulars at local events and charity fundraisers, such as the UPS plane pull. Some took on regular jobs to keep busy and earn extra money. Lisa Marie Varon, who wrestled in WWE as Victoria, went one step further. The entrepreneurial diva owned a pizzeria and later opened a custom auto shop.

"She was a regular at Plato's Closet," says Erin James, who worked at the store during college. "As mean as she was on TV, she was such a girly girl when she came into the store. She loved to shop, and she was always a lot of fun!"

In 2007 the WWE decided to break ties with OVW, moving all their developmental talent to Booker T's training school in Florida. OVW would miss the WWE connection and the money that came with it, but in many ways the change was welcome. No longer would the WWE interfere with story lines by arbitrarily pulling talent out of Louisville at will. Danny Davis and Al Snow had full control of the school and the promotion, and the WWE continued to keep tabs on the students at OVW.

It was no small benefit that several OVW legends returned to continue developing their skills and stay busy while waiting for their next break. Nick Dinsmore and Rob Conway may not have become box office gold at the WWE level, but the Louisville fans were thrilled to see the hometown heroes return. The new students at OVW benefited from working with the veterans, and OVW continued to craft new stars eager to get their shot at the big stage.

A DRIVING TOUR

If a wrestling fan were to take a driving tour of Louisville, they would likely be disappointed, as many of the major historic sites no longer exist.

The Buckingham Theater where Ida Alb and William Muldoon appeared is long gone. The second Buckingham Theater, which was renamed the Savoy and ended its life as a porno movie house, was destroyed in 1983 as part of the city's purge on adult businesses downtown. The Columbia Gym that not only played host for the Allen Athletic Club but was the home gym for young Cassius Clay, is also long gone, replaced by an outdoor basketball court. Parkway Field, where the Allen Athletic Club held shows in the summer, became the home of the University of Louisville baseball team but was later abandoned after the university built a new baseball field closer to campus. The site of the old outdoor Sports Arena between Preston and Burnett is now directly beneath I-65.

A few sites remain with real significance to Louisville's wrestling past, and present, and it's in the present that we will start our driving tour.

The Davis Arena, located at 4400 Old Shepherdsville Road, remains a vital part of Louisville's wrestling present. OVW relocated to Louisville during its stint as WWE's developmental territory. The WWE hated the dilapidated Quadrangle, so they found a new location in Kentucky.

Davis Arena is still the home base for OVW's training school and television production. They also host the monthly Saturday Night Special and other spot shows throughout the month. Many of the early OVW success stories were gone before OVW moved to Old Shep, but the list of stars who wrestled in the industrial park location is still impressive.

The Quadrangle, home to the old Davis Arena, has undergone a major renovation since OVW moved out. The once abandoned square of red brick buildings found a second life as offices and restaurants. There's no sign of the old arena, but plenty of nice places to eat.

If you're going to eat on your driving tour, you might as well head a little ways north of the Quad and visit Clarksville Little Seafood. Founded in 1970 as the Cape Codder, the tiny gray house with the simple furnishings inside has long been a favorite of wrestlers and managers alike. The menu is as short and simple as it gets: fish, shrimp, scallops, clams, oysters, chicken, and burgers, with fries and onion rings and sodas. Fans of the restaurant will swear that you can't find a better piece of fish anywhere on either side of the river.

In the 70s and 80's Clarksville Seafood was a Wednesday ritual for many of the Memphis talent. After the Louisville show on Tuesday, everyone stopped in Clarksville for lunch before making the trip to Evansville. Clarksville Seafood remains a favorite of Kenny Bolin, who can often be found inside enjoying not one but two fish dinners. It's also very close to Jammerz Rollerdrome, where UWA, Evolution Pro Wrestling, and IWA Mid-South have run shows in recent years.

The most hallowed stop on the driving tour is the last one: the Madison Square Garden of the South, Louisville Gardens.

When the Gardens first opened in 1905, it was the Jefferson County Armory, home to Kentucky National Guard's First Regiment. Also known as the Louisville Legion, the First Regiment traced its roots back to 1839. The Regiment first saw action during the Mexican War and had distinguished itself in both war and peace time duty.

George Beuchel was the first wrestling promoter to utilize the building in 1914 when he promoted the inaugural Derby Eve show with Yussif Hussane and Stanislaus Zbyszko. The building would also host some of the biggest names in boxing, including Jack Dempsey, Joe Louis, and Cassius Clay before he took the world by storm as Muhammad Ali.

In addition to playing host for the annual Derby Eve wrestling and boxing shows, the Armory was used by the Louisville Cardinals basketball team from 1945-1958, when Freedom Hall opened. The Kentucky Colonels of the ABA and several other minor league basketball teams used the building, and a few minor league ice hockey teams came and went as well. The basketball floor for the Kentucky Colonels is still beneath the Gardens in a storage area.

Jerry Jarrett was the first promoter to make use of the building full-time. The Armory had become the Convention Center by the time Memphis came to town, but when the Commonwealth Convention Center opened in 1975, the name changed again to Louisville Gardens.

The Gardens that played host to Memphis wrestling was a much different place than the one that first hosted the likes of Strangler Lewis. The main arena was originally all open, with metal arches extending from the side walls over the seats and meeting up at the top center of the building. All that open area vanished when a drop ceiling and press boxes were installed to better accommodate sporting events. Still, the building was well kept and well suited for not only wrestling, but basketball, boxing, concerts, and other major events.

Frank Sinatra played the Gardens. So did Elvis. Harry Truman and Martin Luther King, Jr., both spoke inside the building. Celebrities would enter the building by car through a garage door on the east side of the building. The dressing areas and locker rooms were all located beneath the main arena, accessible from the underground parking and a stairway at the far end of the arena out of sight from the crowd.

One night a bad storm rolled in just before Sly and the Family Stones were set to give a concert. A tornado warning was issued for downtown, and frantic security had to evacuate the building. The crowd was no problem, but the band was another matter. Security banged on the door that opened to the stairway leading to the dressing rooms for several minutes. The door finally opened, and a cloud of pot smoke rolled out the door. Security informed the band members about the tornado warning and the need to evacuate, but the smiling band members politely declined. "It's cool, man, we'll wait it out down here." The door closed, and the band waited out the tornado warning in the bowels of Louisville Gardens.

Of all the surprises and secrets still hidden within the Gardens, the biggest is probably the organ. An antique, one man band, pipe organ once used during ball games and other events still resides at the far end of the arena. The four level keyboard sits above the floor in an alcove. When in use, the organ player's back was to the arena, but two mirrors installed over the keyboard gave the organ player a view of what was happening. About thirty feet away from the organ player's perch is a room filled with metal pipes, wooden pipes, and a number of percussion instruments, all controlled from the keyboard overlooking the arena.

The Louisville Gardens was added to the register of National Historic Places in 1980, and it is now in the custody of the city of Louisville. The local government took possession of the building right before the recession hit, and the city has been hard pressed to find a new tenant. They continue to search, and to keep the lights burning, hoping someone will breathe life into one of Louisville's most important pieces of sports history. The Gardens meant something special to everyone in Louisville, whether they were wrestling fans, boxing fans, basketball fans, or music fans. The biggest names in wrestling history all appeared here: Strangler Lewis, Joe Stecher, Jim Londos, Jim Mitchell, Haille Samara, Mildred Burke, Bill Longson, Lou Thesz, Buddy Rodgers, June Byars, Jerry Lawler, Andre the Giant, Hulk Hogan, Bret Hart, Stone Cold Steve Austin, the Undertaker, Brock Lesnar, John Cena, CM

Punk. It would be a shame to see it go the way of the Old Buck and the Columbia Gym.

IS IT REAL?

Although the fans who packed Louisville Gardens to see the Memphis stars in the 1970s and 1980s took their sport very seriously, there are few people, other than the very young, who truly believe that the sport of professional wrestling to be 100% real these days. The one question that remains is just how much is scripted and how much is real?

The answer depends on who you ask, who you believe, and whom you are discussing. There are those in the wrestling fraternity who have never so much as laid a punch on anyone in the ring. Then there are men like Louisville favorite Mad Man Pondo who takes great pleasure in hitting his opponent with all manner of implements of destruction on "Fans Bring the Weapons" night.

There are things you can fake, like punches, kicks, and crippling knee injuries. Then there are things you can't fake, like falls from a ladder and the impact of steel chair. Having witnessed JBL's Clothesline from Hell up close, no one could ever convince me a man doesn't feel that pain the next day.

To answer the question, I give you a story relayed to me by a co-worker, who attended a football party that was also attended by Doug Basham, who wrestled as The Machine at OVW and one half of the Basham Brothers on WWE TV.

> One of our other friends is a huge wrestling fan. When Doug came in, he was completely star-struck. He knew Doug had wrestled at OVW and had seen him on Monday Night Raw.

He asked our host if he thought Doug would be willing to give him a chop across the chest. At the end of the night, our host mentioned it to Doug, who turned to our wrestling fan buddy with a smile.

"You sure you want to do this?" asked Doug.

Our buddy said yes.

"Okay," said Doug. "But if we're going to do this, we have to do it right. You need to take your shirt off."

Our other friend didn't even question it. He took his shirt off, stripping down to his bare chest.

"Now, how do you want it?" Doug asked. "You want forehand or backhand?"

"I don't know," said out other friend. "I guess whatever you prefer."

"Okay," said Doug. "Do you want to know it's coming, or do you just want me to hit you?"

"How about if I count to three?" said our friend. "Then when I get to three-"

That was as far as he got. Doug hit him right square in the chest, knocked him down, knocked the wind right out of him. When he stood up, he had this huge hand print right across his chest. We all laughed our heads off.

The handprint lasted several days. When it finally went away, our buddy still had a painful bruise on his chest. It was dark purple, and he finally got worried enough to see a doctor.

Turns out he had had a cyst in his chest! When Doug chopped him, he hit so hard he actually burst the cyst. Our buddy had to have surgery to get it taken care of. Doug might have saved his life because if he hadn't done the chop, our friend would never have known about the cyst.

"I always told the boys, do not chop fans, even if they ask for it," says Cornette. "The last thing we needed was a lawsuit!"

Is it real, partly real, or fake? It's real enough that anyone who wants to believe can suspend disbelief and enjoy themselves as long as they like.

OVW standout Jamin Olivencia.
(Photo courtesy Jamin Olivencia.)

OVW stars Rob Terry and Jamin Olivencia.
(Photo courtesy Jamin Olivencia.)

Heidi Lovelace, Mickie Knuckles, and Crazy Mary Dobson test their strength. IWA Mid-South has never shied away from giving the ladies the spotlight.

(Photo courtesy Marked Out Photography.)

Maniacal manager Jason F'n Saint supporting his client in a toy box deathmatch at EPW.

(Photo courtesy Marked Out Photography.)

Current EPW/IWA Mid-South star Reed Bentley takes a boot to the head from IWA Mid-South legend Chris Hero.

(Photo courtesy Marked Out Photography.)

Louisville's own Hood Ninja, IWA Mid-South star Hy Zaya.
(Photo courtesy Hy Zaya.)

The high flying, deathmatch veteran Crazy Mary Dobson, who isn't afraid to mix it up with the guys either.
(Photo courtesy Crazy Mary Dobson and Ichiban Drunk.)

WHAT'S OLD IS NEW (AGAIN)

When I began work on this book in December of 2012, my primary purpose was to shine a light on wrestling past. As 2013 progressed, it became abundantly clear that wrestling's present in the Louisville area is bright, and the future may be even brighter. If you want to get a glimpse of that brightness for yourself, you need only look on the Sunny Side of Louisville, where pro wrestling is still less regulated than Kentucky and thriving.

In 1941 just as the Allen Athletic Club was beginning to heat up, a group of fight enthusiasts went into business for themselves across the Ohio River in New Albany, Indiana. They created their own promotion, known as the Hoosier Fistic Club, to promote boxing and wrestling across the river. The Hoosier promotion did not last very long, but more than 70 years later, a handful of smaller promotions continue the effort to make Southern Indiana as much of a wrestling destination as they did.

The origins of Destination One Wrestling go back to 2010, when Michael Ewing ran the first show across the river from Louisville in New Albany, Indiana. Now under the direction of former IWA talent Rick Brady, D1W produces monthly wrestling programs in New Albany.

At the heart of D1W is a desire to put on a family oriented show that families can afford. "We keep our ticket prices and concessions low," says Brady. "And we stick to mostly family friendly booking. We like our babyfaces good and our heels bad."

D1W blends a mix of local talent and nationally known indie stars with stars of yesteryear. Tracy Smothers, who did battle at Louisville Gardens back in the 80's, joined the promotion in 2013. He then shocked the fans by turning heel and beginning a classic Southern heel program.

"We believe in old fashioned storytelling," says Brady. "And we love surprises. No one expected Tracy to win the belt, but he did. No one expected him to go heel, but he did. We're always looking for ways to keep the fans guessing."

D1W also keeps the fans coming back, drawing well even on nights when OVW runs shows across the river. It doesn't hurt that they continue to bring in former ECW and WWE talent like Tommy Dreamer, Sabu, Brian Christopher, Nikolai Volkoff, and Tito Santana. Big names like these helped the promotion draw a crowd, but the talented workers on the undercard built their fan base.

The same can easily be said for another newbie promotion known as Evolution Pro Wrestling. Run by indie stars Reed Bentley and Christian Skyfire, EPW isn't as large as some of the other Hoosier promotions, but it offers a wider range of matches and wrestling styles than you'll find at most small promotions. EPW gives its fans a little bit of everything - old school, technical wrestling, women's wrestling, tag teams, hardcore, and very recently, a toy box death match.

"We're a little bit of everything," says Bentley. "When you come to our show, you're going to see something for everyone."

EPW has featured a few legends as well, including Superstar Bill Dundee and former Orient Express member Pat Tanaka, and with each show they keep adding new wrinkles. The young promotion doesn't draw the numbers of the other promotions in the area. That, says Bentley, is more of a positive than some may think.

"The great thing about this is I can try new moves, new tactics, new gimmicks, and if they fail, they fail in front of a few hundred instead of thousands," says Bentley. "It's a great place to experiment, to try new things, and to perfect something that can help me elsewhere."

For Bentley, elsewhere includes Ian Rotten's promotion IWA Mid-South. The rise of EPW proved to be a boon for both EPW and IWA. The two promotions share resources and talent, with EPW acting as proving ground for aspiring young performers. By early 2014, both promotions were running monthly shows. IWA continues its tradition featuring legends of the hardcore scene with some of the most promising newcomers on the indie circuit. In late 2013 they welcomed back one of IWA's most popular stars, Chris Hero, after his release from the WWE. In the spring of 2014, Ian Rotten announced the return of their signature event: the King and Queen of the Deathmatch Tournaments.

Ian Rotten likes to refer to the IWA wrestlers and fans as a family, and he's got good reason to do so. Many of the fans who still pack his shows have been following the promotion from the beginning. Kids who attended shows at the old Kmart building in the 1990s are now grown-ups bringing their own kids to the shows. What's more, a number of the wrestlers now wrestling for IWA, including Ian's son Johnny Rotten Sixx and the Hood Ninja Hy Zaya, grew up watching IWA Mid-South.

And let's not forget the little old ladies of IWA Mid-South. After a few shows you'll spot them in the same seats on the front row, stealing hugs from the babyfaces and cussing at the heels. At a May 2014 show one of them got into it with Gary Jay at ringside, waving her cane and flashing her old school IWA T-shirt. "If you ain't hardcore," she screamed at Jay, "You ain't s---!!"

His fans are loyal, much of his talent is very loyal, and while controversy always seems to follow Ian Rotten, the man books a highly entertaining show.

While new legacies are forged on the Indiana side of the river, the legacy of excellence continues at the Davis Arena in Louisville. Danny Davis and his training staff, which still includes Rip Rogers and Trailer Park Trash, continue their weekly TV tapings, house shows, and training classes, offering aspiring wrestlers a second to none opportunity to learn wrestling the old fashioned way.

New students, both beginners and those with experience pack the house at every announced tryout in hopes of taking the next step toward their dream.

The methodology may be old school flavor, but that doesn't mean OVW is stuck in the past. In 2013 Nick Dinsmore wrestled at the May Saturday Night Special against student Jonathan Ramser who is deaf. Instead of calling the match audibly, like he normally would, Dinsmore worked out a way the two could communicate with touch and hand signals.

Dean Hill continues to lend his voice to OVW television, although his role, too, has changed. No longer the play-by-play man to colorful partners like Jim Cornette and Kenny Bolin, Hill now offers color commentary and mentorship to Gilbert Corsey, an Emmy award winning local television anchor who moved to Louisville to become a wrestling announcer.

In 2012 OVW signed a new developmental deal with TNA - Total Non-Stop Action Wrestling. The deal brought another influx of promising young talent to Louisville including Rob Terry, Jay Bradley, Rockstar Spud, Jessie Godderz, Crimson, Lei'D Tapa, and the Blossom twins. Long time announcer Dean Hill even got a call up to TNA Impact one week, when he came out as the attorney for Bully Ray (the former Bubba Ray Dudley of ECW/WWE fame). But what started as a promising new partnership faded away as TNA's financial problems grew. TNA cut ties with OVW in the fall of 2013, and several TNA stars got their release around the same time.

The TNA and WWE banners may be gone from Davis Arena, but the passion for old school wrestling hasn't diminished in the crowd or backstage. Every Wednesday night, fans fill the seats of the arena for the weekly TV taping. When the music hits and the show begins, the fans are on their feet, cheering the babyfaces and booing the heels.

"You're going to lose!" a front row fan shouted to Jay Bradley during a dark match with fan favorite Rob Terry.

"Shut up, Redneck!!" the heel retorts. "I'm winning!"

A moment later, Bradley takes a little verbal abuse from a ten year old female fan. The Chicago native fires back at the little girl. "Who dresses you??" he screamed. "That's the ugliest dress I've ever seen!"

Bradley's comments sent the girl into a rage, but in the end, she was the one laughing. Rob Terry made his comeback, the heel was vanquished, and the heel as he left in defeat. It made her night. I wouldn't be surprised if it made Bradley's night either.

It's moments like these that keep the fans coming back, week after week, year after year. Yes, the finishes are pre-determined in professional wrestling, but it still happens live, with no re-takes and no edits. Nothing can match the thrill caused by these spontaneous moments of joy, shock, exultation, disbelief, and laughter.

OVW was born and grown in the post territory era, long after the last of the big territories shut their doors. They benefited greatly from their developmental contracts with WWE and TNA, but it's largely the leadership of OVW staff that has kept the territory thriving for almost two decades. Danny Davis, is an "old school" guy, and his crew teaches their students the same way they were taught.

It's certainly not the WWE way. But it still works. Since OVW opened its doors, more than one hundred wrestlers made their way through OVW to the WWE, but there's another number Danny Davis touts as a testament to their success.

"Fifty-nine. That's the number of people who came in our door, started in the beginner's class, and found work with the WWE. That's wrestlers, referees, announcers, and even office staff. Fifty-nine people. Not WWE developmental talent, but people who walked in our door and started as OVW."

It's a legacy that grows more impressive the more you step back. More than 100 people in total came through the Davis Arena on their way to the WWE and TNA. If you add in the people who wrestled for Ian Rotten and IWA, the number grows higher still. To this day, the WWE is top heavy with superstars who left their mark on Louisville: John Cena, Brock Lesnar, Randy Orton, Batista, Daniel Bryan, Cesaro, Seth Rollins, Dean Ambrose, Dolph Ziggler, Damien Sandow, Cody Rhodes, Santino Marella, Zack Ryder, The Big Show, Mark Henry, Kane, Rey Mysterio, Zeb Colter, Paul Heyman, and so on.

As time goes on, the number of superstars who visited Louisville on their way to the top will only grow. Just as I was beginning to put the wraps on this book, Ian Rotten announced that Drake Younger, a beloved member of the IWA Mid-South family, had signed a coveted WWE developmental contract. Hundreds of fans packed Jammerz Rollerdrome for his last show to bid farewell and wish him good luck. That same night, Jeff Jarrett came into Clarksville to wrestle Reed Bentley and scout new talent, just five days after announcing the start of his new promotion Global Force Wrestling.

"The superstars of tomorrow today," isn't just a slogan on the outside of Davis Arena. It's the legacy of Louisville wrestling, a legacy that stretches back more than 130 years. OVW, IWA Mid-South, Memphis, the WWA, the Allen Athletic Club, and all those who came between played a role in shaping the most unusual, unique, and enduring entertainment industries in the world. Louisville witnessed it all - the big names, the big promotions, the big matches.

The Louisville promotions of today are not just a place to see "tomorrow's superstars today." They are a link to the past. They are a reminder of the past glories of Ida Alb, William Muldoon, Strangler Lewis, Heywood Allen, Lou Thesz, Jerry Jarrett, Jerry Lawler, and hundreds more. Professional wrestling is one of the few businesses where respect for the past and those who came before really matters. You can see it in the moves handed down from generation to generation - the leg scissors, the stranglehold, the Irish whip, the Lou Thesz press. You can hear it in the old school promos where good guys are good guys and bad guys are jerks. You can see it in the eyes of the young wrestlers who look up to the veterans, their trainers, and their heroes.

TUESDAY
April 21

The 248-Lb. Giant Who
Unmasked Ole Supe

CHAMPION ORVILLE

BROWN

*PROMISES
TO UNMASK*

SUPER
MAN II

*Newest hidden horror,
5-time winner here*

**Can Brown Do It??
Is Supe Champ Longson??
See Tuesday!!**

THESZ vs. SEXTON

Little Wolf vs. Joe Dusek

45c, 55c, 75c, $1

DERBY EVE
Fri., May 1

3 WORLD'S
CHAMPIONS

Champion Bill Longson
Vs.
Ex-champ Sandor Szabo

Champion Mildred Burke
Vs.
Miss Mae Young, Chicago

Negro Champion Samara
Vs.
Ex-champion Claybourne

2 Prelims

THESZ Vs. LITTLE WOLF

Herb WELCH Vs. Buddy KNOX

Ringside $2.75, Terrace $2.20,
Main Floor Gen. Adm. $1.65,
Bal. Reserved $1.10, Gen. Adm. 75c

**10% Off If Bought
Before April 25**

Box Office: ALLEN CLUB, Seelbach No. 325 — JA 1131

AFTERWORD
A parting shot from Kenny "Starmaker" Bolin

Well, pro wrestling fans, I had originally considered it a tremendous honor when I was asked to write the afterword for the book you apparently just read, but after reading through the transcript myself, I can honestly say I have never been more shocked and disappointed in all my life.

First, I find out a second rate talent like Jim Cornette had been asked to write the foreword for this book. I was apparently third choice, after Cornette and Dr. Isaac Yankem, D.D.S. Secondly, I see that the at least 15 chapters of wrestling knowledge, past memories of matches and inside dirt and scoops on many people in the wrestling business including WWE, TNA and OVW that I provided to Mr. Cosper have been condensed to a mere 3 chapters or so!

HELL! Me and my son, the Prince, ARE wrestling history in Louisville! We cover over 30 years combined in wrestling in this market. Think of all the legendary careers I helped to launch: Sean O'Haire, Rico Costantino, Mark Jindrak, Lance Cade! My stories should be marked as separate treasures of this industry and not tossed in a garbage can. We are truly hurt by this action and feel, you the wrestling fan, have been short changed by this.

I Have NO Doubt that Jim Cornette, who is so old he was actually at ringside in 1882 when William Muldoon came in to wrestle the dinosaurs, begged on his hands and knees not to print my stories because he would be blamed for telling me in the first place. Plus he still loves and adore Danny Davis and OVW (about the only company that would ever hire him back), and I assure you he did not want my stories getting out killing any chance he would have of returning there.

When I confronted John about this he said he was doing the right thing because he did not want a negative book! WHAT! Now you tell me! I guess I should have known you weren't taking notes on the good stuff. Every time I started in on something that's really worth publishing, you were too busy shoving the Golden Corral macaroni and cheese that I purchased for you down your throat to write anything down!

Well..that is okay and fine with me and the Prince. This has only inspired us to write our own book about Bolin Services and the TRUE history of wresting in Louisville Kentucky. No editing, no filtering, just the truth as known by the Bolins. And that is the truth, regardless whether you can handle the truth or not.

If it were me, I wouldn't spend the money on this book, mostly due to the censoring of the Bolins. He'll probably censor THIS part too! But fear not! The Prince and I will soon be out with our own book telling the real story of Louisville wrestling – namely, US!

BITE MY ASS, John, and wait till the Bolins come out with OUR book! We will blow your little book completely out of the water, pal! Good Day!

Kenny Bolin
Bolin Services, Louisville, Kentucky
May, 2014

The book in your hands (or on your tablet) was written for two audiences: those who love wrestling, and those who love Louisville, Kentucky. Those who fall into the latter category may very well find themselves confused by some of the terms used in this book. For those who do not count themselves among the many "marks" and "smarks" who eat, sleep, and breathe wrestling, here are some definitions to keep you from getting lost.

Kayfabe. An old carny term used by wrestlers to refer to the secrecy of the business. A wrestler who steps out of character, or admits something is unreal or scripted, is said to be breaking kayfabe. Kayfabe used to extend far beyond the mat. As recently as the late 90s, Jim Cornette would fine wrestlers if a babyface and heel were spotted in public together.

Babyface. A "good guy" in the ring. Not always the nicest guys if you meet them in public.

Heel. A "bad guy" in the ring. Almost always the NICEST guys if you meet them in public.

Heat. The negative reaction a heel gets from a crowd. A heel's goal is to create as much heat as possible so that the audience wants nothing more than to see the babyface kick his butt.

Pop. The reaction a crowd gives to a wrestler when they enter, good or bad. Most of today's wrestlers have a theme song that begins with a stinger - a signature note, sound, or phrase - intended to enhance the pop when a wrestler enters. If you want to see how it works, sneak up behind your favorite wrestling fan and just play the sound of the glass breaking from the beginning of Stone Cold Steve Austin's theme song. You are guaranteed one heck of a Pavlovian response.

Work. A match, interview, or speech that is pre-planned or scripted. 99.9% of what you see on television these days is worked.

Hippodroming. The nineteenth century equivalent to saying a match was worked. The act of staging a wrestling match or other sporting event that is not on the level.

Go Over. To "win" a wrestling match.

Put Over / Job / Do the Job. To take a pin and let another wrestler get a victory over you, as in, "Beau the police dog would not put Randy Savage over in the Waffle House."

Shoot. A match, interview, or speech that is 100% real and NOT scripted or pre-planned. A number of former wrestlers have given "shoot" interviews that can be found on the Internet. You almost never see shooting on television, but the very best of the best wrestlers can, at times, make you suspend disbelief. CM Punk's "pipe bomb" speech, in which he discussed his real life contract expiration and threatened to take the WWE title belt and leave the company, is one of the best examples of this and the reason he became a true main event star.

Mark. A wrestling fan, especially one who has no idea what he's seeing is not 100% real. The guy you see in public with the John Cena matching shirt, hat, and wristbands is usually a mark.

Smark. A "smart mark" a wrestling fan who, in the eyes of those in the business, thinks they know everything but still doesn't know half of what's going on. This is usually the loud-mouth know-it-all sitting in your section at a wrestling show.

Shooter. A wrestler with legitimate wrestling skills. Not one to be trifled with. Shooters were the men and women who would take on all comers in a crowd in the carny days and pioneer days of the sport. They could also easily defend themselves from attempted screw jobs during matches that were supposed to be worked. Kurt Angle and Brock Lesnar are both considered modern day Shooters.

Hooker. A shooter skilled in holds and moves that can temporarily or permanently disable another wrestler. In the early days, hookers would take on the biggest and most serious challengers from a crowd. In later years, hookers would weed out wannabe wrestlers who showed up at the gym with dreams of being a wrestler. The late Stu Hart, who trained nearly every wrestler to come out of Canada for more than 50 years, was known to "stretch" prospective wrestlers in his basement training center, known as "The Dungeon," in Calgary. His children tell stories of seeing their father gleefully lead young men down into the basement and hearing those young men scream for up to an hour before Stu would let them go.

Promo. Speech given by a wrestler, manager, or other wrestling personality to further story lines and sell more tickets and pay-per-view buys. Heel promos are also used to generate heat with the crowd, usually by offending or insulting the locals. Wrestlers with strong mic skills usually deliver, or "cut," their own promos. Wrestlers with no mic skills or personality are often paired with a manager or valet (female manager) who will cut promos for them.

Go deeper into Louisville's wrestling past!

Thirty-five years before Memphis came to town, the Allen Athletic Club set the bar for wrestling entertainment in Louisville. *Louisville's Greatest Show* takes you year by year through the history of this golden age promotion, bringing you the stories of national and local stars who made Louisville a wrestling city. Order your copy from Amazon.com

ACKNOWLEDGEMENTS

A book like this takes more than one man's effort, and credit and thanks are due to a number of people who helped make this possible.

First and foremost, thank you to my wife Jessica for not hesitating to say, "Do it!" the moment I mentioned this book. It's because of this non-wrestling fan (who is in reality a closet Rey Mysterio/ CM Punk fan) you hold this book in your hands.

Second, thank you to my old friend Jason Lindsey, aka Chris Alexander, for sharing his stories and putting me in touch with many of the people interviewed for this book.

Thanks to Erin Rea, another long time friend and familiar OVW face connected me to a number of folks from OVW including Dean Hill, Danny Davis, and Rip Rogers.

A big thanks to Jim Cornette, who not only wrote the foreword and supplied a number of photos, but has been a huge encouragement since the day we met. Jim assisted me with some of the library research on the book, and many of the stories from the Memphis days came from the notebooks that teenage Jim kept back in the 70s and 80's. Jim's mind is a living encyclopedia of wrestling history, his insights were invaluable.

Thank you as well to Kenny Bolin, who, despite contrary opinion and the nasty things he wrote in this book, is one of the friendliest guys ever to grace the squared circle. It's true what they say; the nastier they were in the ring, they nicer they are out of it. Thank you to the Prince, Chris Bolin, as well for sharing his memories of growing up surrounded by past and future wrestling legends.

Thank you to Steve Yohe, whose research on Louisville results helped lay the foundation for the section on Heywood Allen. Steve's work and insights can be found on the message boards at wrestlingclassics.com, including his unpublished bio of Strangler Lewis.

Thanks, too, to Tim Hornbaker for his research on Heywood Allen, the Allen Athletic Club, and the early 1900s. Tim's work can be found on legacyofwrestling.com.

Additional web thanks to Chris Parsons, Indianapolis wrestling historian and webmaster at rasslinrelics.com for his insights and research into Bruiser, Snyder, and the WWA.

Thank you to George Rugg and Sara Weber at the University of Notre Dame Library for their assistance finding some of the old photos in the Jack Pfefer Collection.

Thanks, to all of the folks who shared their stories or helped me connect with others who played a part in Louisville's wrestling history: Dean Hill, Danny Davis, Rip Rogers, Bobby Fulton, Rich Jones, Ian Rotten, Alvin Hampton, Reed "By God" Bentley, Christian Skyfire, Rick Brady, Ben Wood, Roni Jonah, and Terry Simms.

Thank you to Ichiban Drunk for the Crazy Mary photo. Thank you to Adam Jordan and Mike Simpson with Marked Out Photography for those use of some of their photos. Thanks to Rick Brady with D1W for the use of their 3rd anniversary show ad.

Big thank you to Jason F'n Saint for some terrific OVW and IWA Mid-South photos and several great memories.

Thanks to Reed Bentley, Hy Zaya, Crazy Mary Dobson, and Jamin Olivencia for allowing me to include their photos in the book. Take a good look, wrestling fans. These may be the stars of the future.

Special thanks to my dad, John Cosper, Sr., for the photo of my grandfather and for doing the first proofread. Thanks as well to Dad and the guys in his office at Louisville Metro, who allowed me to get a look inside

Louisville Gardens. It really is a special place, and someone needs to save it before it's too late!

Thank you to Addie Williams for staying up late to do one of the many proofreads on this book. Nothing like spending an evening watching *Buffy the Vampire Slayer* with an old friend while she keeps reading your ridiculous typos aloud for your wife.

Last but not least, thank you to Randy D. Pease, who shared his wrestling book and video library with me for several months back in 2004, took me to my first Wrestlemania in 2011, and ignited my interest in wrestling's past. Enjoy the book, buddy.

The Gold Bond Mafia: Chuck E. Smooth, Dave Prazak, Colt
Cabana, and CM Punk.
(Photo courtesy Jason Saint.)

ABOUT THE AUTHOR

John Cosper is a wrestling blogger and historian whose credits include *Louisville's Greatest Show: The Story of the Allen Athletic Club, Eat Sleep Wrestle, Lord Carlton: Wrestler, Artist, My Father, I Probably Screwed You Too: The Mostly True Stories of Kenny "Starmaker" Bolin*, and *Don't Call Me Fake: The Real Story of "Dr. D" David Schultz.* His favorite match of all time is Triple H vs. Stone Cold Steve Austin in their Three Stages of Hell match from No Way Out 2001. He lives in Southern Indiana, not far from Louisville, with his wife and two kids.

Visit his website at eatsleepwrestle.com

Made in the USA
San Bernardino, CA
13 December 2018